VIETNAM,
FULL CIRCLE

VIETNAM, FULL CIRCLE

A Combat Veteran Returns

Martin J. Dockery

Cover Photos:

The top photo is of my fatigue shirt, which I wore in 1963 when I was the only American with a 500-man South Vietnamese infantry battalion. The silver bar on the collar above my name indicates my First Lieutenant rank, and the two white flowers under U.S. ARMY are the South Vietnamese Army equivalent. My parachute badge shines immediately above U.S ARMY. My Combat Badge is not shown because it had not yet been awarded. My name in white under the silver bar is smudged by the blood of one of my South Vietnamese soldiers who died in my arms while I was bandaging his wounds.

The bottom photo is of me teaching in a Vietnamese grammar school, which I did without pay from 2002 to 2012. Parents pay school fees as public schools are not free. The students are practicing the words "touch your ears."

An Old Soldier Press Book

All rights reserved under International and Pan-American Copyright Conventions. Published by Old Soldier Press and Martin J. Dockery.

ISBN 978-0-578-43245-8

Book design by Martin P. Dockery

Manufactured in the United States of America by IngramSpark.

First Edition: April 2019

© 2019 by Martin J. Dockery

All Rights Reserved

This book is dedicated to

Thao Dockery and our children, John Martin Dockery and Eileen Ivy Dockery, who were born in Vietnam on Christmas Eve, 2004.

CONTENTS

★

ACKNOWLEDGEMENTS

I began writing this book in Vietnam 15 years ago. It has been revised numerous times to reflect the comments of many persons, including Eddie Philips, John Brown, Mike Blackwell, Martin P. Dockery, Timothy Dockery, Una Dockery, Eileen Mathews, Emmett Dockery, Richard Joynes, and Thao Dockery. My friend David Joiner edited the book. He read it top to bottom numerous times. His comments and suggestions improved each page.

I have read many books and articles about Vietnam and this book has benefited from them, including: The Birth of Vietnam by Keith Weller Taylor (University of California Press, 1983); After Sorrow by Lady Borton (Viking Press, 1995); Vietnamese Tradition on Trial by David G. Marr (University of California Press, 1981); Dragon Ascending by Henry Kamm (Arcade Publishing, 1996); Understanding Vietnam by Neil L. Jamieson (University of California Press, 1995); and Reporting Vietnam: American Journalism 1959-1969 (The Library of America, 1998).

While writing this book, I kept a detailed list of sources. That record would have allowed me to acknowledge people and credit sources. Alas, the list disappeared during my travels. My memory has allowed me to acknowledge only a portion of the people and sources on that list. I ask understanding from those I have not recognized.

★

PREFACE

Old men ought to be explorers.
-T.S. Eliot

The uniformed immigration officer at Tan Son Nhat Airport, Saigon, pushed my passport over the scanner at his desk. After consulting his monitor, he remarked in English, "Welcome back, Lieutenant." I acknowledged his greeting while puzzling over why he knew I had been in Vietnam during the war. The officer spoke to a junior official at the desk and in Vietnamese said, "Look at this American. He is old but still handsome." It was my turn to surprise him—payback can be sweet. I answered in his language, thanking the captain – "Cảm ơn nhiều đại úy." Our eyes met. He dipped his head and smiled. I entered his country, stamped passport in my hand, somewhat baffled by our exchange but exhilarated at what lay ahead.

From August 31, 1962, to September 1, 1963, I served as a combat advisor to a South Vietnamese infantry battalion. I witnessed the beginning of, and participated in, that conflict. Vietnamese soldiers were my mates; I lived and fought with them. I volunteered for war back then for a reason quite convincing to a young male: I wanted the excitement that combat promised. I was not disappointed. It was the most exciting and influential year of my life.

Since then the years have gone by in the blink of an eye, but not the memory and excitement of what then was new and unexpected.

My book, Lost In Translation (Random House, 2003), describes my experiences as a combat advisor. This book, Vietnam, Full Circle, tells of my life in Vietnam from 2002 to 2012.

At 23, I was too young to have forged my own personal history, developed a sense of time, or been able to imagine that I could or would later revisit my past. After working in New York City for 35 years, and in the wake of the 25th anniversary of the war's end, Vietnam again pulled at my sleeve. In 2002 I returned to Saigon, where I had agreed to teach English for one year in an orphanage for blind children. Other organizations that served the poor and needy readily accepted my offers of help. Most of my work was without pay, but I was compensated in other ways. The Vietnamese showed me great respect and I was able to help them. I felt good about myself and went to bed every night thankful for that day's experiences. Every morning I awoke to wonder at the new adventures awaiting me, thus my one-year commitment stretched into ten years. Usefulness and adventure are possible upon retirement and that is a silent theme of this book.

I had left a good job, one that I had enjoyed and prospered from, to return to Vietnam, once again as a volunteer. Upon retirement I expected a letdown, a feeling of not being needed, and a diminishing change. However, what I made for myself in Vietnam was every bit as exciting and satisfying as the legal career I'd left behind. It was not what I imagined it would be from one day to the next, but it was exhilarating. My wartime memories were of little help. This experience was far different from my military tour. This time I lived and worked with civilians who told me their life stories. Surprisingly, my having been an American soldier in the war opened Vietnamese doors and hearts – and loosened tongues.

The Vietnamese were remarkably candid. They answered my endless questions, no matter how silly or intrusive, with intelligence, honesty, and great patience. They exhibited trust and goodwill that I never anticipated.

During wartime, I discovered a great deal about myself but little about Vietnam, its people, or culture. This time, during peace, I learned about these things, and also that love late in life is a wonderful gift. Thao, a wonderful woman I met in 2002, has filled my life with warmth and delightful twins, John and Eileen.

These pages provide perspective about contemporary Vietnam, the people and their values. I have mingled anecdotes with what I have learned about Vietnamese customs and taboos. The origins of many of these cultural artifacts are obscure. Notwithstanding, they can help the reader grasp a deeper understanding of this country.

Many of the narratives about foreigners highlight the differences between Vietnamese and Western values.

The situations and individuals I describe reflect the strengths and weaknesses of this country. Tales about human nature and the difficulties of life are told through ordinary happenings involving common people. As with most such stories, they take us beyond the events themselves to reveal painful truths and delicious ironies. What one assumes about human behavior is not always consistent with people's actions. At times, I looked on aghast at Vietnam, its people, and my fellow expats.

Sometimes knowledge exposes hidden reality, and as we get to know ourselves better we are able to learn what causes us to do what we do. Self-interest and personal motives give meaning to our actions. We can only guess at the motives of others. My reasons for wanting to return to Vietnam were, and still are, unclear to me. I'm sure wistfulness for an exciting time in my life, when I was strong and free of encumbrances, played a part in my decision. Whatever my motives were, it was a fortunate choice for me.

I will never really understand the Vietnamese and their 4,000-year-old culture. I am just looking in, a shadow on the wall. There are too many barriers and not enough time to understand. It is not possible. I have learned a lot and I understand some of it, but not enough to go about life in Vietnam error-free, fully informed, and completely accepted. Interestingly, Cervantes tells us, "Sometimes one sees best in a dim light."

Today Vietnam is experiencing robust economic development. Foreign economic and social investments are providing the country opportunities as well as challenges, such as rampant inflation and corporate insolvencies. Traditions and family ties are being tested by the influence of foreign ideas, which are appealing to many, but not necessarily superior. Although less so in the cities than in the countryside, where 75% of the population lives, traditional values still prevail in Vietnamese society. Even today, largely, age-old truths and values govern how the people act and react, and they explain and control the consequences. Rural Vietnamese are the keepers of traditional values and are appalled by the lifestyles of their less conservative brethren in Saigon and other urban areas.

Vietnam is divided into regions: North, Central, and South. Northerners, the stern and increasingly insecure rulers of the country, view Southerners with hostility and distrust. Southerners feel the same towards people from the North. This ancient and entrenched North-South tension is a sensitive matter for the government because it undermines authority and is an obstacle to the goal of a truly unified Vietnam.

There are many secrets in this country and mysteries within mysteries. I took very little at face value. Even greetings and good-byes can be ambiguous. My people, the Irish/Americans, are paranoid about revealing personal information, but the Vietnamese are even more cautious. Em Thy, my landlady, told me: "People try know you. Don't tell anything; not about job in America, or you teach free, or you soldier in Vietnam. They no understand and people try cheat you soon."

I speak Vietnamese poorly, and some of my contacts were able to speak only a few English words. However, with body language, repetition, and raised voices we were able to communicate rather well. We understood what the other said and intended, even though at times the exact meaning of the words escaped us. Some of the dialogue in this book is based on my limited understanding of the Vietnamese language.

Accurate information is difficult to come by in Vietnam. Sometimes there are conflicting versions of data and incidents. The costs of goods and services stated in this book have not been adjusted for inflation; prices are higher today then at the time those events took place. I have culled facts from individuals and from sources published or available in Vietnam, which are subject to government censorship. Criticism and negative information about the government, the Party, or their leaders is suppressed – the people are protected!

Vietnam is a relatively open society. Although the media is controlled, people are reasonably free to say what they want among themselves, but it would be folly to speak about politics or criticize authorities in any sort of open forum. I have altered names and certain information to conceal identities. Even so, everything has happened as described.

The differences between Vietnam and the United States are huge. Our cultures and values are not the same. In fact, they sharply contrast and are astonishingly unique to themselves. However, as humans we tend to act, respond, and reflect alike. As you read this book, these universal qualities will surface. Priorities, frailties, and inducements in each country will appear indistinguishable. We are all very much the same. Certainly, many of the problems faced by Americans and Vietnamese, as individuals and as societies, are similar.

Nonetheless, even with common goals, human conduct differs. Culture constricts behavior. Many things that happen in Vietnam could not happen in America and vice-versa.

MJD

Rye, NY

One

A TURBULENT HISTORY

History is a nightmare from which I am trying to awake.
-James Joyce, Ulysses

An old adage holds that Vietnam is like a one-room house with doors on every side. Dirt and dust blown through one door exit out a different one, leaving the house as it had been before. This saying expresses the idea that invaders come and go, but Vietnam remains intact. The observation is accurate. In spite of the profound influences exerted by China, India, and France, Vietnam is an independent, sovereign nation, and the Vietnamese are a culturally unified and distinct people. They have their own national identity.

Vietnam has had a turbulent history. There have been few periods of prolonged peace. At almost every point, nationalist groups have contested foreign invasion and rule. In the 20th century alone, Vietnam resisted and fought wars against China, Cambodia, France, Japan, and the United States. From 1954 to 1975, a savage civil war devastated the country and resulted in millions of casualties. Except for a short period in the early 1800s, Vietnam had never been a unified, sovereign country until 1975.

*****

BEFORE 1975: For over 4,000 years, Vietnam has been engaged in cultural, political, and military struggles with its huge northern neighbor. China ruled Vietnam from 111 B.C. to 938 A.D. and introduced the Vietnamese to Sino-science, medicine, education, arts, literature, and value systems. During this period, the Vietnamese absorbed many other aspects of Chinese civilization, including an organized governmental system, Buddhism, Taoism, Confucianism, wet rice cultivation, characters for writing, cooking styles, and construction methods.

Throughout its 1,049 years of imperial rule, China referred to Vietnam as Annam, which meant the "Pacified South." This was wishful thinking; Annam was far from pacified.

Even after defeating the Chinese in battle in the 10th century, the Vietnamese, ever fearful of the colossus on its northern border, agreed to pay China an annual tribute. After receiving approval from the emperor of China, the name Nam Viet was changed to Viet Nam, thus mollifying the Chinese who had been humiliated militarily by their "younger brothers," the Vietnamese. The new name would not remind them of their defeat at the hands of their inferiors. In 1428, two years after defeating the Chinese in battle yet again, Vietnam was recognized by China as an independent state. However, to keep on China's good side, Vietnam continued to make yearly payments to the Chinese emperor. Over thousands of years, the Vietnamese have been skillful and remarkably lucky at keeping the Middle Kingdom at bay.

The Vietnamese also were one of the few peoples to withstand the Mongol hordes. The Vietnamese defeated the invading armies of Kublai Khan in 1258, 1285, and 1287.

Just like America, Vietnam had its own Manifest Destiny. In the 15th century Vietnam began expanding to the south, defeating the Cham (an Indian-Hindu kingdom) and the Khmer-Cambodians. Over the course of centuries, Vietnam steadily moved its influence and control southward. Some Vietnamese scholars maintain that but for the arrival of the French in the

19th century Vietnam would have continued to expand to include within its borders present day Cambodia and Laos.

From 1558 to 1772, a protracted bloody war took place between the southern Nguyen and northern Trinh families. Foreshadowing the boundary between North and South Vietnam established by international accords in 1954, the Nguyen constructed a huge wall in the 1630s across the narrow waist of Vietnam at approximately the 16th parallel. The Southerners won and imposed severe sanctions on the Northerners, including the mortifying requirement that Northerners wear the Southern national dress, the áo dài (literally, long gown). In return for its aid, France received from the Nguyen court economic and other concessions, which, together with internal political conflict, eventually led to total French control of Vietnam in 1861.

The Japanese occupied the country from 1940 to 1945 and brought about widespread famine and death by villainous policies, which have not been forgotten in Vietnam and remain a factor that influences relations between the countries.

A Japanese-funded study of this period, headed by Professor Tao of Hanoi University, has documented that the French colonialists and Japanese authorities had a policy of not using guns to fight the nationalist guerrillas, otherwise known as the Viet Minh (Việt Minh Độc Lập Đồng Minh Hội, the League for the Independence of Vietnam). Instead, they controlled the food supply, hoping to keep the people in check and eventually weaken their revolutionary ambitions. They forced farmers to supply rice to Japan: 700,000 tons in 1941, 1,050,000 in 1942, and increasing to 1,125,000 in 1945. Furthermore, a ban on transporting rice within Vietnam was imposed.

French and Japanese authorities further limited the domestic food supply by the wanton destruction of rice, maize, potato, and bean crops. In their place, peanuts and other plants, which could be substituted for petroleum in the production of gunpowder, were required to be cultivated. These policies, together with crop pests, caused famine throughout the country, especially in the north. Professor Tao's study concluded that in 1945 two million Vietnamese died of starvation.

After the United States triumphed over the Japanese, the French returned to govern and exploit Vietnam. The French were defeated in 1954 by communist forces led by Ho Chi Minh. After 90 years, the humiliating experience of French colonial rule in Vietnam finally ended.

Following negotiations in Geneva, competing Vietnamese political groups and self-interested world powers divided Vietnam at the 16th parallel into two independent countries: the Democratic Republic of Vietnam in the north and the Republic of South Vietnam in the south. War between the newly formed countries ensued until 1975 when the North, supported by China and the Soviet Union, defeated South Vietnam and America.

In 1962 the U.S. Army assigned me as a combat advisor to an infantry battalion of the Army of the Republic of Vietnam (ARVN). For eight months I walked the rice fields and jungles of the Mekong Delta tracking the elusive Viet Cong. During this time desertion, sickness, and enemy action reduced the battalion's strength from 500 to 400 men. Most of the time, I was the only American with the battalion. As I lived and fought beside them, I learned to like the South Vietnamese soldiers as individuals, but was constantly dismayed by their lack of motivation and soldiering ability.

The Viet Cong were South Vietnamese. They fought in their provinces and their villages. The North supported and controlled the Viet Cong. The conflict was a civil war.

The character of the war changed in 1965 when the North dispatched regular army infantry battalions and large-scale supplies to the South by way of the Ho Chi Minh Trail. Hanoi realized that combat soldiers and massive supplies from the North would be necessary to defeat the ARVN. The Viet Cong could not do it alone. America responded to this escalation by increasing its commitment. By 1969 half a million U.S. soldiers were stationed in South Vietnam. Although the American military performed well, this escalation did not end the war. Soldiers from the North fought bravely, too, and casualties increased on both sides; U.S. Air Force General Curtis Le May advised that we bomb North Vietnam back to the Stone Age. This was not done, but his words mirrored the frustration of Americans.

The United States eventually grew weary of the war. American citizens did not understand why the United States was involved in a war halfway around the world, and its government could not bring itself to do what had to be done to win. Many Americans were incensed that so many privileged, wealthy, and well-connected young American men were able to avoid the draft while the poor and less educated went into battle. Unfairly, legislative deferments and influence peddling meant that if a young man had something better to do he did not have to go to war. By 1972, America had withdrawn its soldiers and, starting the same year, gradually reduced its logistics support to the Republic of South Vietnam. The United States abandoned its South Vietnamese ally.

In 1975, North Vietnamese divisions crushed the ARVN and unified Vietnam. A fully equipped army of 17 conventional divisions supported by 700 Soviet tanks conducted a cross-border attack on South Vietnam. These divisions were trained and provisioned by China and the Soviet Union. Their troops were not insurgent peasants from the South fighting a civil war in recycled rubber sandals. Instead, they were an invading army whose ranks consisted of Northern officers and conscripts. They were from the North and they were hell-bent on conquest.

There was never a general uprising of the populace against the Southern regime. The people of South Vietnam were confused, uncertain, and fearful of Northern rule. Indeed, their concerns proved to be justified. The reality of postwar Vietnam was horrific for the people of the South.

AFTER 1975: After the war, the North Vietnamese treated harshly those in the South who had supported the South Vietnamese government and the United States. Accounts of cruelty and hardship are common. Tens of thousands of people were imprisoned indefinitely. Housing, food, medicine, employment, and education were denied to former soldiers, their wives and children, and to others who worked for the old regime. Such reprisals do not continue today, but lists are kept, favoritism is rampant, and Northerners and their children prosper because of postwar policies, which exclude the war's losing side. This reality fans regional distrust and has made goodwill between Northerners and Southerners difficult to achieve.

Poverty, despair, and a daily search for food were the fate of Southerners after 1975. The "victors" from the North confiscated their property and divided it among themselves. In the aftermath of a civil war, the winner's treatment of the losers largely determines the success of reconciliation and the country's future well-being. The seeds of resentment are rooted deeply in the psyche of Southerners. The North's failure to follow more humane policies after the war was a tragic mistake because it has prevented the formation of a truly united Vietnam. The war had united the land, but not the people.

However, the postwar imprisonment of ARVN officers and other supporters of the former regime stopped effective armed resistance groups opposed to communist rule. In that regard, the so-called re-education camps, where prisoners (when not forced to clear the land) were required to listen to lectures on the virtues of communism, were successful. Since 1975, various groups of overseas Vietnamese have sponsored sporadic armed resistance. They have been uniformly unsuccessful because of the diligence of national security forces and the lack of support of the Vietnamese people.

In addition to deliberate retribution against their former enemies, the Democratic Republic of Vietnam instituted policies that forestalled reconciliation between Southerners and Northerners and caused grave suffering and economic harm to all its citizens. For example, the government decreed that it owned all land, businesses, and institutions, leaving the people with nothing.

Shortly after the war, one million Southerners were moved to new economic zones located in jungles and swamps, which they were forced to clear and farm. City residents and others without farming experience were expected to produce crops in soil that prior generations had refused to cultivate. Their ancestors had known the land was unproductive. Those who were moved soon found themselves hungry, sick, and resentful, and it was not long before most of them rejected the government plan. They resisted and escaped back to the cities where they had lived. Government enthusiasm for the economic zones dissipated in the face of adamant individual and collective opposition. Over time the policy was discarded, and people who had escaped were no longer hunted down and forced to return.

The desperate years ended in 1987 when the government, threatened by famine and insurrection, opened its doors to foreign investment and undertook substantive efforts at reconciliation. By 1987, twelve years of doctrinaire communist policies had produced a backward, desperately poor country. Soldiers, police, and politicians who were ignorant about economic development and beneficent social policies dominated the new regime. Today, in 2018, forty-three years after the fall of Saigon, Vietnam remains one of the world's poorest countries.

Vietnam and Cambodia have been traditional enemies based on long-standing territorial disputes and significant cultural differences. Most of Vietnam lying south and west of Saigon was once Cambodian territory. Today, the area is still referred to as Lower Cambodia by the tens of thousands of ethnic Khmer-Cambodians who live there.

During the Cold War a struggle developed between the two communist giants, the Soviet Union and China, over influence in Cambodia. Before 1975, at the bequest of Russia and in its own self-interest, North Vietnam supported the communist Khmer Rouge, who eventually came to power.

In April 1975, Pol Pot, the homicidal Paris-educated leader of the Khmer Rouge, captured Phnom Penh and swiftly emptied the city of its two million residents. Driven by an extreme form of nationalism, a murderous desire to reclaim lost territory, and sensing a weak Vietnam, Pol Pot launched a series of attacks in 1976 on Vietnamese cities, killing thousands of civilians. At the same time, his followers massacred thousands of ethnic Vietnamese living in Cambodia. In retaliation, the Vietnamese army invaded Cambodia in 1978 and toppled the Khmer Rouge. Pol Pot's forces retreated to the Thai border where they continued to resist into the 1990s.

Comparisons between the Vietnamese situation after 1975 and the communist regime in Cambodia are revealing. After years of vicious warfare, the prevailing governments of both countries promptly and zealously promoted bizarre, unproven, and cruel policies that were detrimental to their people.

One policy common to both communist countries was the forced relocation of people to new economic zones. Vietnam abandoned this policy when it became clear that it was a failure. Although the people sent to the zones thwarted the policy, the rulers of Vietnam, when the time came to push enforcement, did not take the same barbaric action as the Khmer Rouge. That regime killed an estimated million-plus of its own people in a tragic and savage attempt to transform Cambodia into a self-sufficient, communist society where individuals could not own property, social class divisions would not exist, and people worked as part of a collective unit.

In 1979, China attacked Vietnam as punishment for its action against Cambodia and, perhaps, for allowing the Soviets to establish a naval base at Cam Ranh Bay, a mere 700 miles from China's southern flank. Vietnam was faced once again with the task of driving from its territory the soldiers of its near neighbor, which fielded the world's largest army. As in the war with America, Vietnam prevailed against both China and Cambodia, but in each case at great loss of life.

Two

THE OLD SOLDIER

In war there are no unwounded soldiers.
-Jose Narosky

Unable to justify the war any longer to its citizens, the United States completed its withdrawal from Vietnam in 1972. Pursuant to the peace treaty between North Vietnam and the United States, the North Vietnamese Army remained within the borders of South Vietnam. The North and the South continued to skirmish and battle. The war did not stop until the fall of Saigon in April 1975.

In Vietnam today every adult's story begins, "Before 1975" or "After 1975." In the United States, we have little idea of the personal disruption, suffering, and tragedies that took place in the former South Vietnam after this year. Executions, jail terms, and communist rule are only part of the story.

For more than 40 years the victors have punished the losers. It has been a long time, even in Vietnam where patience is encouraged and praised, and long departed ancestors are cherished and prayed to. Many Southerners have volunteered to me that life has improved since 1987 when the country instituted Đổi Mới (renovation policies) and slowly embarked on efforts to reintegrate with the international community. Still, Southerners feel persecuted in subtle ways, and lost opportunities still rankle.

*****

BIG TẾT: Most Vietnamese words derive from the Chinese language. Tết is one and literally means "the joint of a bamboo stem." In an allegorical sense it means a new beginning, a new season. There are several Tếts during the year, but the most important is Tết Ca, which means "Big Tết." It marks the beginning of the Lunar New Year.

During Big Tết, city residents return to their ancestral villages, which they refer to in English as their "countryside," "homeland," or "motherland." Relatives and friends visit and relationships are renewed. The extended family enjoys a lavish feast; they "eat Tết" (ăn Tết). Saigon becomes quiet and less crowded. People say four-fifths of the population leaves the city for the villages from which they, their parents, or grandparents originally came. Respect for ancestors and traditions sends the city people back to their place of origin.

THE OLD SOLDIER: On January 30, 2003, I traveled by motorbike to spend Big Tết with the family of Thao, a woman I'd become close to over the past year. It was my third trip to the home of Thao's 70-year-old father, Phong, who had been a major in the ARVN. This short, sturdy man with a full white beard greeted me warmly. He showed me around his homestead, obviously proud of the fruits of his efforts. From drawers he pulled photographs of himself with American soldiers. Pointing at a photo of an American captain he said: "He live Vermont." Phong and Huan, his wife of 50 years, survive on an $800 annual income from their cashew and cassava harvests.

I was thirsty, tired, and dirty when I arrived. Phong showed me my bed, the only one with a mattress, and the makeshift outdoor shower. Some people sing when they shower; I drink beer. Before washing the road dust from my body, I requested one. On the days that followed, I did not have to ask for a beer; it was given to me as I made my way to the spigot they had rigged high on a banana tree.

Phong had come south in 1954, alone, at the age of 19, as part of an exodus of one million people fleeing communist rule. Most of them were Catholics who feared persecution because of communism's antipathy toward organized religions. Phong, a lifelong Buddhist, has never explained to his wife and children why he left the North, nor has he told them about his childhood (except that he was raised by monks until the age of 16), or who his parents were. He has promised to do so before his death; "If God allows it," he says. They take this to mean he will never tell them.

It is unusual for anyone anywhere to hide his or her past. In Vietnam, where ancestors are revered, it is incredibly strange that a father would not reveal the identity of his parents and grandparents to his children. His four children, understandably, speculate about his early life and wonder what shame, embarrassment, or allegiance is hidden there. His two daughters described this mystery to me and admitted that they have no idea what secrets their father is hiding. There are things in my past that I do not want my children to know about, but none is as basic as where I came from.

In time, Phong became my father-in-law.

FIRST TẾT VISITOR: The three-hour trip on Thao's gift-packed motorbike had been eventful. The highway traffic was hectic and dangerous as bicycles and ox-carts competed with buses, trucks, motorbikes, and automobiles for limited road space. Low-paid police supplemented their incomes by stopping vehicles at random and demanding payment for passage. No tickets were issued. No receipts were given. Drivers who refused to pay were ticketed and subject to long delays.

At one point traffic slowed, stopped, and then moved slowly ahead again. We passed an unconscious middle-aged woman stretched out on the road, her head resting on her extended right arm. Blood flowed from her left temple into and out of her eye socket and down the side of her nose to pool on the pavement next to her chin. She was still bleeding, a good sign. No one else was injured. Her upturned motorbike was nearby. A policeman was on the scene trying to care for the victim, direct traffic, and find witnesses.

Within feet of the fallen woman, the drivers of two motorbikes brushed against each other and quickly exchanged insults. They backed off, eyed their opponent with terrier-like commitment, no words now, and then closed on one another, fists flying. The police officer, busy with other things, did not intervene. Others crept by to continue their journeys. Holiday travel is stressful everywhere.

Neighbors, friends, and relatives visit one another on the first day of Tết. At Phong's house, each time someone arrived he introduced me as an American who lives in Saigon, teaches English to blind children, and drinks beer in the shower.

The first Tết visitor determines a family's luck for the coming year. In the event of tragedy and suffering during the ensuing year, blame falls on that person. There is a lot of stage-managing to ensure that the initial caller is rich and in good health. With winks and nods Phong's family decided that it was correct to consider me, their house guest, as their first visitor that Tết. All Americans are considered rich.

SHOT TWO: In 1975 the North Vietnamese Army routed the Army of the Republic of South Vietnam. ARVN military units disintegrated. The roads to Saigon were choked as civilians and soldiers fled. Phong spoke of the defeat and of the harrowing road trip to Saigon from Nha Trang, his home of 11 years. In normal times the trip took 12 hours, but then, when anarchy ruled and gunshots echoed throughout the land, it lasted seven days. He commandeered a jeep, loaded it with two 50-pound sacks of rice, jerry cans of water and gasoline, and 11 family members. His two brother-in-laws rode shotgun and fought off soldiers who tried to take the jeep. "Shot two," Phong said.

However, Saigon offered no safety. It fell three days after the family's arrival. Phong burned his uniforms and documents. He and his family returned to Nha Trang hoping to find refuge but were turned away by soldiers from his former command that had taken over his house. The soldiers said Phong's family would be safe if they did not move back in. Phong had been an officer who supported the Americans and must go to jail. After another dangerous and eventful trip to Saigon, Phong was captured while hiding at his wife's cousin's house. "Neighbor tell," he remarked.

Phong was placed in a jungle prison. His term was indefinite; he was told he would stay in jail until he had been properly reformed. He was charged with no crime. Phong and his fellow prisoners cleared the jungle 12 hours a day, receiving little more than four bowls of rice daily and all the water they could drink. He became sick from this regimen and contracted bệnh sốt rét (malaria, aka jungle fever) and amoebic dysentery. The government released him to an economic zone to die, but his family nursed him back to health. With no money to buy Western malaria medicine, they resorted to traditional remedies of boiled roots, tree bark, insects, and sun-dried lizards.

A PINCH: The daughters shared stories of their father's imprisonment and the difficult life they all had. They told me of traveling six hours by bus with their mother to see their father in prison. Four visits a year were allowed. Hundreds of people (prisoners, wives, children, and guards) gathered in a large field. Families talked and ate, but prisoners were forbidden to eat food brought by loved ones because it suggested that the authorities were not feeding them properly. One daughter remembered her father being beaten with a stick because he had stuffed in his mouth food they had brought.

Prisoners were allowed to have sex with their wives during the visits. Phong and Huan sought privacy under an old poncho while their children played nearby. Their daughters said they knew something was going on but did not know what. They pretended to play but kept glancing toward the poncho. All around, the field was covered with preoccupied, cloaked couples, quietly playing children, and leering guards.

The youngest daughter, Man, told of one such visit. She and her mother had been unable to board the return bus. They started to walk home but soon grew tired and sat beside the deserted dirt road. A military jeep carrying a North Vietnamese Army captain and his driver spotted them and stopped. Huan knew that if she said she had been visiting her husband in prison they would not get a ride. When she lied about where they were coming from, she pinched her nine-year-old daughter on the arm. The good-hearted captain gave them a ride.

During the journey the driver interrogated Huan further and she lied some more. Each time, Huan pinched the small arm next to her. Man was inexperienced and would have admitted the truth if the soldier had questioned her. She did not know why her mother was lying, but she knew the pinching meant she was to listen and keep quiet. The captain and his driver transported them to the province border and said goodbye. After sleeping in bushes, walking, and other hitched rides, Huan and Man returned to their home the following day.

COUSIN LUCKY: Twice after his release from jail Phong tried to escape from Vietnam with his family. Each time, Nha Trang fishermen took his money, loaded them onto a boat, and motored a short distance before turning back to shore. Police boats were nearby, they claimed. Phong believes the fishermen tricked him out of his money. Naturally, he had no recourse; what he was doing was illegal.

Phong's cousin, Ho, left Vietnam in 1978 even though he had not planned to. One night this 19-year-old lad was delivered into the amazing hands of fate. While walking on a beach in Nha Trang he came upon a group of people loading onto a boat. Afraid that he would inform the police, they shanghaied him. Ho was taken out to sea and forced to bail water for his food and drink. Seven months later, his wife received a letter from him. Three years passed before she and their son were able to join Ho in Paris where he was working as a dishwasher; "A small job," remarked Phong. They live in France today. "Cousin lucky," he told me.

BICYCLE ARREST: When he first came to the jungle, Phong did not know how to get food or make money. He was a city boy. He and his family had to learn by trial and error and by observing those who were already settled there.

Phong built a shelter of broad leaves and sticks over a dirt floor. He and his family suffered from monsoon rains, non-potable water, insufficient food, insecurity, and uncertainty. They lived with snakes, scorpions, and insects.

To survive, Phong's family supplemented their meager diet by scouring the jungle for edible roots, leaves, and beetles. As Cervantes advised, "We must remember the next time we dine that hunger is the best sauce."

Phong learned how to make charcoal and where to sell it so they would have money to buy salt, cassava, chilies, and rice. His family collected wood from the jungle, placed it in a pit, set it on fire, and covered it with banana leaves and dirt. The wood smoldered for a day. When the oxygen-starved burn was over, they uncovered the pit and spread the charcoal on the ground to cool before taking it to market the following morning.

However, his first attempt at charcoal making was unsuccessful. For three days Phong dug the pit, collected the wood, and made his first batch, but all his work was for naught. He had mistakenly cooled the charcoal before the burn was complete. He had uncovered the pit too soon. Early in the morning, when the family went to collect the charcoal, they found only ashes. There was no laughter as he related this tale to me. For days, he had to rely on others to feed his family.

Making charcoal in the jungle was illegal, so Phong and his family had to hide their business from the "jungle police," who were only low-level patrolmen from the North and yet had ultimate authority, which Phong never dared challenge. Before dawn, while the police were still asleep, his family carried baskets of the fuel on their backs to where they had hidden their bicycle. They loaded the baskets onto the bicycle and pushed it for miles to the market. If they got there late, they received a low price because buyers had already purchased what they needed.

One time the police caught them, but they had seen the police coming and had hidden the charcoal. The police were angry at not finding contraband on them, so they "arrested" the bicycle, as Phong put it, and took it to the "police house." The next day Phong sent Thao, his 14-year-old daughter, to ask for the bike. He knew they would not give it to him. One policeman demanded sex for the bike but the daughter refused. Not knowing what else to do, she waited three hours in the sun on the road in front of the police station. Finally a police captain came out and asked her why she was waiting. When she told him, he gave her water, rice, and the bicycle and sent her home. There are good men everywhere, but often they are hard to find.

Phong and his family escaped from the economic zone in 1978 and moved to a different part of the Mekong Delta. He cleared three acres, built a two-room bungalow, and planted cashew trees and cassava. The small house, which he still lives in, is clean and comfortable.

IN THE DARK OF NIGHT: When the communists took over in 1975, they confiscated all land in Vietnam and instituted collectives for farming. Everything belonged to the state, including food, plants, and animals. The state also took the farmers' profits. The peasants vigorously objected, refused to work the land, and Vietnam went from being an exporter of rice to an importer. What the farmers did produce they sold on the black market. As a result, people in the cities did not have enough food. Vietnam returned to being an exporter of rice only when land ownership, through 100-year leases, and the country's produce and animals, reverted to the peasants. The state retained ultimate ownership of the land.

People were not allowed to slaughter cows or pigs without permission. The meat could not be sold in the market if it did not have an approval stamp indicating that a government tax had been paid. Phong explained how he and others had killed their animals in the dark of night. Neighbors would gather in secret to help with the slaughter and then buy the untaxed meat. To avoid detection the animals had to be killed quickly and silently.

By the flickering light of the bánh Tét (a special Tết treat) cooking fire, Phong outlined in the dirt the head of a cow and, after fetching a sledgehammer from his kitchen, showed me where one blow would kill the animal instantly. "Otherwise, the dying cow make loud noise and everyone know what you doing."

GOVERNMENT LOAN: In 1985 the land ownership policy changed. Phong was able to buy the three acres he lived on with a cash gift he received from a friend who had prospered under the communists. However, he lost some of his land in the late 1980s when he was unable to repay a 14% government loan.

Vietnam has an extensive public school system, but education is not free. Attendance is mandatory unless a child does not have a birth certificate or his parents cannot afford the tuition and fees. Phong's four children were young and he did not have enough money to take care of them. Income from his farm and charcoal sales was not enough to pay their school fees and other family expenses.

Phong had used the government loan to buy an ox and cart. His land served as collateral. He hoped he could haul freight and earn enough to feed the ox, repay the loan, and school his children. Unfortunately, his business plan failed. The ox was too expensive to keep and he had few customers. The government took the ox, cart, and an acre to satisfy the loan's unpaid balance. Only one child, the youngest son, finished high school.

Are You Going To Take A Shower? Huan and Thao sat on the floor of the main room and prepared bánh Tết, a mixture of sugar, pork fat, fish sauce, bean flour, sticky rice, salt, and pepper. The mixture was then packed in triple-thick banana leaves and tied securely with bamboo twine. The eight-inch square packages were cooked in a cauldron of boiling water for 20 hours. Thao told me bánh Tét will stay fresh and unspoiled without refrigeration for 10 days, but if not cooked for 20 hours it will go bad in three days.

A folk story explains that at night men must tend the bánh Tét fire to guard against bad spirits stealing the women of the house. During the dark hours, in the yard behind the house, the old soldier, Thao, and I tended the wood fire and added water to the pot. Banana leaves, floating at the top to slow evaporation, turned the water black and added flavor. From time to time Phong placed pieces of half-burnt wood in a second pot. With the lid in place, the oxygen-deprived fire made charcoal for kitchen use in the days ahead.

Under the stars, we talked about his life since 1975, of Orion and the Dippers, and of how to find one's way in the jungle at night. In theory, one can feel on which side of a tree trunk fungus has grown and, presto, lickety-split, ascertain compass points. Of course, like many things in life, it is easier said than done.

I asked for a beer and Thao responded quickly, "Are you going to take a shower?" Her brilliant smile, quick wit, and sweet nature captivated me.

ANIMAL FEED: Cassava, the source of tapioca, is a tropical plant whose roots can be eaten boiled or steamed, or made into flour for sweets. Since it is low in nutritional value, more frequently it is fed to animals. Because of the failed agricultural policies instituted after 1975, there was a shortage of rice in Vietnam for years. All around, people were hungry; often Phong's family and other Vietnamese had only cassava, chili, and salt. Many Vietnamese refuse to eat cassava today.

Phong cultivates cassava and uses the stalks to regrow the plant in the succeeding year. Six-inch sections take root when planted in the rich soil. His small house is cramped and stuffy; it has a distinctively earthy smell because he stores harvested cassava there. Old rice bags packed with the root are stacked floor to ceiling against the inside walls. He will not send his cassava to market until the season is over, when he will get a higher price.

MAN'S PLEA: Phong told me it was good that Vietnam is unified and that foreigners did not rule the country anymore, yet he did not like Vietnamese people from the North. They steal from the South, he explained, and their thinking spreads poison in the hearts of all Vietnamese.

He was also angry at America, which he said he'd fought for, but which had abandoned him and will not pay him a pension.

Retired American soldiers get money, he said. Old soldiers from the North and their families receive monthly payments from the Vietnamese government. Why should he not receive retirement money from the United States? "If America no let me come America, it pay me."

Surely, this is a revisionist view. He was fighting for South Vietnam, not for America. Interestingly though, if he and the South Vietnamese soldiers thought they were battling for America and not their own country, it explains largely why the North won the war.

Many people sought to flee South Vietnam after the war ended in 1975. The United States accepted thousands of refugees and instituted programs to allow qualified Vietnamese to immigrate. One such program permitted those who had supported the United States, and had been imprisoned for at least three years for this "crime," to resettle in America. Phong did not qualify because, mortally sick, he had been released from prison after 14 months.

Phong's daughter, Man, wrote a letter in English to Mrs. Clinton requesting a U.S. visa for her father. This 1998 letter highlights both the desperate years after 1975 and the strength of its capable and determined author. (See Note 1.)

Man's plea went unanswered. Maybe the President's wife never got the letter, maybe the ever-vigilant Vietnamese censors confiscated the reply, or perhaps Mrs. Clinton needed a larger staff. Life is a village, don't you know?

American resettlement programs did not benefit everyone who had supported South Vietnam and the United States during the war. It was not the intent of the United States to do so. Too many people would have qualified for residency so the U.S. Congress set requirements and restrictions. Sadly for Phong and his family, they were not eligible.

Three

COUNTRYSIDE TALES

Tell me the tales that to me were so dear
Long, long ago; long, long ago.
-Thomas Haynes Bayly

Throughout the ages, agricultural societies have marked the beginning and end of seasons with formal sacrifices and festivals. People hope for good crops and, ever mindful of fate and the gods, pray for splendid karma. Farmers and others living close to the land celebrate the Lunar New Year, pausing to reflect, take stock, and start again. The Vietnamese people, in a serious and determined way, continue to follow the Tết tradition and act to reinvigorate themselves and their destinies during the Lunar New Year.

In Vietnam, Tết is the most important holiday of the year. We have nothing like it in America. It is an occasion for mortals and rice paddies to relax. The Vietnamese say they work hard all year so they can enjoy this short holiday. Officially, Tết lasts three days, but businesses and government offices close and most people celebrate for seven to ten days. Good deeds are performed. Arguments and misunderstandings are resolved or forgiven. Quarreling spouses reconcile. Even the most shrewish and defiantly proud mother-in-law is moved to make peace with her overmatched and cowering daughter-in-law. Gifts and alms are distributed, debts paid, special foods prepared.

Small sums of money wrapped in red, the color of luck, are presented to children. A bonus, equal to a month's salary, is given to employees. This giving and receiving of "lucky money" is a cherished custom. My red envelopes contained a U.S. $2 bill, much sought after by young and old alike.

Families visit ancestral graves before the old year ends: they clear weeds, plant flowers, and affix prayer paper to tombs.

Plum trees with yellow flowers decorate homes of Southerners during Tết. People from the North favor pink-flowered kumquat trees. Everyone knows the region of the country you are from by the flowers of your potted tree. Throughout Vietnam, a branch of peach blossoms is often placed in the house to ward off evil nocturnal spirits. If the residents are lucky, it will bloom on New Year's morning.

*****

AN INVITATION: High, out of easy reach, and affixed to an interior wall of the jungle home, was an altar shelf. Still clear and bright, old photos of Huan's parents and grandparents, some in mandarin dress, looked down from the altar. Flowering peach and plum branches added color to the room. Phong explained, "I have no photo of ancestors, but not important because invitation and prayers will reach them."

Bánh Tét and a pyramid of bananas, grapefruits, oranges, tangerines, and persimmons decorated the forebears' shrine. The fruits represented the ancient Sino-concept that the universe is made of five elements: metal, wood, water, fire, and earth. Days later, we ate the fruit. Phong's eyes twinkled with amusement as he told me that the spirits had not accepted the offering. "Not because angry, but because happy and no hungry."

Each morning and evening during the holiday, Phong and his wife honored their ancestors. The fragrance of burning incense filled the small room as they whispered prayers. Phong bowed, hands together in prayer, as he thanked them for their help.

"I believe my parents and grandparents are always near," he told me afterward. "They look after me and help and I make gift. I invite them the Tết celebration."

They had been invited back from the spirit world to observe the passage from the old year to the new.

Phong placed sticks of sugarcane against the wall under the altar. He said the old, hunched ancestors would use them to walk around the house and garden when they came to visit.

KITCHEN GOD: When we arrived at the small cottage, preparations were already underway to welcome back the Kitchen God.

Seven days before Tết, the Kitchen God and the Land Genie return to heaven to report to the Jade Emperor about the family's behavior during the past year. A good report ensures household happiness and prosperity in the New Year. The Jade Emperor will punish the family if the report includes accounts of selfishness, disrespect, or greed. Prior to the gods' departure, the family prepares new clothes and a feast for the two deities, hoping to influence the report. On Tết Eve, the family invites them back from heaven with fruit and other offerings.

School skits performed before Tết feature mandarin-robed 10-year-olds acting the part of the Kitchen God and reading humorous accounts from a scroll of an errant family's activities. Students have written the stories. As transgressions are recounted, punishments to follow in the New Year are meted out by a costumed, stern-faced, 12-year-old Jade Emperor. There are many stories about the Kitchen God, but the central theme of them all is accountability. Repeated year after year, these stories reveal unacceptable behavior and teach children that they must be responsible for what they do.

NO TROUBLE WANTED: Life is better for Phong now, but the communists still will not leave him alone. Among other indignities, he must get approval to host a foreign visitor. When he reported to the local police that I would visit him for Tết, they gave him a Vietnamese flag and told him he must fly it during the holidays. He refused.

"It is VC," he grumbled to me.

I told him the war ended a long time ago and to forget that stuff. "It is your country's flag now. Fly it."

"It over for you, Martin," he replied, "but not me."

The next morning, I came upon Huan tying the flag to a bamboo pole in front of the house while her husband cooked rice for the dogs in the back. When I left two days later, it was still there. She flies the flag every year. It is how this cautious, tiny woman avoids trouble with the authorities and her husband maintains his dignity.

On the morning we departed for Saigon, we ate grilled bánh Tét sprinkled with sugar. It tasted like you would expect sugar, pork fat, fish sauce, bean flour, sticky rice, salt, and pepper to taste after being boiled in banana leaves for 20 hours.

SOON WE EAT THEM: The old soldier keeps five dogs to warn him if someone is stealing his crops. He feeds them rice with fish sauce twice a day and gives them table scraps. Four of the dogs are tethered about the property. The dogs' locations are changed each evening so they will stay nervous and alert and so thieves will not know where they are. One dog runs loose. If given the opportunity, thieves will take the dogs because they are valuable as food or can be sold as watchdogs. When one dog barks, the other four join in. The dogs break the jungle's nighttime quiet often, and if their barking continues, Phong grabs his machete and walks his land to investigate.

One of the dogs acts as a stud for the area. People bring their bitches to be impregnated by old Spot. If puppies are the result, Phong gets the pick of the litter or $15, whichever he wants.

The dogs stop making noise when danger passes, but not the monkey, which is chained to a tree in front of the house. For 10 minutes or so after the dogs have calmed down, the monkey continues to rattle his chain and scream. Phong doesn't mind feeding and caring for all the animals because they protect him, his wife, and his crops. "Anyway," he said, "soon we eat them."

Butchers and restaurants that sell dog meat are clustered in Saigon's Tan Binh District. Impaled canine heads over entranceways announce a shop's specialty. In the window display, amidst buzzing flies, are headless carcasses, hindquarters, ribs, organs, and tails. Poor Spot.

Dogs do not run free in the streets. They are housebound. Upon seeing an unleashed dog my local companions would invariably say "dinner" and laugh.

The Vietnamese say, "Two men and a dog are a party." Restaurants serving only canine meat advertise seven different dog dishes: soup, sausage, boiled, stir-fried, grilled, baked, and minced. A stinking, fermented, bitter shrimp sauce accompanies the meal. Men drink beer, joke, laugh, and sing late into the night.

ICE FOR SALE: In 2003, shortly before Tết, the government ran a power line by Phong's house, and for a fee he was able to hook up to the line. Phong and Huan's children bought them a television and I bought them a refrigerator. They were installed side-by-side in the main room. It was the first time since 1975 that they had had electricity. Thirty years earlier they also had running water, lights, and a fridge. He told me he felt young again and their lives would be easier as they grew older.

In order to pay for electricity, which cost 14 cents per day, Huan sold ice. No one nearby had a fridge. A handwritten sign at the gate to their property advertised five teacup-sized ice cubes for three cents. Each day since installing the fridge, she has realized more than 14 cents.

The availability of electricity caused some tension with a neighbor who, in order to avoid the $62 hook-up fee, which is a lot of money in this poor country, asked if he could connect a line to Phong's meter box and pay for what he used. Fearing the loss of electric service if the power company discovered the unauthorized connection, Phong refused. He explained to me that in the jungle you must help others if you can but0 that this man was asking too much.

Phong's well has water eight months a year. He relies on a different neighbor's well and his generosity during the dry season. Dry well holes dot Phong's farm. When money allows he calls in the well driller to try again. After 20-odd years, there is still no reliable water supply. However, the driller discovered that beneath Phong's land is a formation of sandstone suitable for house building. Phong sells bricks cut from the sandstone to all comers. Two eight-foot-deep quarry pits and six dry well holes add to the security provided by his animals.

Tết Eve is very much like New Year's Eve in the West. People drink, sing, feast, and are entertained by fireworks and televised cultural programs. On Tết Eve at Phong's house, dinner was over at seven p.m. and the old folks settled in for a nap. We got up at 11:30 p.m., dressed in our best clothes, turned the television on, and opened a bottle of tepid champagne. We toasted, hugged, and wished one another a prosperous New Year. By one a.m. we were all back in our beds fast asleep, the doors locked and the mosquito nets in place.

Sometime later I awoke to a dog and monkey chorus. The barking and screeching continued, and I saw the old soldier, machete in one hand and flashlight in the other, slip out the back door. I joined him, unarmed but determined, and so did Thao with a stick in her hand. However, there were no intruders, only a drunken man at the gate standing on his motorbike seat out of reach of the snarling dog; he had been treed, so to speak.

The man wanted to buy ice. When told it was too late, he pointed to the "ice for sale" sign and said, "That means always and now." He did not get any ice but the sign was changed in the morning.

YOU DID GOOD: New Year's Day is a day for receiving visitors and for visiting friends and neighbors. In anticipation, Phong and Huan dressed in new clothes and prepared tea and cakes. They tidied up their house, but no one cleaned the floor. The doors were open, allowing dust and leaves to accumulate inside. Thao told me an old legend about a rich trader who swept the Goddess of Fortune out of his house without realizing it and subsequently became poor. Today, as in ancient times, a woman will not sweep her house on New Year's Day because she fears angering the Goddess.

Seventeen people came to pay their respects to my hosts. Young and old alike consumed the warm champagne that Phong had opened on Tết Eve. They exchanged toasts to prosperity in the New Year and I gave my best rendition of "Happy New Year" in Vietnamese: Chúc Mừng Năm Mới. I was rewarded with smiles and words of encouragement.

Among the visitors was a well-dressed couple in their forties. They were friendly and respectful but I noticed a certain formality not present with earlier guests. "You do good," Phong said. "No say wrong." The well-dressed couple added something in Vietnamese, and Phong translated for me. "They say you a nice American. You humble, not arrogant." Phong had told the couple that I was the director of a charity in Saigon and that his son worked for me. The man, it turned out, was a police officer. Phong was embellishing my activities and our relationship to elevate me in the officer's mind. "They investigate my foreign visitor. No worry."

In the afternoon, Phong's family left to visit friends. They asked Thao and me to stay, explaining that since they now had a television and a refrigerator someone must always be in the house. Otherwise, robbers might steal them. Before, this elderly couple went to the market together every morning for fresh food. Now, one must stay at home to guard the appliances while the other shops. They are prisoners of their possessions now, like many of us.

BAD TOBACCO: The entire family and I sat down for breakfast on the second day of Tết. Huan complained that the dogs had made it difficult to sleep, and she asked me, "You sleep well?" Always sensitive to the feelings of others and the importance of being truthful, I answered, "Yes, I slept well when I was asleep."

The four of us had slept in one room with the TV, fridge, and motorbikes. I told them I had dreamt of a beautiful woman who had walked around the room. She had stopped to open the refrigerator door. The fridge light had shown her counting and rearranging the ice cubes. She had noisily dropped some and then hit her head on the open door as she rose to place them back in the freezer. They all laughed, including Huan, because at 3 a.m. we had all awoken to Huan checking on the ice.

Huan explained that after 1975 she had left her family in the jungle to try to make money in the city. She sold tobacco, gasoline, medicine, and fruit on the streets of Saigon for years and sent money home when she could. To be successful one had to have good merchandise, be prepared, and be lucky. On the night she woke us up, Huan had been checking to make sure there was enough ice to sell the next day.

Huan also told a story of how she had been "captured" one night in 1982 by the Saigon police for selling bad (smuggled) tobacco. The police searched her basket because she had been selling mangos at night. It was suspicious because no one buys mangos then, as they are less likely to be fresh. The police found the tobacco under the mangos and wanted a small bribe to let her go, but Huan refused and shouted anti-government insults at them. The next day her daughters had to pay a large bribe to get her and the "bad" tobacco out of jail. They made excuses for Huan until a policeman relented and told them that their mother must keep her mouth quiet. "All night she say bad things. I hit your mother if she not already old."

TIN WHISTLE: On Saturday nights in Saigon I often listened to a Vietnamese band play Irish jigs, reels, and rebel tunes at Murphy's, an Irish pub. Trim Vietnamese waitresses sang these songs in a sweet brogue. As I watched and listened, I wondered who these musicians were and what circumstances had brought them to Murphy's.

A plump, older Vietnamese woman played the band's tin whistle. She had good posture, dressed well, was courteous to all, and spoke English and French. She was an important and accomplished member of the band and always she smiled. On Tết Eve in the old soldier's jungle home, I learned more about this woman.

We were watching the Tết celebrations on the newly installed television. The show consisted of traditional dances and songs, fireworks, patriotic messages, and commentary, commentary, commentary, just like in America. The camera turned to the dignitaries seated in the privileged seats, and there in the first row, two seats to the right of the party chairman, sat the tin whistle musician. She wore the uniform of an army colonel, and her blouse was covered with medals and ribbons. Three times the camera showed her and three times the same bright smile that lights up Murphy's lit up the screen. The following Saturday night, at Murphy's, I approached her and asked if that had in fact been her on TV. When she admitted that it had been, I asked why she played the tin whistle at an Irish pub. "I like the music and the excitement at Murphy's," she told me, "and the pay is good."

PATROLLING THE HIGHWAY: Thao and I made the return trip from her parents' home to Saigon early in the morning. We wore hats, sunglasses, and long-sleeved shirts to protect us from the sun. Surgical masks covered our faces to keep the dust and pollution from our lungs. Thao explained that police patrol the four-lane divided highway to collect fines because Tết was a holiday when people traveled with money. At one point during the ride, we were pulled over by a baton-pointing policeman. As we rolled to a stop Thao instructed me, "Martin, let him see. Take off hat, glasses, mask." I did and we were brusquely waved on.

I learned that foreigners usually are not stopped because of the language barrier and because the police do not know how they will react. They might complain and cause a problem. That would mean filling out reports and meeting with superiors. The police do not want to spend their time on paperwork and attending legal hearings when they could more profitably spend it patrolling the highway.

On another occasion, while taking me to the bank on her motorbike, Thao was stopped by a policeman for an imagined traffic infraction. After examining her driver's license and registration, which were in order, the officer levied a fine equal to $4. If Thao refused to pay, her motorbike would have been held at the police station for a week or longer, until a magistrate made a decision. Not wanting to be without her bike and fearful that it would be stripped of its parts while in police custody, she argued, pleaded, and negotiated. They finally agreed on $2, which the policeman put in his shirt pocket.

Facetiously the police officer complained that the money would only be enough to pay for his morning coffee. All this occurred in the open with other people nearby. There is nothing remarkable about this tale of petty corruption except that it was so blatant, matter of fact, and accepted. The people resent the extortion and complain to one another about the widespread corruption and theft.

CARDS GREEN: Phong asked me to write to the American government to help his youngest daughter, Man, get a student visa. She was determined to go to America and find a husband. I explained that a letter from me would not help, but he requested a second time. To please him I did as he asked. (See Note 2.) Phong's thank-you letter, with its appealing Tết invitation and evocative reference to two old soldiers, is the product of a gentleman and student of human nature.

I told him I was surprised that he could still speak and write English after living apart from native English speakers for so long. In explanation, he showed me an English-Vietnamese dictionary and confided that he listened to BBC every day.

Man was turned down for a student visa. She did not meet the enrollment requirements at qualified U.S. educational institutions. However, a few weeks later she mysteriously received a three-month business visa. Phong believed I was responsible but I told him no, it was only chance at work. I do not know anyone who can grant visas, I explained. Nevertheless, he asked me to get visas and "cards green" for his wife and himself.

This family and many others want to leave Vietnam, the country I came to live in. They believe life will be easier for them in America. They say, almost as an afterthought, that they will have freedom there. These people are right about more freedom, but no immigrant, or citizen for that matter, is assured of an easy life in the United States. For my part, the absence in Saigon of comforts that I had been accustomed to in America was offset by the excitement and adventure of my life in Vietnam. Living in Vietnam was easier for me than for most Vietnamese because I was a foreigner whose money and status allowed for a fortunate and favored life. Foreigners are usually treated with respect and, in most situations, given the benefit of the doubt. The words, "Earn dollars, spend dong" reflect the fact that the cost of living is lower in Vietnam than in the West, and thus a foreigner's money has more value in Vietnam than in his own country.

CHICKEN DISEASE: Before we departed, Huan served a lunch of vegetable soup, chicken curry, rice, and a garden salad. I was hungry, and the food was good. While we ate, Phong told us that he and his neighbors had lost all their chickens to disease. I listened with interest to his description of the sickness and how these people dealt with the problem.

The farmers knew the disease. It was an old problem. At intervals it returned to kill all the chickens in the area. They knew that when the birds drank a lot of water, got lethargic, started staggering, and collapsed they would die soon. Phong told me that the flesh could be eaten if the chicken is killed before it dies from the virus. Chickens that die from the sickness, and the organs, head, feet, and bones of sick chickens that are killed before they expire, are buried in deep holes away from dogs and pigs, which would die if they ate them. When an outbreak hits, all the chickens in the area die and the people must wait three months before buying new ones.

Phong informed me that the chicken we had just eaten was his last sick chicken. If he was awaiting my reaction, he must have been disappointed. I showed no outward concern. However, for the next few days I mentally charted my bodily functions and every discomfort, ache, and pain.

Scientists feared that the virus would mutate into a disease communicable between humans. Medical authorities were concerned that if that happened, a pandemic similar to the 1917 influenza pandemic, which killed 20,000,000 people, would occur.

At this time, governments were stockpiling a drug that might be a cure for the disease. However, in 2003, it was not known if it would be effective; it had not been tested on humans, only on laboratory animals.

This chicken disease was most certainly the bird flu that six months later spread like wildfire across Southeast Asia. Governments destroyed millions of birds, including caged songbirds, in an attempt to control the epidemic. Human lives were lost, including nearly 100 in Vietnam. The economic cost was incalculable. During this time there were no poultry or eggs in Vietnamese markets. Selling them was illegal. This resulted in a rise in the cost of all food. However, farmers did not surrender their poultry willingly. They had too much invested and, anyway, their chickens seemed healthy enough. Families with caged birds, rather than destroy them, moved them out of sight to back rooms or rooftops.

One could buy "black eggs" and "black chicken" if one wanted to risk it, and many did. One needed only to ask in the market and illegal birds and eggs were brought out of hiding; eggs that cost six cents apiece before the ban later cost 24.

Ben Thanh Market is one of the largest markets in Saigon. It has hundreds of stalls packed together under one roof in an area the size of a football field. Thousands of people move from stall to stall through narrow, ill-lit passageways. Nearly everything one can imagine is for sale and every price can be negotiated. Personal space is non-existent and one quickly learns to tolerate the pressure of surrounding bodies, and to keep one's hand on one's wallet.

Three weeks after the government prohibited the sale of poultry products a new item appeared in the market. Transparent plastic bags clearly marked "5 kilo" and "50,000 VND" ($2.50) were for sale. Neither the contents nor the name of the company was identified. The bags in one box held a yellow powder. In the other, the powder was white. A crowd questioned the vendor who stood behind the products. It is "chicken egg dust" from India, the seller announced. He claimed that the white bags held egg whites and the yellow ones the whole egg. Sales were brisk, two or three bags per buyer. I watched and wondered at their trust. The bags may have contained powdered eggs from India, but I would not buy or consume them under any circumstances.

After five months, the poultry ban was lifted. The affected countries had destroyed infected stock and vaccinated or quarantined healthy birds. The policy, although on a much larger scale, was similar to the actions taken by Phong and his neighbors when all their chickens died. They knew what to do, how to get rid of the disease. Governments did not, or if they did, they acted too slowly. Globalization, expanded world trade, and faster transportation had spread the bird flu quicker and more widely than ever before. Phong and his neighbors know that in time the flu will be back. Indeed, it has returned on a number of occasions to Vietnam and other Southeast Asian countries.

NOT MELLOW YET: In August 2003 I paid another visit to the old soldier's house. I shared the three-hour round-trip taxi ride with his diminutive daughter, Man. She was leaving for America, perhaps forever, and it was her farewell visit. Her plan was to get a long-term student visa or, if that was not possible, meet a good man and get married before her three-month business visa expired. I asked if I would be in the way, and would her parents prefer a last visit without a guest present. Her father was excited that I was coming to visit, Man told me. Furthermore, she confided, "There will be no criticism of me if a foreign guest is in the house."

Upon our arrival, Phong gave me a folded piece of paper. He had written in English to the family in New Jersey with whom his daughter was going to stay. It was a touching and surprisingly well-written plea asking the family to take care of Man. The part I remember is, "Please take care of my daughter, she is not mellow yet."

Phong and Huan walked with their daughter after lunch, giving advice I am sure. I sat in the taxi until Man returned. As we drove away, she kissed her fingertips and waved good-bye.

This ambitious and determined young woman fulfilled her dreams. Mere days before Man's three-month visa was to expire, she married an American. Photographs of the wedding ceremony adorn her parents' cottage. They are pleased that Man escaped to America.

Four

LANDLADY

Save me, oh, save me, from the candid friend.
-George Canning

My landlady, Em Thy, was a commie. She and her husband were from Hanoi, where the husband's father was a high-ranking party official. In 1975 the war's winning side gave the father a splendid house; the previous owner had been an ARVN officer. The victors had confiscated it and given it to one of their own. The son, an army colonel and party member, now owns the house.

Em Thy's father was killed during the "American War" when she was one. Her mother died before she was three from what Em Thy called "the sickness." Her grandmother raised her. "I sad when I think about suffering, but not mad at Americans. It long times ago." I turned to this woman often for advice during the 14 months I rented her house. I trusted Em Thy. She was my friend and looked after me. She never let me down.

* * * * *

NO WASH YET: When I arrived in Saigon in February 2002, I stayed on the fourth floor of a local hotel. My daily $10 rate included breakfast, but no elevator. I spent a lonely month there.

The hotel workers had keys to my room. They came and went when they had jobs to do. One day the laundry woman was going through my dirty clothes. She picked up two shirts, smelled them, and hung them back in the closet. She spoke simple Vietnamese words slowly and used hand gestures so that her meaning would be clear: "No wash yet, wear more." I wore each shirt again and put them in the laundry pile afterward, hoping I'd finally gotten them dirty enough to be washed.

The bats in my bathroom made no noise. While peeing early one morning I looked up and saw four mouse-sized creatures looking back at me. It was light outside and they had returned from their nocturnal hunt. They were hanging upside down from a screen covering a 4" x 6" ventilation hole in the bathroom wall. A protruding cement cover kept the rain and sun out. The bats spent the day in the dark under the shield. They roosted on the screen and kept insects out of the bathroom.

Shortly after arriving in Saigon, I began teaching at a convent. I told one of my students, a Catholic nun, that I wanted to find a house to rent. We went house hunting the next morning. I sat behind her as she drove her motorbike from one rental property to another. Within an hour we had found a house we both liked. I had liked others we had seen, but she had not approved. She had warned, "No safe," "No nice," or "Expensive."

FULL OF MILK: Em Thy was 30-ish, 110 pounds, beautiful with a quick, unforced smile, and full of milk. Her delicate, light-boned arms and thin fingers held her infant as she told me her rental terms. I countered and we began to negotiate. The discussion lasted an hour and included three phone calls to her English friend, Paul, as well as baby breaks. Paul spoke Vietnamese and was able to clarify issues and explain what each of us thought we had agreed to. During one call, he told me to negotiate harder. "It's a sport for them. She will get the better deal." Finally, I agreed to rent the house for $500 a month, paid six months in advance. In addition, she agreed to clean the house and do my laundry in return for two hours of English lessons per week. As we parted she stated that I was the most eligible non-bachelor in Saigon.

The house had three bedrooms, three bathrooms, a roof garden, balcony, kitchen, and living room. Nearby, Em Thy, her two children, and a nanny lived in a cramped three-room apartment. Her husband lived with his regiment near the Chinese border. The area where I would live was safe. Best of all, it was patrolled 24 hours a day by private security guards. When I moved in she winked and declared, "Martin, show me the money." I paid while she explained that she had learned that American expression in Malaysia when her husband was stationed there. Out of the blue, and not as part of her agreement, she cooked me a hot meal twice a week. Em Thy was just being kind to an old bachelor. Protecting your assets is an important principle of capitalism. She indicated that I was the most eligible married bachelor in Saigon. There was enough irony in this arrangement to satisfy anyone.

My house stood along a row of houses in a quiet alley. The alley abutted a soldiers' barracks and for this and other reasons was considered a safe area for foreigners. The houses were attached and looked alike. A glass and metal door opened into my living room from the street. A folding iron gate rolled across the door for security.

Every morning from my roof garden I saw soldiers marching and drilling under the watchful eyes of their officers. There was always some young soldier out of step, going the wrong way, or with his rifle in the wrong position. That is true in all armies. The purpose of the interminable drilling and training is to condition the troops to obey commands instantly so that in the heat of battle everyone acts together and goes the same way. Moreover, it works. Soldiers expose themselves to mortal danger when told to advance under enemy fire. They are trained to put themselves in danger when the natural reaction is to hide or run away.

Em Thy was bright, strong, controlling, and a keen student of human nature. She was also rather protective of me: "Don't be open, Martin, people try control you," she would tell me. "Not nice girls know you here. They young. They beautiful. They come you house and get you. They take you money and go. Close you door. Not let them in house. Say no, Martin, say no." I put a string on my finger.

My students and Vietnamese friends gave me similar warnings. "Be careful, Martin, be careful. Thief man come." I heeded their warnings, but Icarus got warnings, too. Read between the lines.

House owners must be licensed to rent to foreigners and are obligated to register them with the police. Required information includes the tenant's occupation and marital status. I told Em Thy I was a bachelor and a retired lawyer. Before departing for the police station with the registration form and my passport, she pointed to the occupation section and laughed softly. She had written my answers to all the questions in Vietnamese except one. In the box for occupation, she had written "Freeman."

My comfortable Saigon house contrasted sharply with the dark, primitive, bamboo and reed hooches where I lived in the Delta during 1963. Those shelters lacked running water and privacy—there was always an entranceway but never a door. The battalion generator powered a single light bulb attached to a frayed cord that hung from the low ceiling. Rats scurried across the floor and stinging insects dropped from the stalk-and-frond roof. A leaf-sided privy was nearby, but there was usually a line to use it. I was totally immersed in a foreign culture and an undeveloped rural environment under wartime conditions, most of the time separated from other Americans. Today, it surprises me that I was able to operate under those circumstances. For some reason I accepted it all matter-of-factly and without the depression and neurosis that is associated with isolation. I was a stranger there, yet I thrived.

FAKE MEN: One afternoon Em Thy answered a knock at my front door. Two unsmiling men dressed in brown uniforms faced her. One of them peered with interest inside my house. The other man held up a piece of paper with numbers printed on it. She took one look, shouted "Go away," slammed the door, and quickly made two phone calls. Afterwards she turned to me and counseled: "No pay fake men. No cyclo men sleep house. No give beggars at door."

The men at the door had been trying to collect the electric bill by pretending to work for the electric company. One of her phone calls was to the electric company and the other to the police.

"Only foreigners pay fake men," she said.

A prior American tenant had let a homeless cyclo driver sleep in the house, and had actually given him a set of house keys. Cyclos are three-wheeled pedal bicycles used to transport people and goods. Poor, and widely considered uncouth and unsavory, cyclo drivers are near the bottom of the economic and social order. After three weeks of sharing his house with the cyclo driver, the American came home one evening and found that the man had left and all the appliances had been stolen.

"If Martin give beggars," Em Thy warned me, "they stay you door and cause problem for you neighbors. Give in street, but no let beggar know where you house."

Em Thy helped me get settled and gave freely of her advice:

- Wash clothes, little soap, little water. Cost less.
- Gas go boom in kitchen, no use, off tank.
- Juice expensive, drink water.
- No eat restaurant, expensive.
- They cheat you in market, go Em Thy.
- Rest in day, you old.
- Careful sun. Wear hat. You skin white.
- No motorbike. No safe. Go taxi.
- Keep fridge cool, cold cost money.
- Tell problem. I fix. I fix.
- You old, but still sweet.

After cleaning the house, she took my garbage away and placed it in front of her own house. "No put street in front foreigner's house," she told me.

A common form of transportation in Vietnam is the xe ôm, which translates as "motorbike hug." The term describes how one clings to the driver for safety as he ferries you about. A "Honda driver" is a xe ôm driver.

One night, after a xe ôm driver dropped me off in my alley, I went to the wrong house and tried my key in the padlock. Several neighbors appeared immediately to inform me of my mistake, and then took the opportunity to instruct me about my inadequate security measures.

"You no use enough lock."

"You must lock when go out."

"Bad men everywhere."

Apparently, my neighbors had taken note of my comings and goings, how many locks I used, and which doors I tried to open. The driver watched all this and later told the nuns I had taught that night.

In New York, I had never locked a door at my house. Em Thy gave me five padlocks, but I used only three at a time, two on the gate and one on the glass door. To confound thieves who had stolen or purchased a key from previous tenants, I was told to rotate the five locks. Every time I entered or left I fumbled through five keys, trying to find which one went with which lock. This was a fitting metaphor for my attempts to comprehend what was going on around me. I had to try different ways to understand this culture and these people.

REST AND RECREATION: Vietnamese lived in the houses on either side of mine. They were friendly young couples from the North with children. In the building 12 feet across from me lived three families whom I thought were Indians. Two of the three men from these families went out every day. The women stayed home with their children. The third man stayed at home to watch the women. He wore a colored cloth wrapped Indian-fashion from waist to ankles, was shirtless, and patrolled the alley and house all day long. He was the keeper of the keys and of the women. I was told that the women had to ask for his permission before visiting the local shops; they never went out alone.

The man stared expressionlessly from his balcony when not walking the alley. My bedroom, with its small balcony, faced the Indians' house. The balconies protruded from our houses so that they were only six feet apart. On my first morning there, I awoke to find him watching me in my bed. I did not like his presence in the alley, nor, for that matter, did the Vietnamese, but he was there and not going away. I gave him big, exaggerated hellos and waves, which he always returned enthusiastically. Later, after the Indians had moved, Em Thy shared with me the neighbors' suspicion that these people were not Indians but Tamil rebels taking a rest from their war in Sri Lanka.

NOW IT COME BACK: My landlady paid me a visit, infant girl in her arms. I put aside my dinner of a peanut butter and jelly sandwich and a Heineken to listen to her. I repeated what she told me and asked if I had understood her correctly. Back and forth we spoke, Vietnamese to English, English to Vietnamese. Her message was, "If police come door no open. But if do, or police talk you on street and ask who you, say you marry Em Thy husband sister."

"But that is not true," I replied.

"No worry," she said. "They write down you marry Em Thy husband sister in America and then no trouble renting house to foreigner."

I was surprised to learn that a party member's sister lived in the United States. Em Thy insisted it was true. Over time, I learned that such family situations existed and were the result of the war and opportunism. Circumstances and allegiances account for much of what we do.

Em Thy explained that an old regulation prevented military officers from renting their houses to foreigners. "It go away, but now come back." I took a long pull on my beer, as she added, "No worry, Martin, no worry it okay. Maybe police no come."

It was just another quiet evening in Saigon.

A few days later she informed me, "Trouble go away. Police my friend now."

MORNING CALLS: Most mornings the sunlight awoke me and I was up and out for a walk before 6:30 a.m. It was a good time to observe and reflect. One Saturday I slept in and was awakened at seven a.m. by my telephone. A nun was calling about a schedule change. Too sleepy to understand what she was saying and afraid I would get the time and date wrong, I told her I would call her back.

As I lay back on my pillow the phone rang again. It was an assistant manager from a street children's organization calling to say she had just received a scholarship to attend a conference and school in America. She thanked me for helping her with the application.

This was followed immediately by a phone call from Em Thy, who announced, "I come cook." The line went dead before I could respond. She was in the kitchen when I came out of the bathroom 15 minutes later. Her infant daughter was asleep on the floor while her eight-year-old son was in my living room kicking his soccer ball. She explained that she had agreed to bring food to her son's school for lunch that day but that she had no cooking gas. In cities, most cooking is done with propane. In rural areas, charcoal is favored.

A LITTLE LEFT: I had been given four 3' x 1 ½' lacquered wooden panels depicting a countryside scene of bamboo, water buffalo, peasants in conical hats, thatch houses, and a red flowering summer tree. My seminarian students had presented them to me amid speeches and applause at the last class before their two-month summer break. During July and August they go to the countryside to live and work with the poor.

Em Thy and I directed her husband while he secured the panels to my wall. First, he had to hold the panels up and move them from place to place while she and I debated where they would look best. It was my art and my rented wall, but I put them where she wanted because I guessed they would not go up unless she agreed. Another commie victory.

The colonel worked from a ladder while his lady critiqued from the couch. He climbed the ladder, measured, drilled, hammered, and then did it all over when Em Thy decided that the alignment was not correct. I was quiet during the process but Em Thy supervised with zeal: "A little left. More right. Move up. Move down." My former foe had a stern master. Revenge need not be violent; it can take many forms.

However, Em Thy's husband was no slouch. He had just returned from a four-week stay in Sweden and Norway where he led a Vietnamese delegation on government business. This important, dour man stoically endured the American's art hanging; no false pride there. Maybe some PhD candidate funded by U.S. government grants and assisted by undergrads wanting to become PhDs can tell us in 800 pages why this episode explains the communist victory in 1975.

STAY LIVING ROOM: Some of the best-paying jobs in Vietnam are in the homes of foreigners, as housekeepers, cooks, or drivers. However, some "foreigner jobs" are more desirable than others. If a Vietnamese woman has an opportunity to choose, she will turn down a job with an Asian family in favor of a Western one. The Western family pays more and supposedly treats its Vietnamese employees better. Newspapers carry stories of beatings, sexual assaults, and other ill treatment of Vietnamese, usually by employers from other Asian countries.

Supposedly, the best Asians to work for are the Japanese. As for Westerners, one experienced Vietnamese woman told me that the French are difficult, the Germans are confused, the English are unfriendly, and the Americans, although friendly, courteous, and generous, change their minds too often.

Mai was 50 years old, attractive, underdressed (if you get my drift), and spoke slowly. She worked six days a week, nine hours a day, as a house servant for an Indian family. It took her 45 minutes to bicycle every morning from the room she rented to her employer's home. She traveled both ways in the dark. Her monthly salary was $42.

She knocked on my door early one afternoon. Someone had told her I gave free English lessons to poor people, and she needed to learn English to keep her job. Once a week, while the Indian family took its siesta, she was allowed to come to my house for lessons. She had purchased an English instruction book for house servants. It contained sections on Greetings, Cleaning, Cooking, Politeness, Privacy, Shopping, Toilet Care, Message Taking, Child Care, and, would you believe, Royalty! She repeated after me sentences I read from the book: "Give the baby a bath. Clean the kitchen. Where is the toilet paper? Get it for me. We are going on vacation next week. Take out the garbage, it smells. Change the bedclothes. The Master wants…"

From time to time Mai vented about her job and the family she worked for. They were not fair. When they took a vacation, they did not pay her. Her pay was too low. The wife spoke unkindly to her and now the children were doing the same thing. "But I must work," Mai told me. "Jobs hard to get and I alone." She said that before 1975 she had worked in a bar and had lots of money and boyfriends. Her hemlines are still a little short and her clothes still a little tight.

Em Thy disapproved of Mai; she was suspicious of her intentions and did not think it was wise for me to teach Mai in my house. "Keep door open and stay living room," she advised.

After two months, Mai stopped coming for English lessons. She gave me neither notice nor explanation. Maybe she lost her job, or maybe Em Thy warned her "stay away Martin house."

Five

LIFE IN THE WARD

Better is a neighbor that is near than a brother far off.
-Proverbs 27:10

Vietnam's population is larger than that of every country in Europe except Russia. Only 12 countries in the world have more inhabitants than Vietnam's 90 million people. By 2050, the number is projected to reach 120 million.

The government has instituted policies to limit population growth. In the past, especially in the countryside, large families were common. Today, city families are smaller due to regulations that permit only two children. State workers who exceed the limit have their salaries reduced. Although restricted to two children, many rural families break this rule, seemingly without punishment.

Vietnam is divided into provinces and municipalities. Each political subdivision is further partitioned into districts. Districts are made up of wards and wards are split into cells.

On Election Day, national, provincial, and local officials are chosen. Citizens get to choose from candidates nominated by the Communist Party. In my district the voters could vote for any three of five such candidates.

Starting at age 18, voting is required by law. If you do not cast a ballot, police come to your house seeking an explanation. Frequently, one family member votes for the others. Proxy voting and police enforcement ensure that 99% of the people vote, thus allowing for government claims of election legitimacy. People understand that it is a farce. There is no real choice. "Elections are not real," were the words of a young student I taught.

*****

WARD MEETINGS: I lived in the same ward for three years. It was a safe area and only a five-minute walk from the center of Saigon. I spoke to everyone I passed in my neighborhood, especially the security guards. Everyone knew me. I was the old American soldier doing charity work.

The ward conducts elections and contracts for enhanced security and sanitation services. The leaders settle disputes, hire security guards who patrol 24 hours a day, and ensure that the national flag is flown from every house on holidays. The ward organizes parades, festivals, and youth activities. Homeowners are levied a small fee for these services.

Once a month, the ward officers hold an evening meeting with the homeowners. In the motorbike parking lot at the back of my house, tables and 25 plastic chairs were arranged, as in a classroom. An electric wire ran from a nearby house to the lamp on the ward chief's table. A young woman sat to his right and recorded what was said. My balcony overlooked the parking lot, which allowed me to observe the proceedings. Problems discussed included rats, prostitution, crime, garbage disposal, illegal businesses, bad neighbors, nighttime construction, and landlord-tenant problems. The homeowners were serious and civil. Their questions included "Where does the ward money go?" and "How is it spent?" They demanded an accounting.

Meeting attendance is mandatory. If homeowners, all of whom are from the North, do not attend, they will be questioned; if their explanation is not satisfactory, they may be fined. At one meeting, people pleaded unsuccessfully that the meetings be held every three months. Meeting every month was a waste of time, they argued.

These meetings are held all over Vietnam. They address local concerns and are part of the control mechanism to ensure compliance with party doctrine and policies.

DRINKING TIME: My door was open and I was sitting at my desk awaiting Thao. A young schoolgirl appeared at the door and then disappeared into the night. When she returned several minutes later, she asked me for water. Her blue and white uniform was dirty and too large for her slight frame. A black book bag hung from her small shoulder. Her initial caution gone, she told me her name was Cuc, that she was seven, and that she was waiting for her mother, who worked for a sick foreign man in a house nearby.

The man's house was empty so she was standing in the dark alley. She wanted to rest in my living room but I told her, for my protection and her education, "No, a girl should not go into a man's house without her mother." I allowed her to sit in the doorway. She pouted a bit while drinking her water and then gave me a long explanation of her predicament. I did not understand most of it. Her words and pantomime for the Vietnamese words "drinking time," "river," "school," "afraid," and "father" mystified me. She accepted fruit and more water when I offered them.

When Thao arrived Cuc began to tell her story again, but she ran off before finishing it. She was back in 20 minutes, showered and in clean clothes. The sick foreign man (an American named Randy) and her mother had returned from buying medicine. Her mother was coming to visit soon, she told us.

Cuc's mother was 42 and tired looking. She was dressed as if she were from a countryside village, in drab cotton pajamas. She thanked me for being kind to her daughter and volunteered her story. Thao translated.

The mother had moved into Randy's house because she could not take the beatings she suffered at home. Her husband did not want Cuc to stay with his wife. He was lonely and insisted that Cuc live with him. While Cuc's mother took care of Randy, her husband was responsible for Cuc. He picked her up after school, washed her clothes, fed her, and made her bathe.

She explained that although this sounded like a good arrangement, her daughter was afraid to stay alone with her father. His "drinking time" began at seven p.m., and that was when he used to yell at and hit his wife. If she were not home, he would hit Cuc instead. Cuc's mother complained to the police, but they said it was a family matter and would not talk to her husband. Cuc was caught between her drunken, abusive father and her fearful mother. She had chosen her mother and safety.

HE IS NOT EDUCATED: Cuc had eluded her father after school that day and retraced the one-and-a-half-hour journey to Randy's house, a journey she and her mother had taken together months earlier. She had successfully negotiated the chaotic Saigon River passage and the dangerous city streets. Adults pay 14 cents for the ferry, motorbikes and bicycles cost 7 cents, and children are carried across free. Cuc's mother did not know her daughter was coming and so the child sought safety in my house when she found herself alone, and afraid, in the dark alley. Referring to me with a quick glance, Cuc told her mother: "He is a good man; I am safe with him." This child had shown remarkable resourcefulness and insight. Cuc had solved her problem, but only for the short term.

"Your father will be angry," her mother said. "He doesn't know where you are and he is alone."

"Tell him you picked me up at school," Cuc replied.

She wanted her mother to lie, but the mother explained that it was wrong for a wife to lie to her husband and for a daughter to lie to her father. The two of them eventually left, but not before the mother called her husband and told him Cuc would live with her now. I could hear him shouting over the telephone that there would be trouble now.

A few days later I spoke with Randy about Cuc's situation. I learned that she was not the only daughter in the family. Cuc had a 19-year-old sister who happened to be Randy's live-in girlfriend. The sister worked in a bar. She wore shorts and a halter, leaving her tattooed arms, back, and legs uncovered. She was pretty, but loud and coarse; Em Thy declared that she was not a Vietnamese lady. Cuc's mother shopped, cooked, laundered, and cleaned the house for the couple.

I expected this real-life drama would continue and I was right. Two weeks later, at 10 p.m., the father placed himself in front of the house where his wife and daughters were living. He bellowed, "Give me Cuc." Repeatedly he shouted the words. Doors nearby opened and neighbors peered about for the angry voice. Many left their houses and stood near the infuriated man, observing silently. Curious, but cautious, I watched from my front balcony as he increased his pitch and the rapidity of his words. When no answer came from Randy's house, he banged on the metal gate and yelled some more. His words turned vulgar.

Finally, a timid response could be heard from the house. "Go home, Daddy, I live here now."

A second response followed, in a male voice that was deep, angry, and American. "She's my daughter now."

Naturally, Cuc's father was not placated by what he heard.

A security guard arrived wielding a red stick and stood between the irate father and Randy's house. Next on the scene was the ward chief. No amount of pleading could quiet the father. Sympathetic words and conciliatory gestures did no good. The police were called.

Six green-uniformed policemen trotted into the alley, nightsticks held horizontally, shoulder-high, in two-handed grips. They carried no firearms; usually, police here are not armed. They sent the spectators home and moved Cuc's father down the alley towards the street. He stopped below my balcony, though, to berate the police captain in charge. The officer chided him for coming into the ward and starting trouble. Cuc's father was told to go home, sober up, and then return during the day to talk to the ward chief. He explained that he had been promised money for his daughter, but the

American had not paid it. He would not leave. The police captain threatened him with jail:

"Bad things will happen there."

"I won't go unless I get money for the ferry."

Randy was persuaded to pay for the ferry and the man left. Em Thy later explained to me that since Cuc's parents had no wedding papers, under Vietnamese law the girl belonged to the mother. The father had no rights because he had not legally married Cuc's mother. Fearing he would not get what he wanted, he caused a scene to embarrass the American into paying him. "He come back drunk," Em Thy predicted.

The neighbors disapproved of the living arrangement at Randy's house. They were scandalized by the behavior of the 19-year-old daughter and her father. Although sympathetic to the plight of Cuc and her mother, the ward residents wanted the situation resolved. Randy was rather large, middle-aged, and, like his girlfriend, tattooed. Only once was he criticized in my presence. Someone said, "He not educated."

Cuc was still at Randy's house with her mother and older sister when I moved to a different part of Saigon. I do not know the outcome of this situation. However, at the time of my move the American was not sure how long he could let her stay. If the father continued to complain to the police that a foreigner has taken his family away, the government might revoke Randy's visa and deport him. In conflicts with foreigners, Vietnamese win disputes, especially those involving family matters.

AN UNNECESSARY APOLOGY: Five xe ôm drivers await fares in the alley, which serves as an entrance to the ward. Even though they compete with one another for business, they join to chase new drivers away from their turf. For a negotiated fee, a driver will take you to your destination. You sit behind him as he makes his way through the perilous traffic.

Minh, a muscular 38-year-old former soldier, was my preferred driver. He was helpful, reliable, and I felt safe with him. He drove slowly, looked both ways, and signaled before turning. He did not attempt to speed ahead of everyone else and did not race to beat others to a spot on the road. Minh bathed and did not smoke while driving, so I did not have to endure the all too common xe ôm curse: a wet dog odor and cigarette ash blowing into my face. He wore a helmet, too, a rarity then in Saigon, and, uniquely, toted a second helmet for his passengers. Em Thy advised me to wear a hat under the helmet to avoid "helmet insect problem." I liked him and gave him my business whenever possible.

In 1992, while driving an army truck, he killed a child who had chased a ball onto the road. He said the brakes had not worked. The army said he had been careless. Minh was imprisoned for six months and then discharged. If he had had money to pay the boy's family, Minh believes, he would not have been jailed.

One night I went to the alley to arrange a ride for the following morning. I was looking for Minh, who had recently taken me to the same address, a two-hour round trip. He knew the way and I knew his price. I told one of the other drivers that I wanted to speak to Minh and explained why. He asked me, "Minh not here in morning, I take you?" I agreed.

Minh was talking to the backup driver when I arrived the next morning. Minh turned to me and we confirmed that he would take me for the same price as before. Our conversation was clear, no ambiguity. A simple transaction, I thought.

That evening, after returning from my trip with Minh, I walked past the backup driver. "Mr. Martin," he hailed me. He was tipsy; too much beer. In a measured, respectful tone, he reviewed our discussion of the previous evening. He conceded that he was to take me on the trip only if Minh was not available, but he was upset that I had not told him I was going with Minh. Apparently, I had slighted him. When I pointed out that he was standing next to Minh when I hired Minh for the trip, he said, yes, of course, but you did not tell me.

For what seemed like the thousandth time in my life, I apologized—not because I had done anything wrong but just to move the situation along. My contrition, however, only encouraged him.

"My life hard. No make big money. Drivers steal customer. They don't help." He ended his venting with the accusing words: "You no tell me."

A crowd of curious onlookers had been listening to his monologue. Someone lightly touched my left arm. A neighborhood security guard was at my side, red stick in hand. He said he had listened to our discussion, and the driver and I were friends. We must shake hands and the crowd must go home. We did and they did.

I tried to make sense of it all later that evening, and concluded that he had confronted me so that I would feel guilty, and perhaps give him future business.

A STRANGE POLICEMAN: Early one evening I answered a tap at my door. A tall man dressed in a long-sleeved black shirt and pressed black pants stood there holding a book. In English he barked, "I am police."

"What do you want?" I answered politely in Vietnamese.

"Money," he responded, again loudly and in English.

"What for?"

He had exhausted his English by this point and answered my last question in Vietnamese. The police were collecting money for disabled children, he said. He showed me their photos and a photo of himself in a police uniform. I sensed something wrong, so I turned him down. He left quickly—a little too quickly, I thought. There were no threats, no pleading, not a word.

When Em Thy heard about the incident she explained that if the ward leaders approve, the police can come and ask for charity money, but they never come alone. They come with a uniformed policeman and a ward official who introduces them.

A security guard investigated; he reported that the man had not asked my neighbors for money and that the ward chief did not know who the man was.

"He is strange policeman or fake policeman," Em Thy said.

I understood "strange policeman" to mean an actual policeman from elsewhere in Saigon who was unknown in our ward.

"You were right to no give," she went on. "But Martin, no open your door to strange people."

This was advice I used to give my children.

At a parking lot near my house, attendants guarded motorbikes 24 hours a day for 14 cents apiece. My front door was in their line of sight. The security guard asked the attendants to call him if there was any problem at my door. The parking lot owner instructed the attendants to look after me.

Two weeks later Em Thy asked if I would teach English, without charging a fee, to the eight-year-old son of a "good" policeman. I thought it a good idea, a little insurance, and she did, too. Spending one hour on Saturday mornings doing what I enjoyed was a small price for additional security and peace of mind.

BUMPTIOUS USHER: Song, dance, and music are integral parts of Vietnamese culture. Thousands here make their living performing traditional and Western-style routines.

I attended a classical music concert at Notre Dame Cathedral. Brahms, Bach, Beethoven, and various Russian composers were featured. Before the music started, a bumptious seminarian in an ankle-length black cassock confronted me. Fiddling with the vertical line of shiny black buttons running down his cassock, he insisted I sit in the front of the church with the other Westerners. I moved but was not happy. The deference that Vietnamese often show to foreigners is annoying. It goes beyond politeness and is unmerited. Why should I get preferred seating because of my white skin and Western face?

Vietnamese who were unaware of the seating priority were turned away when they tried to sit in the front seats. There were some ugly scenes; a few local people demanded to know why the best seats were reserved for foreigners. Other Westerners did not seem bothered, but it made me uncomfortable.

I attended many artistic performances in this country and each time was amazed at the amount and decibel level of audience noise. Being quiet and attentive are attitudes not expected or required. Performers play right through all sorts of raucous distractions: mothers meeting sons not seen in 30 years; a child lost months ago, suddenly found; cell phones ringing; keys dropping; worlds colliding. Anything goes, or so it seems. No dark-suited attendants reprimand noisy guests.

The 30-piece orchestra began with a Bach double concerto, followed by a piano solo—a simple, peaceful melody. Three singers, in turn, sang from famous operas. Mid-aria, the day-release crowd from the respiratory floor of a nearby hospital decided to compete with the singer by coughing, hacking, and clearing their throats. The singer was resolute, indomitable, and determined. It was the loudest rendition of this aria that I had ever heard.

GREAT GRANDMOTHER: An 84-year-old great-grandmother from Hai Phong, the North's second largest city and main port, lived near me with her granddaughter. She spent her days on a stool in front of her door tending a cooking fire, preparing vegetables, sleeping, and talking to her four-year-old great-granddaughter. I waved and said hello in Vietnamese whenever I passed, and both she and the little girl responded in kind, but we'd never had a conversation. She saw everything that went on in the alley.

One Sunday morning, when I opened my door to walk to church, I found her waiting for me. She was pale, bent, and fragile-looking. A single black tooth protruded from between her dark lips. Betel nut chewing and time had taken the others.

"Where are you going?" she said in Vietnamese. When I explained, she asked, "Can I go with you next Sunday? I can't go alone because my eyesight is poor and I am afraid of being injured by a motorbike while crossing the streets."

I thought of my mother who died at 93. In the last years of her life, I took her to Mass on Sundays and I still feel the warmth of her presence and the joy of those mornings.

The following Sunday we walked arm-in-arm to church, the great-grandmother in her blue-and-white áo dài, and me in dark pants and white long-sleeved shirt. She talked all the way there and back, in a whisper at times, but loudly when excited. She pointed with bent forefinger and raised thumb, and jabbed the air with her fist to add emphasis to her words. While her free hand gesticulated, the other vigorously pulled and jerked my arm. People stared, obviously puzzled by our relationship. During Mass she was quiet and attentive.

We had our photograph taken in front of the church. Later that day the photographer delivered three photos to my door costing 14 cents each. The old woman wanted them to show to her friends in Hai Phong. She hoped to return there soon, but she said her granddaughter would not let her. Later I asked the granddaughter if this was true, and she explained, "Yes, it is true because there is no family to care for her in Hai Phong and her friends are all dead."

FOUR SETS OF LIPS: Most Vietnamese households do not have computers. However, there are numerous Internet cafés where for three cents per minute secondhand computers procured from industrial countries are available. Communicating by email can be a frustrating experience because the infrastructure in Vietnam is inadequate and the computers are quirky. In addition, one must contend with gangs of children playing computer games at adjacent terminals.

Foreigners and wealthy Vietnamese frequent upscale Internet cafes at double the normal cost. These cafes offer modern equipment, broadband access, air-conditioning, and beverages. Cigarette smoke and the babble of people making Internet telephone calls fill the air.

The Internet café I used was a four-minute walk from my house. It was clean, air-conditioned, and the staff was competent and friendly. Nightspots lined the street. There was something for everyone. Sometimes, after wrestling with the Internet in the early evening, I would stop to have a beer at a lively bar. The Vietnamese musicians were good and the sax player excellent. One night I ordered a bottle of beer and the barkeep asked for $1.75. "Too expensive," I said, and he responded, "Okay, $1.65." He lowered the price to $1.55 when I still objected, and finally to $1.50, but only after checking with his boss.

Japan is a major investor in Vietnam. Many Japanese businessmen and their families live in Saigon. They stand out because they are taller and lighter-skinned than the Vietnamese. Japanese women are easy to identify because of their distinctive style of dress. The Japanese are respectful and well behaved. The area I lived in is sometimes called "Little Tokyo" because of its many Japanese restaurants, clubs, and food stores.

Across from the Internet café was a French restaurant with an accomplished jazz pianist. One evening I sat at the bar to have a draft and listen to the music. The only other customers were a table of seven jolly Japanese businessmen. They were gradually making their way through the cocktail menu; every 15 minutes or so the waitress would go from their table to the bar with a new selection. The three bartenders, all young girls in short dresses and flimsy tops, were having great fun preparing the drinks. They laughed, giggled, and tasted the concoctions as they mixed them.

The waitress would take the last sip and had the last word on what ingredient to add. She had to deal with the men. "More red," she said, and quickly the barkeep added red liquor from a bottle behind the bar. The mixture was poured into martini glasses and one of the bartenders winked at me and said, "007." The men were too far-gone to remember what they had ordered or to know what they were drinking. Alcohol is a disinfectant, I knew, but I wondered if it was potent enough to kill the germs left by four sets of lips. Although alcohol kills harmful microbes, I have been told it nourishes romance. All the while, the piano player played on and I watched from my stool.

KILL HIM NEXT TIME: After the war ended in 1975 a united Vietnam was impoverished and destitute. The country's infrastructure was in ruins and the countryside strewn with unexploded munitions. The Vietnamese Communist Party turned to Russia, its socialist brother and war ally, for assistance. Russia responded with material aid and thousands of expert advisors—engineers, technicians, economists, agronomists, doctors, planners, and military specialists roamed the country. Russians, like their American predecessors, spent their time telling the Vietnamese how to grow rice. In return, Russia received long-term use of the former U.S. Navy base at Cam Ranh Bay.

After 1975, Russian language courses were offered in schools and many young, ambitious Vietnamese mastered it in the hope that it would lead to success. Although many learned Russian, it became obsolete when the Russians were asked to leave and Vietnam opened its doors to foreign investment in December 1987. One of my English students, a 50-year-old vice-director of a university, confided that although she is fluent in Russian it is no longer of value to her or her country.

Many Russians stayed in Vietnam, one of whom was my neighbor, Ivan. Barrel-chested, 6 feet 3 inches tall, bald, always shirtless and in shorts and sandals, he lived with his 4-foot 11-inch Vietnamese girlfriend, Hoa. She came from District Four where, my neighbors told me, all the robbers, murderers, mafia, and prostitutes live. Ivan moved into her house shortly after her husband disappeared. The husband had not been seen in four years and neighbors speculated that he had been killed.

Ivan had six dogs, all the same small breed, and he exercised them two at a time, a leash in each hand. Six times a day, forty-two times a week, this formidable man and his animals annoyed everyone. The pooches fouled the alley, barked noisily, and challenged people on foot, seated on doorsteps, or on motorbikes. Ivan pretended to set the hounds on people and then slowly pulled them back, laughing as he calmed the animals. He cussed and shouted at anyone who complained. The couple was greatly disliked. Neighborhood women pointed at them to show disrespect.

Em Thy told me the police usually would not come when called about them. "Police say Ivan small problem they can't fix." She related how, one day before I arrived, Ivan had fought with two Vietnamese men. Their motorbike had scared his dogs. He had overpowered them, locked their motorbike in his house, and would not give it back. When the police arrived at his door, Ivan met them, the bike owner, and onlookers with a raised sword. Hoa held a hammer. They were ready. There was cursing and heckling but no one was hurt. It took an hour to sort it all out. Apologies were exchanged and the bike was returned. Ivan was admonished in front of the crowd, and in a loud voice the police officer in charge told the neighbors not to call the police again about the Russian. "Kill him next time."

These words were intended to scare the Russian and make him behave. However, the words emboldened the neighbors as well. Some problems have many solutions, my landlady explained.

DISTURBING THE PEACE: My students parked their motorbikes in my living room. The bikes were safe there. The living room opened directly onto the alley via wide doors that swung inward. Every house had a concrete ramp in the middle of its steps, which made it easy to bring motorbikes inside. Some students dismounted at the door and pushed their bikes in; others rode directly into the room.

One morning I was teaching English in my living room to two young women. Their motorbikes rested on kickstands next to an interior wall. I had left the door open to catch the afternoon breeze. At one point in the lesson I became aware that they were glancing toward the door. From the alley could be heard the gruff, then shrill sounds of human conflict. I looked and saw Ivan dragging a small Vietnamese woman by her hair into a nearby house. With his free hand he beat her, and she screamed with each blow. Ivan then returned to his own house and closed the door. Neighbors hurried out of their houses to tend to the woman. They discussed the situation, muttered, and pointed towards Ivan's house.

Em Thy came to my door and stepped inside. As she walked to my telephone she said, "I call police." The three of us listened to her speak excitedly into the mouthpiece, describing what she had seen and asking them to come. "Police come," she said as she left, and then, from the alley, as an afterthought, I heard her add "again."

Many families have a live-in house servant. Some have several. For less than $50 a month a woman will live in your house to clean, shop, cook, and care for your children. Ivan had a servant who was also required to clean up the filth left by his dogs. Van, the servant, told the neighbors that no amount of cleaning could get the urine smell out of the floor and that she did not want to work there anymore. Van gave notice and told Ivan that she had taken a job in the countryside. However, it was not the truth. The day after saying goodbye to Ivan the woman began working three doors away. The insult was too much for Hoa. She attacked the servant on the street, raining blows on her head and face. Ivan intervened when Van began winning the fight and that was when I saw him drag her into her new employer's house.

A policeman arrived 20 minutes later in a 30-year-old U.S. Army jeep. He questioned the three persons involved and the eyewitnesses. Van refused to press charges because she was afraid of retaliation. The police officer made Ivan pay for Van to be patched up at a hospital, and then he fined the three of them $12 each for disturbing the peace. Because of this and other incidents, the neighbors petitioned the official in charge of the ward to evict Ivan. The neighbors did not think it would happen because of Hoa's mafia connections in District Four.

Late one afternoon, the difficult couple challenged the lady who had filed the petition. The woman stood her ground in front of her house as they shouted back and forth. Ivan placed himself between her and his wife to keep Hoa from hitting the lady. Then he would get excited and turn on the woman and Hoa would have to keep them apart. For 20 minutes, back and forth, the argument and the carefully synchronized dance continued. No blows landed. The woman was not intimidated.

The following morning Em Thy reported to me the parting exchange between the woman and Ivan's wife:

"I know who and what you are," the woman had shouted. "We all know. You are a bad person and a bad neighbor."

"Yes," Hoa responded. "I am both and there is nothing you can do about it. You are all afraid of me and my family."

A final story about Ivan reveals that the local folk have had enough of him. He knocked on my door one evening after the Tết holidays. His face had been bloodied in a beating administered by three men. A young Russian man was with him and they were trying to recruit Western men to go fight the Vietnamese assailants. After thoughtful consideration, I politely declined the invitation and advised him to get his face bandaged. The police arrived while we were talking and took Ivan's statement. They sent the young Russian home and told me to close my door. The police and Ivan cruised the neighborhood looking for the Vietnamese men, without success. I never found out what caused the incident, and the neighbors either did not know or would not tell me.

Six

SIDEWALKS, STREETS, AND VEHICLES

Chaos is the score upon which reality is written.
-Henry Miller

One day someone will write a learned paper about how the streets and sidewalks of Saigon reflect the soul of the Vietnamese. The Vietnamese do not act as if they live in a police state; they seem to do what they want without concern for the consequences, especially when they are in or on a vehicle. They are free-spirited, determined, and dreadful drivers.

Saigon is by far the largest city in Vietnam, covering 760 square miles, a large portion of which is rural. The number of people living in Saigon is unknown, but most estimates exceed eight million. Although several explanations are offered, the derivation and meaning of the word Sai Gon is lost in history. One theory holds that it means "the wood of the kapok tree," another "the forest of the emperor." Northerners refer to it as "Ho Chi Minh City," the name they gave the city when they conquered South Vietnam in 1975. Southerners call the city "Saigon" out of habit, or as a rebellious political statement.

*****

BUILDING NUMBERS: The city is divided into 26 districts; some are identified by number and some others by name. Buildings are numbered in order most of the time, beginning usually with one. Even numbers are normally on one side of the street and odd numbers on the other.

Often, the name of a street will change as it crosses into another district. Even if the name remains the same, the numbering may begin anew at a district border. Consequently, some streets have two or three buildings bearing the identical address. Therefore, it is important to know in which district a building is located before looking for it.

After 1975, many streets were renamed, and then 15 years later some reverted to their original names. Sometimes an avenue has two names, one for one side and another for the opposite side. The house at 17/22 Le Thanh Ton is directly across the pavement from the building at 8A/C1 Thai Van Lung. Bewilderingly, 15B/31 Le Thanh Ton and 8A/E1 Thai Van Lung are the addresses of adjacent houses.

CHAOS: Most buildings are attached, without front, back, or side yards. A small business often occupies the ground floor. Living space is on the second and third floors. During the mornings, families virtually live on the sidewalk. It is their living room. Some cook, eat, and conduct business there. Some take siestas in hammocks tied to whatever is convenient while others stretch out on hemp mats. Still others snooze while reclining on the seat of a parked motorbike.

Motorbikes are repaired on the sidewalk, where shoes, food, and clothes are often displayed for sale. A section is often roped off and used as a parking area for motorbikes, but only after making financial arrangements with the local policemen. For 14 cents one can leave a motorbike, confident that upon returning hours later it will still be there. On retrieval, cautious owners inspect it to see if inferior engine parts have replaced the manufacturer's original equipment.

Hammock and awning ropes attached to poles, trees, and parked motorbikes cause pedestrians to stoop, turn, and step aside. In many places walkways are so crowded that people must trudge in the street, being careful to dodge traffic and garbage tossed from houses and food stalls.

The sidewalks belong to the city, but homeowners treat them as their own. Many are tiled with baked clay; some are made from cement or brick, some from dirt. Adjacent segments are often at different heights; pedestrians must keep their eyes down to avoid stumbling. At 10 p.m., tables, chairs, food stalls, goods for sale, portable repair shops, and motorbikes are taken into houses overnight for safekeeping. Barber and ear-cleaning chairs remain on the sidewalk, secured to immoveable objects by heavy chains.

Tall leafy giants line city roads and parks. Each tree has a white inventory number painted on its bark. The bottom four feet of tree trunks are painted white. I asked people why and received the following answers.

- To make it safe for motorbike drivers.
- To keep insects away.
- To beautify Saigon.
- To protect the trees from the sun.
- To create shadows.
- To keep rats away.
- To employ people.

Downtown Saigon has few public parks. Most are small and consist of flowerbeds, stone paths, sculpted bushes, and grassy areas.

One night on my way home, I noticed that the street had just been cleaned. It was peaceful until suddenly, out of the houses, young men appeared wearing only shorts. They divided into teams and began to play soccer. The road was their pitch and sandals marked their goal lines. Play was competitive and fast. They did not stop for the occasional motorbike or truck that roared by, or for the cyclo driver pedaling his passenger home. It was a dangerous combination: bare feet, broken and uneven pavement, passing traffic, and the recklessness of the young.

The city is quiet at 5 a.m. Vehicles are few. Young people converge on the widest of streets to play soccer. Instead of roaring traffic, one hears boisterous players shout and cheer while chasing a soccer ball. Laughter and curses energize and taunt the players. Games end at about six a.m. when the streets are no longer empty.

VENDORS: Seven days a week the vendor arrived before noon and parked under a tree in front of a restaurant where I sometimes ate lunch. His two-wheeled pushcart was piled high with coconuts sitting atop mounds of ice. The ice melted slowly in the shade. From time to time he rotated the coconuts so the ones on top were moved next to the ice at the bottom. He removed their husks and shaped them with a few deft strokes of his machete—the bottoms cut flat so they could be placed on a table. Customers paid 12 cents for a chilled coconut and straw. The vendor departed by early evening when most of his wares had been sold. Space was limited in front of the restaurant and I wondered by what arrangement he used it all day. Did he rent the space from the city, the police, or the restaurant owner? Would another vendor take his place if he did not show up one day? What profit did he make for his labor?

Men and women operate ear-cleaning businesses under jerry-rigged awnings. Atop a high stool, a man decked out in a miner's lamp goes about this delicate business. Thin bamboo slivers, topped with cotton dipped in fragrant oil, are inserted into the customer's ears, twirled, and withdrawn; inserted, twirled, and withdrawn. Entrepreneurs solicit the seated customer, offering nail care and limb massages. As the day advances, nail clippings, discarded instruments, discolored cotton swabs, and food bits collect in an oily stain seeping from beneath the armchair.

Small boys walk the streets banging spoons together. The sound advertises soup for sale. They take your order and return in five minutes from a back alley kitchen with a bowl of hot noodle soup. Later they return to retrieve the empty bowl. Dishes and cutlery are washed at curbside in buckets of cold soapy water, and then rinsed in a second bucket of water and drip-dried.

Other boys point with disgust at your feet and offer shoeshines. If hired they will depart with your shoes, returning them ten minutes later gloriously polished. However, a prudent man waits for the return of the first shoe before giving the shoeshine boy the second.

Old rotary phones wired from nearby buildings sit on curbs, available for use. Old people tend the phones, charging pennies a call. Motorbike owners buy compressed air for their tires from curbside vendors. High-backed scales are wheeled along the sidewalk to the accompaniment of bells and whistles. For a small fee, one's weight and height are given. Young boys bang bamboo sticks together, announcing massage services.

Day and night, people of all ages and in all conditions hawk lottery tickets. Amputees and others unable to walk ride the streets beneath canvas-covered push-pull carts; one hand clutches a wad of lottery tickets for sale while the other pushes and pulls a wooden bar that moves the cart.

Five-, six-, and seven-year-old children, some in school uniforms, peddle gum, trinkets, flowers, and lottery tickets late into the night. Hoping for a score, they congregate outside restaurants and bars that cater to foreigners. Parents place them there to earn their keep.

In the early morning and late afternoon, motorized wagons deliver bathtub-size blocks of ice to sidewalk vendors. Often nothing is placed between the ground and ice; on top, burlap coverings prevent the inventory from quickly melting away. All-day and late into the night, vendors chop the blocks. Streams of customers emerge from noodle shops, restaurants, and homes to purchase ice at two cents a pound. They take the ice away in plastic bags to use (after being washed, one hopes) for cooling food and drinks. To order a beverage "có đá" (with ice) is an expression of absolute trust and naive hope. Many established restaurants serve ice cubes with holes in the middle. Supposedly, this means the water for the ice does not come from Saigon's polluted waterways but from a certified hygienic source, and therefore is clean and safe to drink.

DIRT JUMP UP: Loose garbage is dumped at the curb. Walls, trees, and poles are often used as urinals, while curbs, bushes, and grassy spots sometimes serve as commodes. Dust, dirt, construction debris, motor oil, and discarded food litter the streets and sidewalks. Mud and stuff stick to shoes during the lengthy rainy season.

Like the Japanese, Vietnamese people leave their shoes at the doorstep and go barefoot in the house. The purpose is to keep dirt and filth out of the home.

On arrival to my house, visitors often asked if they could wash their feet. In explanation I was told, "Dirt jump up" and "I wash so slippery go away."

LOTTERIES: Every province and major city is authorized to conduct weekly lotteries. They are an important source of revenue for local governments. Ticket sellers make seven cents on each ticket they sell. By custom, the owner of a winning ticket gives the seller a small share. Small children, aged women, the disabled, and the homeless buy lottery tickets from government offices for resale. Unsold tickets may be returned up to one hour before winning tickets are drawn. An upsetting sight is an aged, bent grandmother rushing to the lottery office just prior to the deadline to receive cash for her unsold tickets. Even more disturbing to see is a distraught, crying child chasing an older boy who has stolen his money and unsold tickets.

Playing the lottery is an immensely popular pastime. A ticket costs 14 cents and the top prize can be as much as $2,500. An illegal lottery operates alongside the official one. Payouts from the "black lottery" (vé số đen) are higher because of lower operating expenses and no taxes.

A CRY SOUNDS THE ALARM: Police periodically interrupt the rhythm of life on the sidewalk. They arrive unannounced and in force, by truck and motorcycle, to remove the wheeled soup kitchens and clear away the street merchants. These entrepreneurs and their customers clutter the sidewalk with benches, seats, and cooking fires. A cry from down the street sounds the alarm and immediately everyone scatters. Owners scurry about to collect their goods and get away. Tables, stools, and braziers disappear into houses. Food stalls are pushed hurriedly into alleyways. Fruit and vegetable sellers, coconut and roasted corn vendors, and hawkers of sunglasses, lighters, combs, and nail clippers make a run for it. However, those burdened with inventory and infants are usually apprehended.

On both sides of the avenue people jump off their stools, grab their food and consume it on foot. Customers stride away, bowl held chin-high, slurping their noodle soup. Ready brooms sweep away bits of toilet paper, which patrons use to wipe clean their spoons, chopsticks, and lips. A roll of toilet paper sits on each table; one tears off what one needs. Discarded chicken bones and vegetables are tidied up as well. The routine is so practiced that it takes just minutes to clear the sidewalk, hide the evidence, and present a "What? Who me?" face to the arriving police.

If the warning system fails, then the merchants and restaurateurs will be caught and their goods confiscated and hauled to the dreaded police station. That very day the owner can retrieve his property and return to the same site, but only after paying what the police call a fine and the people call a bribe. If not caught, vendors are back within an hour. They must return; it is how they support themselves and their families.

The police cannot raid every sidewalk every day. It just is not possible. Lacking the resources, frequently they resort to driving their black trucks slowly through the streets, relying on the warning cries to clear the area. At these times they will not stop to confiscate goods, but people do not know that and business is disrupted as owners and customers flee. At other times, and to the same result, an open police jeep will cruise by while the officer in the passenger seat thoughtfully scans the sidewalk. At carefully timed intervals, he focuses on some egregious violation and ostentatiously raises his pen and writes in the book resting on his lap.

In this city of eight million people, where nearly everyone at some time during the day plays, eats, or sleeps on the sidewalks, it does not seem possible that the police can keep them clear. Big cities everywhere face this problem. I have seen the same cat-and-mouse game between police and street vendors in New York City. However, in Saigon, because of the ubiquitous sidewalk eateries, it just seems so much more colorful.

QUIVERING AT CURBSIDE: Vietnamese watch in bemusement as newly arrived foreigners try to cross the street. Minutes tick by as they stand at the curb, confounded, frightened, and quivering; people of all ages cross in front of them, while they hesitate, fret, and ponder. Soon they realize there are no breaks in the traffic. Eventually, with lungs full and teeth clenched, they check the traffic, place a foot on the pavement, and withdraw it; then determined to cross they lurch into the oncoming traffic.

A slow, steady walk is safe. Drivers adjust their speed and direction based on where they calculate the pedestrian will be. Drivers do not want accidents. They worry, "Police come. Pay money. Motorbike break. People hurt." The uninitiated traverse in a frenzy of darts, dashes, and stutter steps. Drivers swerve and slow down to avoid them, but sometimes they do not and pile-ups occur. At times tourists lose their courage mid-road. They stand there terrified, afraid to go forward or back, as cars, motorbikes, trucks, cyclos, and freight-movers whiz by. If they wait long enough a kind-hearted citizen will often take them by the hand to safety, but if they panic and bolt, people all around are put at risk of injury. People joke that an old stooped grandmother carrying a bowl of steaming soup is the safest person crossing a thoroughfare. All vehicles give her a wide berth.

Experienced locals proceed with caution. They cross in groups, or alone with an outstretched hand, or behind vehicles. Whenever possible, people keep something between themselves and the traffic.

One morning near a hospital I passed a doctor and nurse in scrubs making the perilous trip with a gurney. They were wheeling across the busy street a middle-aged man lying face up with his limbs exposed. Intravenous bags hung from poles attached to the wheeled bed. The physician and his assistant were careful to keep the patient between themselves and the oncoming traffic.

HOLD ON TO SOMETHING: Vietnamese women are concerned about the sun. They are quick to say, "Men like light-skinned girls, not girls made dark by the sun." It is sad to hear these sentiments in Vietnam, the land of women "not yellow, but just a little brown." To avoid the sun, most women wear jeans or an áo dài, shoulder-length gloves, sunglasses, wide-brimmed hats, and surgical masks or scarves that cover them from nose to neck. They fret about their children's skin color and take precautions to keep them out of the sun. Pregnant women drink soybean milk in the belief that their children will be born with white skin.

Visitors to Vietnam often ask, "What do motorbike passengers hang on to?" Well, it depends on their relationship to the driver. Uninvolved and unrelated passengers rest one hand between their legs and one behind their back, where they clasp the aluminum hold-on bar. Passengers who are friends of the driver place their hands on his shoulders or hips. Older married couples and couples with a young child on board travel this way too. Young couples often turn the ride into an affection-sharing experience. The girl wraps her arms round her boyfriend's waist, resting her hands between his legs. She has to hold onto something. Of course, it is dangerous—his mind is not on the traffic, he is steering the bike erratically, and he is off to quick starts. How can the young man drive safely? Passengers on other motorbikes incline their heads toward the amorous couple and smile and wink to one another. Paradise is where you have been, always.

This takes place in a culture that disapproves of public signs of affection. Few couples hold hands and there is no public kissing. Lack of privacy in this very crowded city and the anonymity afforded by speeding traffic explains the contradiction.

Privacy is not easy to find. Generations within a family share a small house, sleeping on floors and under stairs when bedrooms are too crowded. Groups of students and migrants from the countryside share tiny rooms in the city and wash at the same tap; rents are high for single accommodations. These young people have no family in Saigon; they are poor and have no choice. They have no kitchen rights and must share a filthy toilet with their housemates. Each person pays as little as $7 per month. Others, depending on their family's financial status, have better accommodations.

Drivers maneuver in and out of traffic. If the passenger does not keep her knees close to the xe ôm driver, she can be knocked off her seat by a passing vehicle. I had to caution a friend who was visiting from the United States to keep her knees together. Women do not often hear that from men.

Controlling the vehicle is easier for the driver if his fare sits close against his back. Westerners unfamiliar with this fact are encouraged to snuggle up, but most will not because they are uncomfortable with the intimacy and the driver's reeking torso. Unwittingly, they choose propriety and comfort over safety.

Passengers in skirts ride sidesaddle. Although certainly modest, it looks precarious. However, I have not seen any of these proper ladies slide from their seat to be dashed on the pavement.

HELMETS NOT SAFE: Riding on a motorbike is frightening; speeding, disorderly traffic suddenly stopping and starting, only just avoiding people and other vehicles, and always moving forward. No one gives an inch.

In 2005 there were 3.3 million registered motorbikes in Saigon. One million bicycles, countless cyclos and hand-pulled carts, and 400,000 cars, trucks, and small freight movers added to the congestion. It was pandemonium.

Beggars and vendors often crowd you at traffic lights. One's senses are challenged by shrieking police sirens, grunting bulldozers, grinding power saws, mindless and incessant honking, putrid smells, and, of course, the wistful glances, methinks, from short-skirted, leggy damsels atop speeding motorbikes.

Traffic is required to travel on the right side of the road. Most times it does, but do not trust in what should be. Stoplights appear to be optional. A traffic policeman, stick in hand, stands near busy intersections to ensure that signals are obeyed. Until 2007, helmets were not required in the city and few motorbike riders wore them. One young man told me, "Helmets not safe. They make me go fast." If a street is marked one-way, motorbike drivers traveling in the opposite direction use the sidewalks to reach their destination.

The streets are sometimes full of pedestrians because long stretches of sidewalks are not passable.

Pedestrians are in danger when they attempt to cross the street. I saw accidents almost every day I was in Saigon. The Times of Vietnam reported that there were 11,000 motorbike deaths in Vietnam during 2005. Injuries were not reported.

I do not drive a motorbike but, judging by what I have seen, the unwritten rules of the road are:

- As between vehicles and people, vehicles have the right of way.
- As between big and small vehicles, big ones have the right of way.
- A spot on the road belongs to the first vehicle to reach it.
- Never stop if you are in an accident; speed away if you can.
- Use the horn instead of the brake.
- Speed up if the green light turns yellow.
- Look before going through red lights.

From the back of a Honda, on the way to an orphanage one morning, I saw a passenger on another motorbike holding a 2' x 5' piece of plate glass. It rested on his thighs and against the back and head of the driver. They moved through traffic that way, a danger to all.

Twelve-foot-long pieces of bamboo or metal pipe are often transported balanced on the driver's shoulder. Such items protrude front and rear. Like knights of old atop brave chargers, these motorbike jockeys race, pointed lance to the front, through crowded streets. No warning flags are affixed and no precautions taken. I have seen no one impaled, but I have no doubt it has happened.

Restaurants produce grease, bones, and table scraps every day. Dealers buy the slop and load it into large, blue, uncovered plastic barrels. They tie the vat onto the passenger seat of their motorbike and sell the contents to pig farmers. Other vehicles give a wide berth to these distinctive containers, not just because of the noxious odor wafting from them but also because they fear being splattered by the sloshing waste.

HONDA KISS: Motorbikes are a platform, so to speak, for another type of business. Brave working girls cruise the streets displaying their wares. Hot prospects negotiate the price of the service and the place of delivery. The Western media, the gauge and guardian of political correctness, has in recent years described such women as "sex workers" instead of using the centuries-old term. It is a new euphemism for this activity. In solidarity, I will not pen the "p" word here. It is likely this laudable sensitivity will evolve to encompass other deleterious activity. Perhaps "bank worker" will come to replace "bank robber" and "child keeper" will be used instead of "kidnapper." English is a living language, always changing. In America, even now, those guardians favor "undocumented migrants" over "illegal aliens."

Honda kisses are hot, sizzling stuff. They exhilarate and endanger, and are difficult to avoid. I have had two. The warmth and heightened sense of awareness are memorable. However, the experience is not available to those in long pants.

Motorbikes in Saigon have a silver-colored muffler stretching along their right side, seven inches off the ground. As hot engine gases pass through the tapered aluminum tube, noise is deadened and the muffler becomes hot enough to burn flesh. Distracted passengers in skirts or shorts often scorch the inside of their right calf when dismounting. Burns on the outside of either calf are the result of "kisses" from other motorbikes that brush against the unwary in traffic. The stench of grilled human flesh fills the air, but it quickly abates and mixes with the exhaust of 3.7 million vehicles. Depending on the heat of the tube and the duration of contact, the resulting mark can be permanent. I thought the oval shadows on the legs of Saigonese were birthmarks. After being burned one afternoon, I learned they were Honda kisses.

A COMMON ACCIDENT: One morning, a hotel owner joined me while I had breakfast at his sidewalk cafe. He said I could use his computer free of charge and his 17-year-old nephew would help me surf the Internet in the evenings. The owner's sister had been killed two years before when robbers tried to yank her handbag from her as she was riding her motorbike. She would not let go, so they pushed her to the ground and she was killed when her head hit the street. Her son and husband now live and work at the hotel with the other 17 family members.

I was enjoying lunch at a curbside restaurant with Pham, the principal of the public school where I taught. When I looked up I saw a toddler fall to the road from her mother's motorbike. Her clothes got caught on the pedal of a motorbike whizzing past and she was dragged five feet, bumping, scraping, and banging her head on the pavement. Her cries lasted only seconds, which I took as a bad sign. Several people rushed to the injured girl and inexplicably rubbed her limbs and head. The girl's mother rushed her by taxi to a nearby hospital. From the outset, Pham told me not to help the girl.

"They know what to do—it is a common accident," he said. "It is no one's fault."

The streets are dangerous, but the sight of a young child riding on the back of a motorbike and clinging to the shirt of an adult is normal. At times, a parent steers with one hand and carries a baby in the other. Sometimes a youngster sits between her mother's legs while she drives holding a cell phone to her ear.

It was noon. I was walking on the street, inches from the curb, when a handlebar nicked my left arm. The laughing schoolgirl on the back waved at me in apology while her teenage classmate struggled to control their wobbly bicycle. Street debris and potholes made it difficult. Their front wheel jerked left, right, and left again. A speeding motorbike passed me and, as it overtook the students, slammed into the careening bike. One of the injured was helped off the busy street and seated against a wall to await an ambulance. The girl who had been pedaling did not move. She lay face down on the dirty road. Blood flowed from a head wound. A passing taxi stopped. Men placed the unconscious girl on the back seat. The driver was a good man, I was told. "He take her hospital, no money."

CYCLO CRASH: My daughter, Eileen, gets carsick. So that she could arrive at school with a full stomach and clean uniform, she, her twin brother,

John, and I traveled by cyclo. For three years the same cyclo driver arrived promptly weekday mornings at 7:15 a.m. This gentle, former ARVN private spent four years in a re-education camp as a prisoner of war. He has been using his strength to move people around Saigon since 1982.

It was not comfortable for us sitting in a narrow armchair seat mounted on the front of the three-wheeled bicycle cyclo. Our situation did not compare with that of our sweating, grunting, 60-year-old, 140-pound, pedaling chauffeur, who struggled with his 220-pound human load. At hills, he dismounted and pushed. During our journey he navigated the streets, avoided darting motorbikes, speeding autos, wandering pedestrians, and construction debris. Only once did he make a mistake.

During one ride to school, the right wheel fell into an eight-inch hole left by a street repair crew. The cyclo overturned and we were pitched to the pavement. I regained consciousness in seconds. As people raised me to my feet, I saw Eileen in the arms of a woman, crying, and John standing with his hands on his hips. He was angry because a motorbike had run over his foot and the man had not stopped to say sorry. They were not hurt. To protect us, a man had placed his motorbike sideways between the overturned cyclo and the oncoming traffic. A woman from an adjacent pharmacy splashed medicine on my cut and bruised head, and then placed a black bandage on the wound. I thanked everyone for their help, shook hands with our driver, and we continued to school in the undamaged cyclo.

TIRE PATCHES: Tires are surprisingly durable given the heat and the rugged condition of the streets. When punctures occur and repairs become necessary, drivers wheel their motorbikes to the nearest repair station. There are many of them, often several at each intersection. An old tire suspended from a stick or a bottle holding a paper funnel marks a station's location and identifies its services. The mechanic does his business on the sidewalk. All he needs are patches, a few hand tools, a pan of water, and an air compressor or hand pump. The cost in 2006 was seven cents to put air in a tire, 28 cents to patch each hole, $2 for a new inner tube, and $13 for a locally made tire.

Drivers observe closely to prevent the mechanic from making additional holes in the tire, which would require additional patches at 28 cents each.

Not wanting to rely on time or chance to deliver customers, some repairmen spread nails and glass on the street. This practice is especially dangerous on highways because a tire blowout at high speed always results in an upturned motorbike and injuries. The nails are sprinkled in the lane used by motorbikes and not in the outer one used by trucks and cars; the men are equipped to fix small tires only. Stopping this dangerous and fraudulent practice is difficult because evidence is hard to find. Nevertheless, from time to time arrests are reported in the press.

SATISFY THE TAXMAN: Bus service connects Vietnam's cities and towns. It is an extensive system with regularly scheduled departures and arrivals. Many buses are privately owned, and a conductor-mechanic accompanies the driver. These buses are unreliable and dangerous. In Saigon, they leave from a station after ticket taxes are paid. The bus does not leave until there are enough passengers to satisfy the tax collector.

A 19-year-old student who returns to his home village twice a year explained that if he buys a ticket at the bus station it costs him $3, which includes tax, but if he boards after the bus has left the station—buses often stop to take on more passengers along the road—it only costs him $2.40, because no tax is collected.

The tax collection process, mechanical breakdowns, police extortion stops, and various unexpected incidents make the schedule unreliable. Taking an inter-city bus is dangerous because the drivers are reckless and the movements of other vehicles are unpredictable. In contrast, local bus service in Saigon is clean, efficient, and safe. New buses transport people over citywide routes at a cost of 20 cents.

Seven

CHILDREN IN NEED

Do ye hear the children weeping, O my brothers,
Ere the sorrow comes with years?
-Elizabeth Browning

Street children are the ones who suffer the most in Vietnam, and the younger the children the more oppressive their situation. They are unable to help themselves and are always at great risk. Their future is limited and dim. Without family support and an education they are attracted by the lure of easy money—not a good thing for young girls and boys anywhere, especially on the streets of Saigon.

Many children are put to work selling lottery tickets, plucking duck feathers, collecting plastic bags from garbage dumps, and other menial jobs. Some beggars rent infants by the day and use them as props to solicit sympathy and money. Desperately poor parents ignore the risks of such transactions.

Before I retired, I did not involve myself in other people's problems. I was too busy with family and work. Instead, I gave money to charity to soothe my conscience. A tax deduction was my only satisfaction. I found in Vietnam that directly helping others is a better reward.

It is wonderful to help improve the lives of others. We must try. However, whether we give time or money, in many cases our efforts are unsuccessful because the problem is too large, too complex, or too entrenched to solve. Often we never learn the results of our charitable activities, and often, when we do, we are disappointed.

*****

CHILD SCAVENGERS: The streets and sidewalks of Saigon are used as garbage pits and toilets. However, they are cleaned every day by brigades of sanitation workers. The workers, mostly female, consider themselves fortunate because the work is steady and they are entitled to vacations, pensions, health insurance, and paid sick days. Disease is an occupational hazard for them. The kitchen waste and trash they pick up are placed in the same bag. Shards of metal and glass are mixed with banana skins and table scraps. Injuries to these workers are common.

All day long, refuse is dumped at curbside. Scavengers, both two- and four-legged, scatter the contents looking for nourishment and valuables. Once a day women in orange coveralls, wielding long bamboo and straw brooms, clean up the litter. Everywhere is relatively free of filth for a short while.

Residents are charged for garbage collection and sidewalk sweeping. In 2002, I paid 75 cents per month, and in 2011, $1. Business owners pay more depending on the volume of trash they generate.

Trucks of all sizes transport garbage to incinerators and landfills. These stinking, barge-like vehicles are avoided by others on the road, but traffic jams are inevitable and I can attest that it is unpleasant to be stuck anywhere near a sun-baked, Saigon garbage truck.

Human scavengers, young and old, pick through the waste searching for items they can eat or sell. Bottles, newspapers, old shoes, broken toys, bits of plastic, rubber, and metal all have value. People who earn their living this way are pitifully poor and only have hope to sustain themselves. It is a mean and desperate life.

Eleven-year-old Mai and Tung, her 15-year-old brother, rode bikes strapped with old rice sacks through my neighborhood looking for discarded cans and bottles. At day's end Mai would sell large glass bottles for three cents; soda cans fetched two cents. Neither child had ever been to school.

Too small for her bicycle, Mai could not sit on the seat and pedal at the same time. Therefore, she pedaled while straddling the crossbar. I befriended these children, providing them food and drink at my door. They got first crack at my garbage, too.

Tung spoke no English. Mai, on the other hand, spoke limited English with an American accent. She always greeted me with this rhyme:

"One, two, buckle my shoe
Three, four, open the door
Five, six, pick-up sticks..."

I learned their story and, contrary to Em Thy's warning, took an interest in their situation. They and their parents lived under a building overhang near my house. In the evenings I saw the mother and father gambling and drinking beer with other homeless people while Mai and Tung, perched on their bicycles, watched television through the open window of a nearby house. Their parents collected from the trash pieces of metal and plastic. Each child was required to give them 50 cents a day from their earnings. In other words, Mai and Tung, instead of going to school, combed through other people's trash in order to support mom and dad's gambling and drinking habits. Em Thy told me that others had tried to help the children but the parents would not cooperate. She said adults could do what they wanted with their offspring. Under Vietnamese law, it was considered a family matter and neither the police nor the Education Ministry would intervene. Even if they had, the parents would not or could not pay their children's public school fees.

THE GIRL HAS A CHANCE: One day I noticed a piece of black cloth pinned to the little girl's shirt. Mai told me that her baby sister had died. Then, realizing her mistake, she said, "No sister, mother die." A few tears ran down her cheeks as she made a hacking sound and pantomimed to explain that her mother had died from a cough two days before.

I asked a social worker I knew to talk with the neighbors to find out about the children's situation. She learned that an American woman was paying for the children's meals at a local street kitchen and that a Vietnamese woman was allowing them to sleep and wash in her house. For some reason, however, the father would not let Mai and Tung continue to accept these favors. She also found out that he had five more offspring living with relatives in the countryside to whom he was required to send $1 per day for their support. Since his wife's death, he had increased the daily amount Mai and Tung had to pay him to 60 cents each.

The father told the social worker that for a payment of $25 per month per child his children could go to school. She advised me against it, explaining that Tung and Mai would have to start in the first grade with the 6-year-olds. Because of the age differences, they would not succeed: they would feel inferior and soon drop out. Furthermore, she added, the father might keep the $50 and make them work anyway.

Her proposal, which he accepted, was that they work for him until 5 p.m. and then go to a nun's school from 6 p.m. to 8 p.m. They would learn reading, writing, arithmetic, and proper behavior, and when suitably prepared they would be enrolled in a daytime public school. I agreed to pay him $20 per child per month. I was elated; I thought I might make a difference in their lives.

I gave the social worker money to buy clothes for them. However, Mai and Hung never showed up to shop for the clothes. When she found them picking through garbage the next day, they told her that their father had changed his mind. They could not go to school and would have to work until 9 p.m. each night. The social worker returned my money. I was aggrieved by my failure. I wanted to help them. I did not want to be just another well-intentioned but ineffective foreigner passing through their lives.

A few weeks later I asked Em Thy if she had seen the children. She answered that Mai was in a boarding school run by a different religious group. The American woman who had been paying for their meals had agreed to the father's terms for the girl and was paying her school fees as well. Apparently, the man had been negotiating with the American woman and me at the same time over the fate of his progeny. They were his assets. He took the best deal.

Years have passed since Mai left the streets. I lost track of her. The American woman had succeeded in changing this girl's life. Hung still scavenges for valuables amid the garbage and trash. He felt too old for school.

CHANGED FOREVER: My friend, Son, is a singer and waiter at an Irish pub. He is also an accomplished but unheralded painter. I own three of his works. He called me one evening and asked me to write a paragraph about him for an art auction catalogue sponsored by Operation Smile, a foreign NGO. He also asked that I attend the auction the following evening and bid on his painting if no one else did.

"All the paintings but mine are by famous Vietnamese artists," he said. "I will be sad if the others sell and mine does not."

I accepted the mission, wrote the paragraph, and bought a ticket, a tuxedo, and shoes, all in the space of a few hours.

The auction proceeds were to be used to pay for cleft palate operations. Volunteer teams of doctors and nurses came from the United States several times a year to perform the surgeries. One thousand were performed in 2003 for $75 each. All the money is raised in Vietnam and no team comes until the funds are in hand.

The event was held at a first class hotel. Men in formal dress and women in elegant evening wear enjoyed cocktails, dinner, and conversation. The auction that followed was well run, and the crowd was in the mood to spend. Action was brisk. An Indonesian man at a table to my right bid on each painting and was the winner of many. Son's canvas was put on the block, but no one bid. I did not want another of his paintings, but I had promised to help him and it was for a good cause. I hesitated also because weeks earlier Son had offered me this particular painting for $300. Nevertheless, I opened the bidding at $1,000, the Indonesian man made an offer of $2,000 and I went to $3,000. The room was silent for ten seconds but then the Indonesian bid $4,000. I was never so happy to lose. Son, who was sitting at my table, cried when the gavel sounded. The charity raised $90,000 that night, 85% of which would be used for cleft palate operations.

The lives of children who have this surgery are transformed forevermore: no longer do classmates ridicule them, no longer do they dribble food and water, and no longer is their speech distorted.

PAY FINE IN ADVANCE: There are probably thousands of street children in Saigon. Some have homes to sleep in but they spend their days on the street. Others sleep on the sidewalk with their parents. Children without parents tend to gather to sleep in parks, and then, in the morning, they disburse around the city to forage for food and beg for money. All of these children are extremely vulnerable to beatings, sexual abuse, and robbery. Frequently they are ill and covered with sores.

Poverty and government policy keep poor children out of public school. Children without birth certificates cannot go to school. Parents who migrate to the city to find work without permission of the authorities are illegal residents, and their children are deemed ineligible for Saigon birth certificates.

The paperwork, cost, and shrewdness that are necessary to navigate the greedy bureaucracy and achieve Saigon citizen status are often beyond the ability of simple people from the provinces. Even if all residency requirements are satisfied, the applicant is only given a temporary permit. After five years, a permanent residency license is granted. One person explained that permanent residency authorization is available after one month at a "secret cost" of $1,000. The cousin of this person worked at the city permit-issuing department. When the relative was asked to waive the $1,000 payment, he responded that it was not possible because too many people shared in the money.

I spent six hours a week preparing grant applications, fundraising reports, and donor correspondence for a local NGO that provided shelter, education, healthcare, and citizenship training for 1,600 street children at seven locations in Saigon.

The NGO gets no state money; it exists on grants and private contributions. Most of the money comes from Japanese companies and individuals. The founder is a former officer in the South Vietnamese Army who spent two years in jail after 1975. While I worked there, the NGO received two grants from American organizations and a scholarship for one social worker to study in New York City. They said these successes were a result of my help. I beamed, but knew better.

Lanh, the director, runs a four-bedroom guesthouse to help fund the organization. For $200 a month, one gets laundry service, air conditioning, a private bathroom, and Internet access. Lanh says it is a good guesthouse. "No prostitutes or Taiwanese allowed in the rooms," he declared. He holds Taiwanese men in low regard because of their reputed brutal treatment of Vietnamese women.

When I asked if I needed police approval to stay in his guesthouse, he answered: "Don't worry about the police. I take care of problem the Vietnamese way. I pay fine in advance." He meant that periodic payments ensure that problems don't surface.

WOUNDED: Shortly after arriving in Saigon I had lunch with Lanh and his office staff of one male and seven females. There was a lot of joking back and forth. They tried to include me in the conversation, but it was difficult. I told them that my son was coming to Saigon in a few days to visit.

"What is his name?" one of the young women asked. When I replied "Martin," she said, "No, that's your name. What is your son's name?" This went on for a while as they laughed and spoke with one another. I then told them my father's name was also Martin, which resulted in more discussion. In Vietnam, no one is named after a relative, living or dead. It upsets the spirits and causes bad luck.

Finally, the girl who spoke the best English said, "We have decided that you and your son have the same name, but we want to know if he is available." She continued: "Does he have a wife?"

"No," I said, "but he has a girlfriend."

She consulted with the others and then, with a lovely smile, said, "No wife means he is available."

Three Vietnamese nuns staff one of Lahn's seven facilities. Two hundred children are registered there. Photographs of Lahn greeting Mother Teresa when she visited are on display. Handicrafts are available for purchase. A table lamp made from shirt buttons costs $3. Colorful cloth wallets are $1 each. Embroidered handkerchiefs, napkins, and handbags are priced by size and detail. The center has classrooms, a kitchen, a library, and 50 dormitory beds for children who live there. The beds are plywood platforms. The nuns explained that four youngsters share each bed, but fewer if the children are older. The older boys sleep in a shed nearby; the nuns were sure I would understand why. Some children are orphans but most are neglected because their parents must work long hours to provide for their families. "When left alone and uncared-for, the children will get problems," one of the sisters said.

One morning a father brought his brave three-year-old boy to the center. It was his first day. The other children took him by the hand and I saw no tears. During recess he wore my hat. While I was speaking with one of the nuns, he returned it. The nun, without breaking our conversation, began looking for lice in the boy's hair, killing the ones she found with her fingernails. I generously presented the hat to the child.

Another young girl, who sold gum on the streets in the evenings to help her family, arrived at 1 p.m. with a bleeding left arm. She had been "wounded," the nun said, in a collision between her bike and a truck. Her shirt was speckled with blood, but she was happy because she had been able to drag the damaged bike to the center. A nun took her by motorbike to the hospital.

One of the nuns asked me if I knew Miss Goldberg from New York City. I told her, "Of course, I know all the Goldbergs in New York City." She explained that Miss Goldberg was from a Jewish American NGO. The organization had supported the children in the past, and recently, after visiting the center, she had informed the nuns that it would continue to do so.

HEIGHTENING THE HOUSE: At the centers, parents learn about childcare, budgeting, saving money, proper work habits, earning an income, interest on borrowed money, and healthcare. Parents must attend lectures on these matters if their children are admitted into the program.

They form into groups of five to implement a microcredit savings program. Every week each family deposits a small sum with the group's leader, whom the participants have chosen. Group members can apply for a $50-$250 loan. Other members of the savings group must approve the loan's amount and purpose as well as its repayment conditions. The loans bear interest at 2% instead of the 25% market rate. Group pressure ensures compliance with the terms of the loan.

"Nguyet's mother is a sewer." I thought it a little strong. I was revising a staff member's letter to a corporate donor in Japan when I came across these words. The letter explained that part of last year's contribution paid for the cost of teaching parents about the microcredit program. Nguyet's mother was an example of a success because she had used her loan to buy a sewing machine. She was earning a living by sewing. She was a seamstress.

Another example given to the Japanese donor was that a loan had been made "for heightening the house." There was no clue as to what that meant so I changed it to "for adding a floor to the house." I pointed out this change to the writer when I returned the corrected letter. She told me nicely that I was wrong and that "heightening the house" meant making the floor higher. By lifting the two-room house and placing it on a 12-inch earthen platform, water would not flood the house during the rainy season.

A final success story was about Miss Yi, "who was now better at conception because of her studying."

ADOPTION REALITY: The willingness to raise orphaned children as one's own is a good thing. Most times the child and adoptive parents receive substantial benefits. The child's physical and emotional needs are provided for and the parents are rewarded by the joys of giving and receiving love. Society benefits, too, because children who are physically and emotionally secure are less likely to engage in antisocial behavior.

Today, almost everywhere, it is illegal to buy and sell people. Slavery is not so distant that we have forgotten that evil. The law in most countries requires that the child's best interest comes first, and that the mother cannot receive payment for her child. On paper, these simple statements are consistent with our values. However, in practice, in Vietnam these rules were sometimes turned on their head.

Until recently, the interests of the birth mother, the prospective parents, the adoption agency, and greedy bureaucrats came before those of the child. It was assumed that if all these people were happy with the infant's placement then the child's interests were well served. Demand for children exceeded supply and money flowed freely from adoptive parents to other parties. It could cost as much as $30,000 for a foreigner to adopt a Vietnamese child.

There were numerous adoption agencies in Saigon. Some were honest, I am sure. The crooked ones paid for protection. They sent scouts to the countryside looking for children to buy. The mother was paid $1,000 and the scout rode into the sunset with his precious cargo. For a fee, another woman pretended to be the birth mother and signed the required forms. Orphanage officials, hospital staff, and government officials all received money to facilitate the process. Those who had to approve documents demanded bribes, and the payments were quickly made.

Some orphanage and hospital administrators would sign statements declaring that an infant was abandoned even though the parents were known. The parents received money for their child and the administrator was paid for the false statement. Certain American adoption agencies and couples worked together to thwart American and Vietnamese law. These practices caused several countries to suspend the right of their citizens to adopt Vietnamese children.

The only entity that prevented adoption by Americans from becoming an open auction was the U.S. Immigration and Naturalization Service (INS). If the adoption process did not comply with United States and Vietnamese law, the INS would not approve a passport for the child. The INS investigated each application, frequently discovering false statements and fraudulent activity. However, it was difficult for the INS in Vietnam, where official cooperation is often limited by self-interest, to verify sworn statements.

Many adoptions in Vietnam were obtained in violation of law. If a child was denied a U.S. passport, the child might be given a new name, birth mother, and identity papers, and offered for adoption a second time to a different couple.

For Western couples the adoption process was lengthy, emotional, tedious, expensive, bureaucratic, and frustrating. However, eventually everything would come together and the necessary papers filed with the Ministry of Justice in Hanoi. Forty days after the filing, and assuming there were no complications, the couple returned to the U.S. with their new child.

For the most part, adoptions in the U.S. are highly regulated and closely supervised by the courts. In the U.S., we have conveniently limited the supply of unwanted children and in this way have exported much of the corruption, and many of the gut-wrenching decisions of birth mothers, to the poor countries of the world. How to reconcile the social benefits of adoption with the prohibition against the trafficking of babies has not been resolved.

Since 2007, international organizations and the Vietnamese government have taken effective steps to control and eliminate illegal adoptions. Today, it is difficult but still possible to adopt a child in Vietnam.

UNLOCK BABIES: Many Vietnamese have proudly told me that you can buy anything in Vietnam.

The men and women who lived across the alley from me (and relentlessly stared at me and tracked my comings and goings) moved out and were replaced by two men, a Vietnamese woman, and a four-year-old boy. This family also included two small dogs that lived on the bedroom balcony. The dogs were short-chained to the railing and rarely given walks. They could lie down but not move around. They ate, pooped, and peed there. Both dogs wore leather half-masks because without the muzzle their incessant barking displeased the neighbors.

In Southeast Asia, Philippine musicians and singers perform at clubs and hotels in all the major cities. They play American pop and oldies and are accomplished and popular. Some people call these bands the single most important export of the Philippines. The men who moved across from me were Filipino singers; they performed every night in Saigon. They were gay and the small boy was their son. They had bought him from an unwed bargirl, who was paid $186 for her out-of-wedlock infant. The Vietnamese woman took care of the child and cleaned the house. My landlady told me there was no government paperwork documenting "who own boy."

I asked Em Thy how she knew about the gay men and their son. The nanny had blathered to the neighbors that she had cared for the boy for four years and when the men did not want the boy anymore he would be hers. Em Thy believed that this arrangement was best for the child because the men would care for him. Further, the biological mother did not take care of her son and did not want him, she told me. However, much to the dismay of the nanny, the mother sometimes stood in the alley hoping to get a glimpse of her son.

What the outcome of this informal agreement will be is unknown, but what is certain is that no one, to my knowledge, has any clear legal rights. If the men want to return to the Philippines, can they get a passport for the child? Can the mother reclaim the boy? Are the men obligated to educate and care for him? Can the child inherit from the men? Does the woman caring for the child have any rights?

Vietnamese have told me that the buying and selling of "out-of-lock babies" and "unlock babies" is common and that informal adoptions occur frequently.

FOURTEEN YEARS: They lined up at the door to the dining hall by height, 110 boys, ages four to 18. It was six p.m. on a Sunday afternoon and they were waiting for dinner. Son, a waiter and singer at an Irish pub, had collected donations to provide the meal. His co-workers and customers at the pub had contributed their time and money. They had been playing with the children at the Buddhist orphanage since one p.m.

The four-year-old boy at the head of the line had been at the institution under the care of the monks since the 14th day of his life. His father had killed his mother 14 days after the boy was born, during an argument about a family problem. As punishment, the father was sentenced to 14 years in prison. The monk who told me the little boy's history said the boy would have trouble at age 14, his unlucky number.

The boys sat 10 to a table; quiet, straight-backed, and disciplined. An older boy rose and recited the orphanage rules. One of the monks spoke for five minutes about patience and its relationship to happiness in life. The little boy was told to inform the others that they could begin eating, and he did so in a loud, clear voice.

The orphanage is a large complex containing classrooms, a kitchen, toilets, dormitories, playing fields, and a large pagoda. The boys sleep on bamboo mats in bunk beds; two to each bed. A mile away, Buddhist nuns operate a similar facility for 140 orphaned or abandoned girls. Both orphanages rely exclusively on contributions to feed, care for, and clothe the children.

I brought with me 110 pounds of rice. I was surprised to learn that it was less than what the 110 orphans and 17 staffers ate in one day.

I told Son I wanted to make a small monetary contribution.

"Should I give it to the man in charge of the dining room?" I inquired.

"No, Martin, don't give that man. You give, he go vacation. Give money head monk."

Son took me to see the monk in charge. I waited with a number of Vietnamese to present money to him. He was of medium height and thin. He sat cross-legged on a wooden, straight-backed armchair, his hands folded. His clean, orange robes contrasted with the glossy black wooden table.

As he poured tea for us, he said in perfect British English, "The children in this orphanage have many problems and their future is limited. There will always be orphanages and there will always be monks to keep the children safe. The children will enjoy your gift. I thank you for it."

Eight

HEALTHCARE

Health that mocks the doctor's rules,
Knowledge never learned in schools.
-John Greenleaf Whittier, "The Barefoot Boy"

A healthcare system funded and operated by the state provides for the public. Patients pay low fees. Care is also available at for-profit hospitals which reputedly provide better service, but at a higher cost. Those who can afford to pay get better care than those who cannot. This is true everywhere.

Saigon has numerous public hospitals. Some are new, but many are old, dirty, smelly, noisy, and crowded. They are often dreadful, abysmal places. Poor service and treatment are commonplace.

The needs of the poor overwhelm the public hospitals. There is not enough money to provide adequate facilities and staff. Training, procedures, protocols, and knowledge are inferior to Western standards. Salaries are low, so doctors and nurses expect to be tipped. Patients who do not are treated last. People say that when a doctor finally sees them he does not listen, is abrupt, in a hurry, and explains nothing. In 2005, a day in a public hospital cost $1.30.

Private, for-profit hospitals occupy new buildings and offer comparatively good service. They attract the best Vietnamese doctors because they pay them substantially more than the state does. A Vietnamese man who I respect on many levels advised me that if I have a serious medical problem I should seek treatment in Bangkok, Tokyo, or Singapore. If that is not possible, he said, go to the best Vietnamese private hospital you can find. The doctors will have extensive medical experience. They will know what to do.

He also told me to stay away from the foreign-owned hospitals and clinics, which have a number of foreign doctors on staff, who he maintains are unable to get good positions in their own countries. They only stay in Vietnam for a year or two and are not experts in tropical medicine, he explained. Notwithstanding this advice, I saw American doctors when I had a medical issue. They are educated to a higher standard than their Vietnamese counterparts, and have always provided me with competent care. In addition, the chance of miscommunication is much reduced.

In 2005, accommodations in a for-profit hospital cost as much as $30 per day and included bedsheets, a pillow, and toilet paper. Doctor's fees and laboratory charges were extra. There was only one patient per bed.

Public hospitals cannot be sued for malpractice but private hospitals can. Frequently, private hospitals will not admit those in critical condition and will quickly discharge patients who take a turn for the worse and appear to be near death. People know this and relatives gather to mourn when a loved one is transferred from a private to a public hospital.

*****

OPTIMISM AND HOPE: There are many newspapers in Saigon. A daily paper costs 10 cents at a newsstand and 14 cents if purchased from a roving peddler. Everyone appears to read them: during breaks the cyclo driver, shop worker, bar girl, and student scan the pages of their favorite publications.

Carefully worded reports describe social problems and policies to combat them. The media regularly features stories on HIV/AIDS, pollution, traffic congestion, public safety, criminal activity, errant Việt Kiều (overseas Vietnamese) and foreigners, education, housing, and (surprisingly) out-of-favor, corrupt police and venal officials. Sections devoted to sports and international news are included, as well as employment notices and advertisements. Publications contain no criticism of the government or party, but only describe social problems and solutions under consideration.

Vietnam receives aid from other countries, foreign charitable organizations, and individuals. Frequently, the English language newspaper, The Times of Vietnam, announces new grants from abroad for infrastructure, healthcare, education, and social service projects.

This newspaper has been called a prime example of "congratulatory journalism" because it constantly reports that every government goal has been achieved. Articles report that the party is responsible for good news, and bad news is the result of natural disasters or criminals, but never government incompetence or dereliction of duty. Vietnam is ranked in the bottom 10 (out of 170 countries) in the Press Freedom Index.

Newspapers report that foreigners give money to build schools, hospitals, orphanages, and wells. The healthcare and education of some Vietnamese are paid for with donated money.

Sweden, through its Swedish International Development Agency (SIDA), supports health-related projects in Vietnam. In addition to funding the construction of hospitals and clinics, SIDA provides scholarships to study hospital administration in Sweden.

In 2004, 25 grants for a three-month hospital administration course were offered to persons from six designated underdeveloped countries. Training would be conducted in English. To qualify, candidates had to be nominated by their superiors and have the requisite experience in the subject to be studied. English proficiency and subject area knowledge would be tested by SIDA officials during an interview and were the determining factors in the scholarship selection process.

Doctor Binh, a 29-year-old to whom I taught English, applied for one of the grants. Binh is short, tightly wound, and good-hearted. He is one of two doctors at a leprosarium near Saigon who care for 1,000 lepers and 2,000 of their dependents. The other doctor is 65 years old. "He doesn't do much," Binh said resignedly.

It is a general hospital because they diagnose and treat not only Hansen's disease, but also a wide range of physical and mental illnesses. On an average day Binh is responsible for 120 patients. When I asked how it was possible for him to see so many patients, he told me that in Vietnam not only doctors see patients, but nurses and healthcare workers do, too. Nurses attend two years of nursing school. Healthcare workers study for three years at a technical college. Doctors study medicine for four years at a university and then undergo three years of on-the-job training. All three examine, diagnose, and medicate the sick. Fifteen to twenty of the sickest people are referred to Doctor Binh each day.

He had been working at the hospital for three and a half years. It was his first job after graduating from medical school. His intent was to gain experience before opening his own practice in Saigon. However, in time, even though his salary was low, he wanted to stay. "I love my job and I love my patients," he told me more than once.

One of his many titles at the hospital was Director of Health Systems. Doctor Binh readily admitted that he had no training for that job and complained that the senior doctor was close to retirement and would not let him make changes. The older man wanted no problems.

Doctor Binh was just the kind of candidate SIDA wanted for a health systems management scholarship. He would benefit from the training; so would the hospital and his patients. Vietnam would also be a little closer to having an acceptable healthcare system. First, he had to convince the Swedish interviewer that he was knowledgeable about health systems management—which he wasn't. And second, he had to demonstrate that he possessed a good command of the English language. Although Dr. Binh could speak, read, and write English well, his strong accent made it hard for others to understand him.

On four successive Sunday afternoons we conducted mock interviews in my living room. We used a book from his hospital to identify questions he might be asked, and then located the correct answers and practiced how to pronounce them in English. Nevertheless, his accent remained a problem and it prevented him from getting the scholarship.

Dr. Binh is a determined young man and will try again. He is optimistic about his chances next time and about his future in general. Optimism and hope are related, and they flourish in this country.

HEAD TO TOE: When I wanted to go somewhere that was too far to walk, I traveled by xe ôm. The same drivers were always for hire at the beginning of my alley. I negotiated a fare, climbed on back, and off we went. Minh was my favorite driver; he was slow and cautious on the road. One day when I asked for Minh, I learned he had been in an accident and was hospitalized with a broken leg.

I visited him the following day. There were four beds in the room, eight patients, and a filthy toilet. He was recuperating in a bed with a man whose leg also was in a cast. Same-sex bed sharing is common in public hospitals, especially in the countryside. The female relatives of these men were at their bedsides to feed, clean, and care for them.

TWINS: Thao, my wife, was admitted to a private hospital. She was 38 years old and seven and a half months into her first pregnancy. Her blood pressure had spiked, and she was pregnant with twins. At midnight two days later she was removed from her room, handed her medical file, put in a taxi, and dispatched unaccompanied to a public hospital. The reassuring explanation she received was that the private hospital did not keep dangerous cases.

At the state hospital, Thao was placed in a room with nine other pregnant women and their relatives. Friends had to bring her toilet paper, soap, and a towel. Jerri Hirsh, an American, visited and was appalled by Thao's accommodations. As Thao's money was in the bank, Jerri promptly lent Thao $1,000 and arranged for her to be transferred to the foreigners' floor, where she had a private room and first class care. Within a few days, six weeks early, she gave birth on Christmas Eve 2004, by cesarean section to a boy and girl. Fortunately there were no complications; all three were discharged five days later in good health. I, who am always in the right place at the right time, had traveled to the States only days before Thao was admitted to the hospital. My intent had been to return before she gave birth. On Christmas Day, my friend, Big Bill, called from Saigon and left a message on my answering machine in New York. The message was in code and short: "Ding and Dong have arrived." Bill is an American veteran who has lived in Saigon for 15 years. His calling card identifies him as Ông Mập, Vietnamese for Mr. Fat Man.

Giving birth is a painful, traumatic, and life-changing experience. When I told Em Thy about the twins and Thao's experience at the two hospitals, she gave me a knowing look and recited this bit of feminine wisdom: "A daughter really only loves her mother after the daughter has given birth."

In Vietnam, a woman who gives birth to opposite sex fraternal twins is considered lucky. Since she has a male and a female baby, it is not necessary for her to go through another pregnancy. I told Thao's envious friends that the method of conceiving opposite sex twins was an American secret, which I was happy to share with them. However, their eagerness to learn disappeared when I told them I had to be there when they tried to conceive.

When twins are of the opposite sex, tradition holds that they should have a wedding ceremony as soon as possible after birth. The belief is that in their prior lives they were a couple that had never married. Their spirits have returned as twins to wed, and their wishes must be honored or else the children will have problems. When older, they obviously must marry others; by then the spirits will have forgotten the infants' marriage ceremony.

Huan, my mother-in–law, arrived at our house two months after the births to officiate at the marriage of her grandchildren. She lit candles and incense sticks and placed them around their cribs. Huan hovered over the twins for 15 minutes, chanting ritual incantations. Thao translated her mother's concluding words: "You are married now, the spirits are happy, and your lives will be fortunate."

BOTCHED OPERATION: Phong, my father-in-law, needed a prostate operation. On the appointed day, he traveled by bus to Saigon, alone, and checked himself into a public hospital. In a large plastic bag, he carried the things he would need that the hospital did not supply. His small room was crammed with beds and nine other patients. Soaking clothes filled the sink and drying laundry hung from wall pegs. The room's lone window had no curtain and there were no screens between the beds—only family members sleeping on the floor. A fluorescent wall lamp lit the room, whose walls and cracked ceiling needed scrubbing. Waste encrusted the toilet in the bathroom and filled the room with an eye-watering stench. Groans of men in pain rang through the room. This apprehensive 74-year-old slept on the floor until a bed in the room became empty. He could not have surgery unless a bed to recuperate in was available. It was hospital policy!

His roommates had been operated on already; they were relaxed and in good humor. When I visited, they were teasing Phong about impotence and incontinence, complications all men fear. His wife arrived before the operation. Huan's job was to wash him and his clothes, buy his food and medicine, and generally comfort him during his hospital stay. A young doctor who had not met or spoken with Phong performed his surgery the next day.

For three days after surgery Phong lay in pain. He was double incontinent. The nurse was slow responding to his pleas for help. She was responsible for 70 patients, she explained, and could not come every time one of them cried in pain or soiled a sheet. One of the patients in the room told Phong to give her 15 cents whenever she did something for him, otherwise the next time he needed help she would not come.

No doctor saw Phong until the third day after his surgery, when the surgeon's friend, a doctor from another hospital, arrived and said the surgeon was too busy to come.

"How are you?" the man said.

"I am in pain. I have trouble urinating and when I do there is blood."

"That is normal. You can go home today."

Phong was discharged and, still catheterized, made the two-hour bus ride home. The following day, this time with his wife, he took the bus back to the hospital. The catheter had clogged. He had not urinated since leaving the hospital. An older doctor performed the procedure again, but this time while the original surgeon observed. Phong learned later that within days of his ordeal three other patients of the fledgling surgeon were operated on a second time. The older doctor performed each corrective surgery while the young one watched.

One month later, back in his jungle home, Phong again found he was unable to pee. The clinic near his home was afraid of being blamed for any complications that might arise. They advised him to hurry back to the hospital in Saigon before his bladder burst. At the hospital, they emptied his bladder and scheduled a third operation. However, on the day it was to be performed the doctors cancelled it without an explanation. Phong was confused and bewildered. Four days later, mysteriously free of his troubling symptoms, he was discharged. When presented with the bill he told them, "You did a bad job." He demanded and received a 50% discount.

Phong's problem is gone. He paid a total of $71 in hospital, drug, and doctor fees, not including the nurse's tips.

A FRACTURED JAW: Late one night, a friend, Karl, was hit by a car. His motorbike skidded out from under him and his head smacked the pavement. He lay in the road for 20 minutes before anyone stopped to help him.

Karl was a foreigner so he was given a room on the top floor of a government hospital. It was a floor with private rooms and several nurses. He got the best care available in Saigon and he paid top dollar. They set his broken left arm and fractured jaw. Fifty stitches closed two deep wounds. He was black and blue, and road rash (a euphemism for torn, scraped, and bleeding skin) covered parts of his body. His two-week hospital stay, including medical care and medicine, cost $1,000, a sum far beyond the means of most Vietnamese.

The hospital elevator worked only during afternoon visiting hours and cost seven cents for a round-trip lift. I was told that off-hour visiting was allowed, but no elevator would be available.

CHILDREN'S HOSPITAL: Saigon is not a quiet city. The roar of vehicles, jackhammers, pile drivers, blaring televisions, street vendors, and crowds of busy people wailing, shouting, spitting, and hacking is jarring. From 6:30 a.m. until 10:30 p.m., a deafening noise hangs over the city.

At eye level, one sees cement and brick, no grass or bushes. The only green comes from the tall trees, which struggle to survive the exhaust fumes and other pollution.

Not far from where I lived, in the middle of the grinding din and unhealthy air, were 20 acres of green tranquility. On the grounds of the state-owned Children's Hospital there are no motorbikes, no litter, no noticeable air pollution, and no pulsating racket. The soothing quiescence is interrupted only by the happy, but sometimes anxious, sounds of children, and the melodies of songbirds.

The hospital was established when Vietnam was a French colony. It consists of a mixture of old colonial-style and modern buildings. Magnificent trees shade stone benches that line paths bordering lawns and flower gardens.

Hospital guards are supposed to allow only staff and patients' families to enter the grounds, but they let me come and go. We nodded to each other as I passed. I would find an empty bench and watch small children, some bandaged, some in casts, others on small crutches or in little wheelchairs, make their way around. Concerned parents assisted them. I hoped for them.

The rooms were dormitory-style; cribs lined the walls, four infants or two toddlers per crib. Doors and windows were open for ventilation. There were no fans or air conditioners. Mothers, grandmothers, or aunts stayed at the hospital nurturing the child. They slept on the floor between the cribs. Male relatives napped outside in hammocks anchored to trees and railings.

The buildings and grounds were clean. The staff acted professionally. Patients were well cared for at this serene and peaceful place. Notwithstanding the circumstances, the employees seemed cheerful and the children happy.

DENTAL CARE: Depending on the dentist and his training and equipment, dental care costs and results vary in Vietnam. However, I have not seen anyone walking around holding their jaw in their hands. As with medical care, if one can afford it, top quality dental care is available.

In pain and not wanting to leave the country, I asked for a recommendation. Six French-trained Vietnamese dentists—four men and two women—staffed the private clinic to which I was referred. The waiting room was crowded. I was the only foreigner. Many of those waiting were Việt Kiều who, when visiting their relatives in Vietnam, have dental work performed at a cost much reduced from what they would pay in America, France, or Australia.

The woman who worked on my teeth was professional, competent, and efficient. I hesitate to add that she had a great bedside manner and better equipment than the male dentists. During the course of four visits spread out over two weeks, I had X-rays, a root canal, a porcelain cap installed, a cavity filled, and my teeth cleaned and whitened. The total charge was $125.

MEDICINES: Government hospitals stock medicines made in Vietnam and other less developed countries because they are cheap. However, patients, with good reason, do not trust these drugs. One job of the relative who stays with the patient in the hospital is to take the hospital medicine to a local pharmacy and purchase an equivalent drug made by a pharmaceutical company from an industrialized country.

Pharmacies sell drugs without a doctor's prescription. One either tells the clerk (many are not trained pharmacists) what one wants, or one describes one's symptoms and buys what the clerk recommends. Either way, one never knows if the medicines one purchases are suitable, or if it is a counterfeit. Knock-offs are common. Upsetting to foreigners, medicines mailed from overseas are confiscated by the Vietnamese government.

Local and foreign drug companies have exploited the drug delivery system and undermined the integrity of pharmacy clerks by paying them to sell their products. The medicine that returns the highest profit is recommended to the customer. This is similar to what happens in America when doctors receive expense-free vacations disguised as educational seminars from drug companies.

Patients are at risk.

BEAR PAWS: Western medicine believes that disease originates from outside the body. Bacteria and viruses enter the body to cause sickness. Doctors trained in the West prescribe medicine to kill germs that cause illness.

According to age-old Chinese reasoning, the universe influences the human body. Organs have cosmic analogues. Man's anatomy and physiology are linked to, and influenced by, the stars, planets, and other astronomical objects.

Traditional medicine posits that disease results from an imbalance between yang and yin in certain organs, and not, as in the West, from the introduction to the body of disease-causing agents. The practitioner of traditional medicine uses his knowledge of medicinal plants and ancient therapies to restore the yang and yin balance. When accomplished, the body's vital energy flows, as before, to the affected organ. Thus, the patient is healed because the organ is in harmony again with the cosmos.

In Vietnam, folk medicine exists side by side with Western medicine. Traditional medical schools provide training in Hanoi and Saigon. Pharmacies sell Western medicines, organic compounds, and medicinal plants—often stored on the same shelf. Since traditional medicine has no concept of infection and no real method of surgery, Vietnamese prefer Western medicine for surgery and bacterial diseases. Non-bacterial diseases, exhaustion, and functional disorders are treated with ancient remedies: pineapple juice cures kidney stones; warm buffalo dung spread on sweaty palms eliminates tension; scar tissue is minimized if one avoids eating shellfish while a wound heals; chicken saliva neutralizes the poison of a scorpion bite.

Generally, poor and rural people rely on traditional medicine because they are familiar with it and it is cheaper.

It is true everywhere that a doctor's competency and a patient's luck are critical factors in correct diagnoses and treatment. Bi, my 55-year-old neighbor, is short and heavy. Her demeanor is just on the civilized side of fierce.

One day I saw her limp in obvious pain from her door to a waiting taxi.

"What happened?" I asked. "Can I help?"

"I fell in my house and hurt my leg. I'm going to the traditional medicine doctor to get a leaf."

That evening she described her encounter with the doctor. He had caused her pain by pulling and kneading her shin. He told her she had a loose muscle and gave her leaves wrapped in newspaper, then instructed her to soak them at home and wrap them around her injured limb. When she asked, "How long should I soak them for?" he sharply said, "As long as it takes."

The visit ended badly.

"How much do I owe you?" she asked him.

"Nine dollars."

"Too much."

"Okay," the doctor said and deliberated a moment. "Four dollars and fifty cents."

His superior manner annoyed her and the deep discount convinced her that he had tried to dupe her. "You cheat. Keep your leaves," she said, then left the stunned and unpaid doctor and hobbled outside to hail another taxi.

Bi went to a public hospital, where an X-ray showed a fractured shinbone. She returned home in a cast and on crutches.

Acupuncture, skin pinching, and massage are common pain relief treatments. Berries, herbs, and pulverized animal parts are mixed with alcohol or water to make potions to cure the sick or make men strong. Men drink wine fortified with fruit, penis, liver, heart, antler, snake, lizard, frog, or bear paw to increase their virility. Oh, if it were so easy!

I asked a friend, an expert in such things, "Why bear paw?" and was told that bears hibernate in the cold months, eating and drinking nothing. They sleep in their dens curled up, knees to stomach, paws to nose, and survive by smelling their feet. They have no nourishment other than the scent of their paws, and therefore the paws must be very potent. When consumed by a man they will make him strong.

Recipes for these tonics vary by region and village. The efficacy of formulas and particular ingredients are passionately debated. Good health and a strong sexual appetite are attributed to one's preferred elixir. Men buy mixtures that have the best reputations.

An order of Catholic nuns I worked for makes a medicinal wine that enjoys a high score. At Tết each year they give a thousand bottles to friends, benefactors, police, and government officials. Not surprisingly, the labels on the bottles only promise good health. Nevertheless, men who believe it boosts their libido seek out the good nuns' wine. I received two bottles as a Tết gift. I can attest that drinking the sisters' wine did not made me sick, nor, unfortunately, did it affect me in any other way.

Snake blood, too, supposedly boosts virility. At snake meat restaurants a waiter will behead a snake at your table and drain its blood into a shot glass. Alternatively, a macho patron may choose to separate the reptile's head from its body using his teeth. In either case, the customer drinks the blood, usually with vodka, while the snake meat is grilled at the table. The man (it is always a man) raises his beer glass and at the count of three washes it all down.

It is said that men who eat snake hearts understand birdsong. I was afraid of being disappointed, so I did not try any hearts.

TOUGH QUESTIONS: A French doctor asked me if I would teach English to his hospital's 55-year-old head pharmacist and her younger assistant. He explained that, notwithstanding the country of origin, pharmaceutical packages contained information printed in English. He was convinced the hospital and patients would benefit if the pharmacists' English improved. As with many of my students, these two women had studied English for years but had never had the opportunity to speak it conversationally. Both had Master's degrees in pharmacology and believed that the Party would solve Vietnam's social and economic problems. They were serious students who came prepared to discuss important topics.

One topic was HIV/AIDS. Toward the end of the discussion, the senior pharmacist read aloud the following sentence from a local English language newspaper: "Women who are raped or who have dry sex are more likely to contract HIV/AIDS from an infected man."

"What does that mean?" she said, turning to look at me. "What does dry sex mean, Martin?"

I do not duck often, in fact hardly ever. I take things head on. It works for me, but not in a discussion about dry sex with these women. "I don't know," was my lame answer.

HEMORRHOID SHOP: Another student, Duc, studied medicine during his three years of college. After graduation, he attended a 10-day hemorrhoid seminar that cost $62. He then opened a "hemorrhoid shop" in a house on a busy Saigon street, but closed it three months later because he was not making money. Duc told me he did not know "how to do the hard jobs."

Duc's next employment was as a private doctor for a 55-year-old Korean man. The man, his Vietnamese wife, and Duc lived at the couple's ceramics factory. At 6:30 a.m. every morning, Duc was required to check the man's blood pressure and heartbeat, and to examine his eyes, ears, nose, and throat. Occasionally Duc was summoned late at night to check the man's vital signs under the watchful eye of his pillow-shrouded wife. Nothing was wrong with the man's body, Duc told me. "He is a little crazy. He needs a monk, not a doctor."

The man's wife would not pay Duc's salary while her husband was away for one month in Europe. She reasoned, "Your job is to take care of my husband. My husband is not here. You do no work. You get no pay." Although the factory owner did not overrule his wife when he returned to

Vietnam, he asked Duc to stay on, but Duc refused. "It not a real job," he told me.

Today, Duc lives and works at a government-run drug rehabilitation camp. The camp is located in the jungle near the Cambodian border, far away from everyone. Addicts are kept there to be punished and hopefully cured. They work in the rice fields. Duc treats 300 inmates. He says his job is dangerous because the inmates are able to get drugs and they rob, fight, and sometimes kill one another. For their own safety, Duc and the other staff live inside a barbed wire compound. The army patrols the camp boundary; there is no fence. The criminals are at-large while the prison staff is confined.

Finding medical personnel who will work at the camp is difficult. If Duc stays four years then the government will pay for the completion of his medical schooling—an important and appealing inducement. Duc hopes he has the strength and determination to stay three more years at the camp. His new wife lives with her parents in Saigon. Duc visits her two days a month and worries about her. "It not good way to begin marriage."

THE JACKSON WASH: For many Vietnamese, the standard for beauty is Western. It is sad to hear them say the Western face is more beautiful or handsome. In the same breath, they say the Asian face is not as nice. Plastic surgeons modify a woman's nose, eyes, and lips to look Caucasian. Dimples are added. Skin is whitened by chemical bath. The process requires three 60-minute soaks. Sometimes the whitening treatment is only partially successful, resulting in large white splotches on lovely brown skin. One can only guess at the long-term damage done to the skin and…psyche. Locals call it the Jackson Wash, after the late American entertainer.

DOCTOR WRONG: Former students of mine, a brother and sister both in their thirties, invited me to dinner at their parents' house. The university-educated siblings had low-level government jobs that brought them in daily contact with foreigners. They spoke understandable English and were keen to improve it. Their parents wanted to thank me for teaching their children. I would get a nice meal, and their offspring would have an opportunity to practice their English.

They picked me up in a taxi. We shared the back seat and talked about different things. At one point, the daughter volunteered the following about a recent doctor's visit.

"I go to doctor. Itch often. Woman's problem. Doctor looks everywhere. You know what I mean, Martin? When he finish, I pay. They give me documents. Documents say I virgin. Doctor wrong. He make mistake. I no virgin. Should I go back, say fix records? What you think, Martin? What he see? Stretch skin? Where is it? I look, see no stretch skin."

Neither her brother nor I responded and the conversation switched to other topics. I have no idea why she felt free to speak about this to me.

Perhaps Cervantes' cautionary words apply to this young woman. "Beware! Careless and confused virgins are a source of trouble."

Doctors make mistakes in every country. Peter, an Australian pilot working for Vietnam Airlines, scratched his right ring finger. It became infected and the sore got bigger. The hospital dressed the wound and prescribed antibiotics. A week later his Vietnamese doctor did the same, but still the infection remained. Worried, Peter flew home for treatment. Two days after arriving in Australia, his finger was amputated. He was released from the hospital after 30 days of treatment; eight times a day antibiotics were pumped directly into his heart. The diagnosis was gangrene due to a bacterial infection. He is back in Vietnam and has regained the 35 pounds he lost during this ordeal.

I HAVE NO FAMILY: I had no serious medical problems in Vietnam. I ate what and where the Vietnamese ate. Like them, I took a de-worming pill every six months. It is the size of a silver dollar. One chews it. Intestinal parasites are killed and one experiences no unpleasant aftereffects.

My son Tim and I were in Hanoi during Christmas 2002. We were sightseeing and generally enjoying one another's company. On our second morning, I discovered that I could not put weight on my right foot. My instep was so painful that I could not walk without assistance. This problem developed suddenly. It had not happened before and I had not hurt my foot. In a guidebook, I found French, Japanese, and American hospitals listed. I insisted that Tim spend the day on the prepaid sightseeing tour, and with the aid of our hotel staff I boarded a cab.

Thirty minutes later my driver pulled up to the address listed in my guidebook for the American hospital. Confusingly, across the front of the building were the words "French Hospital." Unfazed, I entered and was assigned the only doctor fluent in English, a 40-year-old Vietnamese woman.

"Your symptoms indicate either gout or arthritis," she said. "A blood test will tell us which."

My wise immigrant father used his money to care for his wife and seven children. Dad once told me he did not go to doctors because they always found something wrong. "That's their business," he stated. "That's how they make money." Understandably, I had not been to a doctor in years, so I asked her to do comprehensive blood tests and a urine analysis.

An hour later she reviewed with me the three-page report. I did not have gout, arthritis, or anything else. The results were normal, within acceptable ranges. She looked me in the eye and said, "You are a perfect man." What a great physician, I thought. Not only did the doctor find nothing wrong with me but she also broke the news in a delightfully pleasing way.

We talked a bit. She guessed that I was an American who had been in Vietnam during the war. "I am a Hue orphan," she told me, and went on to explain that her parents were killed in 1968 during Tết and that after 1976 she and other orphans were cared for and educated in Hanoi. "I have a good job now," she said, "but I have no family. They are unknown to me. I don't know who I am."

To grow up as an orphan in Vietnam where one's family is paramount must have been difficult. I could only imagine the anxiety and despair she had experienced over her lifetime.

"Now your foot must be X-rayed," she ordered, ending talk of the past as quickly as it had come up.

I wanted to respond to her story with kindness and understanding, but she did not give me the chance. I silently watched her turn and leave the room.

My X-ray showed no broken bones. She prescribed an ointment for my swelling and pills for my pain. I left the hospital with the cream, pills, X-rays, a copy of my test results in French, and a receipt for $110. It is a lot of money anywhere, but in Vietnam, it is a fortune few can afford. Two days later my foot was normal again and has been ever since.

Tim and I checked out of our $14-a-night hotel the following morning. We were returning to Saigon. While waiting for our taxi to the airport a policeman entered the lobby and spoke to the manager who then reached into the cash box and gave the officer money. The manager explained to us that he must pay every month because if he does not then the police will cause problems for his business and will not come when he needs help.

FRESH BUT UNSAFE: One feature of Vietnamese culture that immediately strikes the Western visitor is food. Vietnamese food and Western food are quite different. Ingredients, preparation, cooking, and eating etiquette are highly distinct. Vietnamese have a varied diet; they eat everything that grows, crawls, walks, flies, and swims. The variety of dishes and subtlety of flavors is surprising. Vietnamese food is not served spicy hot; one can add chili peppers if that is preferred. Rice, fish sauce, green leafy vegetables, fish, chicken, and pork are staples. Soup and fruit are part of many meals. The taste and smells are amazing and enjoyable. The food is healthy and low in fat. Notwithstanding, expats eat Western food when possible. Every night they crowd the Western restaurants, which are numerous in Saigon, Hanoi, and other large cities. Vietnamese in America experience the same longing for their country's food.

Women go to the market every morning. What they buy they eat that day. The markets are large, city-operated areas under a single roof. They are crowded with produce, merchants, and customers. Every fruit and vegetable available in the United States is also grown here. The names may be different but the food is the same. The Vietnamese name for asparagus, măng tây, translates as "Western bamboo." Food unknown in America can be purchased, too. Edibles are displayed in baskets, on stall shelves, or on the cement floor. Buyers look for quality and haggle over price.

The day's first customer is believed to bring good luck and is given a discount. If she is pregnant, however, this is considered bad luck and she may not be served.

Bargaining is a contest of knowledge and wits. However, to engage the seller, negotiate, and take up her time and then not buy something is considered rude. If you do not buy, the seller may shout and call you names.

In addition to city-sponsored markets, sidewalk markets exist in every neighborhood. Poultry, fish, vegetables, and fruit are displayed on the sidewalk, oftentimes forcing people to walk in the streets. Buyers handle the meat and poultry to see if they are still warm and therefore fresh. If cool to the touch or off-color, they will not buy them unless the price is discounted.

Specialty vendors take goose egg orders from pregnant women. A goose lays 8-10 eggs. The first egg laid is believed to be the most nutritious, and the woman who eats it is thought to be lucky, so expectant mothers pay extra for it. With unbridled trust, mothers-to-be rely on the peddler, who relies on the farmer, who relies on the goose, to verify that the egg they are buying is indeed the first-laid.

Unscrupulous vendors adulterate food to increase their profit. To make food appear attractive and fresh they routinely add substances that have not been tested or approved by the government, risking their customers' health.

In Hanoi one evening I watched a peasant woman force-feed chickens on the sidewalk. She held each one by the neck and pushed white powder down its gullet. Subsequently, I learned that the powder makes the birds retain water and thus it will weigh more in the morning at market. She was fattening her chickens to increase her profit. However, shoppers know the trick; if they feel a hard stomach they refuse to buy, or they demand a discount.

Prices for most things are negotiable, but a warning is in order. Do not negotiate too hard in the market. The seller wants to make a sale, but if the buyer bargains too hard the vendor is likely to deliver bad goods or use a scale that favors her. To ensure fair weight, many women bring their own scale when shopping for food.

Woeful sanitary practices at food establishments are a health risk to all. Beverages, boiled vegetables, roasted corn, sandwiches, pork spreads, sweet sticky rice treats, soups, clams, fish, and meat are purchased for pennies a serving from bicycles and small wagons that serve as mobile food vendors throughout the city. Preparation takes place in home kitchens or on the street. No one inspects the cooking or storage facilities. Since Vietnamese recycle every possible thing, and in this culture where "rice is gold," it is certain that yesterday's leftovers are mixed with the next day's products. Inadequate refrigeration, vermin infestation, and generally poor sanitation habits result in tainted food, which cause intestinal disorders. When friends or students disappear for days, the explanation is usually the same. Three days of diarrhea leaves one weak, sore, and disoriented.

When a foreigner chooses to live in Vietnam, risk of serious sickness must be accepted. When I was a soldier here, I ate all my meals with the Vietnamese. There was no baked Alaska, lobster fra diablo, or pasteurized milk; mostly I remember eating only fish and rice. After eight months I was diseased and emaciated and had lost 40 pounds. I was flown, on a stretcher, to a US Air Force hospital in the Philippines. I spent five weeks there recovering from hepatitis, malaria, worms, and amoebic dysentery.

Frequently, monosodium glutamate (MSG) is used to flavor Vietnamese food. This white, crystalline powder is added to many dishes. No one in Vietnam attributes vague discomforts to the chemical. Most restaurants and house kitchens keep bags of MSG next to the sugar and condiments. The Chinese, Japanese, and Koreans consume large amounts of the chemical as well, with no apparent ill effects. Many Americans believe MSG causes health problems and refuse to eat it. Vietnamese wonder how something they have eaten all their lives without causing them to be sick can be harmful to Americans.

Reckless and criminal acts endanger the food supply. The misuse of pesticides is common. The seminarians I taught were rushed to a hospital after an evening meal; victims of pesticide poisoning.

Animals that die of sickness or unknown causes are promptly BBQ-ed and honey glazed. The attractive, orange-tinted meat is sold to the unsuspecting.

Nine

EDUCATION

Without a teacher you are nobody.
-A Vietnamese saying

In Vietnam, education is a national ambition. It is viewed as the key to an individual's success. Parents sacrifice to pay the costs associated with their children's education. The state promotes a modern educational system, which is strictly standardized and politically controlled. Although underfunded, the system, according to the government, has produced a national literacy rate in excess of 90%. Underlying this statistic is the assumption that any child who makes it to the second grade is literate.

The Vietnamese respect for education and its rewards derives from the teachings of Confucius.

To study and then apply what you have learned...
What greater source of pleasure?
To discuss with friends from distant quarters...
What greater source of delight?
-Confucius in the Analects

In addition to respect, duty, and virtue, Confucius set a high value on the obligation to learn.

Those who are born wise are the highest type of people;
Those who become wise through learning come next;
Those who learn by overcoming dullness come after that.
Those who are dull but still won't learn are the lowest type of people...
I won't teach a man who is not anxious to learn and I will not explain to one who is not trying to make things clear to him.
If I hold up one corner of a square and a man cannot come back to me with the other three, I won't bother to go over the point again.
-Confucius in the Analects

Age is no excuse for not learning. An infant's smile is considered a sign that the baby has just acquired knowledge from God. Contrariwise, a crying tot indicates that the little one failed to learn.

One's educational level has a direct bearing on one's status. A common motif in folk tales is the sacrifice required to educate the oldest or brightest son. Even if not formally schooled, people who are respectful, virtuous, and loyal are considered educated. To call someone uneducated is a grievous insult in Vietnam.

*****

TEACHER'S DAY: In 1076, the National University was established in what is now Hanoi to educate the sons of royalty and elite families. In later years the exceptionally bright sons of peasants attended. A student's success on difficult local, regional, and national exams determined his future. A high score on the palace exam, which the king administered, ensured a high mandarin status and government position. The monarch and his aides questioned the candidates and graded their answers. The sovereign sent those who passed the test home to their villages in a celebratory cavalcade. Motivational posters of these triumphal processions appear in schools throughout Vietnam today and are a common artistic and educational theme.

In times past, the teacher was revered just under the king and ahead of father, monk, soldier, farmer, and merchant. Today, in keeping with traditional philosophy, educators enjoy a high social status. On National

Teachers' Day, November 20th, there are no classes but students are required to go to school to thank their teachers. Pupils present fruit and small gifts.

Although respected, teachers are not paid well. After informing me that poets and novelists are also honored annually, an elderly educator solemnly advised me not to let my daughter marry a man whose profession is honored by the government once a year. "She will always be poor," he confided.

Teachers supplement their meager salaries by charging for extra lessons held after-hours in their homes. Critics complain that the real teaching takes place during these sessions and is available only to children whose parents can afford to pay; or worse, that students get high grades because the instructor has been paid. Many public school teachers also work nights and weekends in private schools.

Most of my students came to my house on Teachers' Day to thank me, and those who did not come telephoned. Every student gave me something. Gifts included a rose, a dahlia, a diary and pen set (pen missing), fruit, medicinal wine fortified with animal organs, a box of corn flakes, a calendar, a desk clock with a company's name printed across the top, and a plaster photograph frame with a mermaid at the base.

On this day students of every age serenade their teachers with "Chalk Dust." The song is a tribute to an old teacher whose hair turned white from her years at the blackboard.

I felt honored by the visits and the gifts and that was the intent. The Vietnamese saying, "One gift is a worry, two are a debt," came to mind. One of my doctor students presented me with a bamboo scroll on which had been painted in ancient Vietnamese script: "You teach me one word, you are my teacher; you teach me half a word, you are still my teacher."

STANDARDS: Parents everywhere do what they can to give their children opportunities and advantages. Most people believe that a top quality education can lead to limitless possibilities and untold wealth.

Private international high schools offer a full academic curriculum at a cost of $20,000-$30,000 per annum. Professional teachers from Western nations earn $40,000 for a one-year contract. Children of foreigners and of wealthy Vietnamese attend these schools in the hope of admission to prestigious overseas universities.

Vietnamese study English and with good reason. It is the language of tourism, commerce, and international organizations. A good knowledge of English is necessary to succeed at many jobs in Vietnam; a premium is paid to proficient speakers. For this reason, English language instruction is required at all public schools beginning in grade one.

There are numerous privately owned English academies in Vietnam. A few have high standards and provide excellent instruction. However, most instructors are Vietnamese whose spoken English is not good. Many of the academies are substandard and a waste of time and money. Unrealistic expectations, ignorance of modern educational standards, low cost, and lack of quality alternatives explain why parents send their children to such schools.

The English academies compete for the limited number of native English-speaking teachers, who earn $15-$25 an hour. A few are hired to impress the parents—a recruiting aid. Most are not professional teachers. Usually they are men between jobs, or on second careers, or who have retired, or they are just travelers. Their teaching ability varies, and many are unqualified and unreliable.

I was asked to monitor an English class taught by a Canadian. Students had complained that they could not understand him. Nor could I. He was French-Canadian and spoke the patois of his people. His Canadian passport allowed him to pass as an English speaker. They let him go when I told the principal the man was not a native English speaker.

AMERICAN HISTORY: A friend of a friend asked me if I would teach at his university.

"Are you a teacher there?" I asked.

"No," Do replied, "I am the dean of the English department."

Do was skeletally thin and of medium height, with a broad smile and piercing eyes. He was disarming, friendly, and enthusiastic. His English was flawless. The government-owned university had three campuses with a total enrollment of 8,000 students. The following day I visited the English department.

What had once been a local jail was now used for classrooms. The three-story building had become too decrepit to house felons so they were moved to a new jailhouse. The university had purchased the lockup ten years earlier. Do allowed that the only money spent on the building since its purchase was to paint the school name over the door.

Every room was dirty, and the walls were cracked and peeling. Narrow steel steps connected the levels. The hallway floors had been constructed of metal grating, thus making it possible to observe prisoners who were out of their cells.

Bits of torn newspaper had collected in the corners of the bathrooms, where there were unwashed and seatless toilets. Instead of urinals, a rusting metal trough hung thigh-high from a grimy wall. Broken faucets made soap and towels unnecessary. There was no toilet paper. Students carried a daily ration in their schoolbags.

Appalled by the school's condition I resolved not to teach there, but I was seduced when offered a position in the Foreign Languages School. I could pick the course I would teach from a list of 43 subjects, and I chose American History. I looked forward to interesting discussions and the exuberance of youth in my classroom. Other subjects required to earn a BA degree in English included: British History, American-British Literature, Sociolinguistics, English Syntax, American-British Society and Culture, and Marxist-Leninist Theory.

I would have 35 pupils in my class, each with a new textbook. Do assured me that my students could speak English. To prepare for the course he gave me a 30-page photocopy of U.S. history materials taken from the Internet. This included a list of historical events from 1776 to 2004, the names of 43 presidents and the 50 states by order of entry into the Union, the dates the 11

Confederate States seceded from and were readmitted to the Union; and the entire U.S. Constitution.

The classroom I was to teach in was the former holding cell where prisoners were kept until processed. It was outfitted with rows of wooden benches. They faced an old, grey metal desk that rested on a makeshift timber platform. Iron bars reinforced the door and large rear window.

When the time came for me to teach, Do introduced me to the class and encouraged students to ask me questions during the course. He informed them that each student was required to submit one multiple-choice question to me before the end of the term. The final exam would include their questions and account for 100% of their grade.

For four years, I taught every Monday morning from 7 to 11:30. Photocopies of the same 30-page set of U.S. History materials that I had been given were distributed on the first day. Boldly stamped in red letters on the cover were the words NEW UNITED STATES HISTORY TEXTBOOK.

I began my second class by reviewing what I had discussed previously. The students were bewildered and with good reason. This group was not the class I had taught earlier. Of great surprise to me, the American History course had two sections. I did not have 35 pupils, I had 70—and many of them did not understand me. Spirited conversations about slavery, Manifest Destiny, the New Deal, and the Cold War would be impossible. Students did not volunteer comments or ask questions. English was a problem for about half of them and, perhaps more importantly, so were the expectations we had of each other's classroom role. In Vietnam, teachers lecture and students slavishly write out their words. The students copied my words the best they could but did not appear to think about what I was saying. Determined to engage them, I walked around the classroom challenging them. "Are you a rock? Talk to me. Ask me a question." As I approached, heads lowered to inspect notebooks. However, students could not hide from a microphone thrust under their nose. As they became comfortable with my teaching method and me, they responded more readily with comments about American immigration, race relations, welfare, social security, and wars.

Twice my lesson got their undivided attention. A low rumble spread across the room as they whispered and translated. That America got its name from Amerigo Vespucci, the 15th-century explorer, interested them. The origin of the Native Americans excited them, too. One thin young lady with bulging, almond-shaped eyes asked, "Did the Red Indians really come from Asia? Did they really walk across the ice to America?" Her voice was incredulous.

These incidents by themselves did not free me from feeling that I was a participant in a conspiracy to defraud the students and their parents. Nevertheless, I taught them a great deal about America, but I wondered what they learned. In the grand scheme of things, the rotten school building, the misinformation, and the half-truths I had been told did not matter. I loved being there.

LAW IN SIXTEEN NIGHTS: In 2006 I taught a law course at an Australian-owned business school. After three years of night school, the students receive a degree in international business management. The degree helps them obtain employment with foreign companies that do business in Vietnam. Competition for these jobs is intense because the companies offer benefits, good pay, and the possibility of travel.

The business law course ran for 16 weeks, meeting every Wednesday from six to nine p.m. Except for two 19-year-old women who attended university during the day, my students worked full-time at demanding office jobs. The 14 enrollees ranged in age from 19 to 54. They were attentive but tired when class began, and exhausted by the time it ended. The two university pupils were also enrolled at a Japanese language school. They said going to three schools was difficult but would be worth it when they finished. When I asked, they told me they were at the top of both their university class and the Japanese language school. Not surprisingly, they were also my best students.

There are two legal systems in the West. England and her former colonies have legal systems based on the Common Law, which developed in England over the course of 1,500 years. Largely it is judge-made law and relies on precedent to provide legal continuity and public certainty. On the other hand, other European nations and their former possessions, including Vietnam, embrace a legal system that harbors the Civil Law, which is based on Roman principles and concepts. The Civil Law judge is bound by the provisions of law enacted by a legislative body, not by previous judicial interpretations. The textbook my class used was Common Law based.

Since 1975, provisions of the hundred-year-old Napoleonic Code have been changed in Vietnam, first by Soviet-style laws intended to implement unbending communist polices, and then after 1986 by laws to encourage business, property privatization, and foreign investment. Those charged with interpreting and enforcing the law are challenged by its conflicting provisions and expectations.

After my discharge from the army in January 1964, I attended law school for three years. The curriculum included core subjects and electives. Some courses lasted one semester; some took a year. My Vietnamese business law students received one night of instruction on each of 16 common law subjects. In condensed three-hour lessons, I taught them the law relating to torts, property, contracts, corporations, bankruptcy, etc. Not once during these 48 hours did a student ask me a question. I knew they did not learn much about these areas of the law in one night. It was not possible to absorb so much law in so short a time. However, the business degree must have had value because students kept enrolling and graduates got jobs with foreign companies. They were trying to succeed by hard work and chance.

The final exam arrived from Australia. The school's Vietnamese administrator asked me to review the questions and answers with my students prior to the test date. "But don't show them the exam," he cautioned me. "It is not allowed." He recognized the difficulty of mastering the subject in such a short time and, I suspect, feared for his job if the students' failure rate was high. Astonishingly, only five students attended the review session. All five of them received passing grades. Six of the other nine pupils failed.

Before retiring from my law practice, my billing rate for legal advice was $500 per hour. I earned $7 per hour to teach this course. Time and circumstances foster humility.

PILOT SCHOOLS: Saigon is divided into school districts, with nearly 500 primary schools and one million students. Children must attend their neighborhood school. Public schools are supervised by the Ho Chi Minh City Board of Education. The school year runs from September to June. Many schools have two sessions: 7 – 11:30 a.m. and 1:30 – 5 p.m. Still others conduct single sessions ending at 4 p.m. Classes last 45 minutes. Some public schools are superior to others and parents do what they can to get their children admitted to the best. A cash payment to the principal of the preferred school ensures admission.

A person in a high government position who I never met did me a favor. He obtained for me a six-year residency visa for $60. No longer did I have to pay $150 every six months for a new visa. I asked my intermediary, a school principal I had assisted without a charge, why this man had helped me. The educator explained that, years ago, as a favor, he had increased the test score for the official's son so that the son could attend the city's top high school.

The primary school I taught at overflowed with 2,600 pupils, but it was well equipped and the teachers and administrators were caring of the children. On the ground floor, a part time medical and dental clinic served the students free of charge. Teachers identified for me the pupils who were police officers' children. I was informed and forewarned.

As the children entered the classroom, they bowed to me with arms folded at the waist and eyes downcast. It was a modified kowtow, the traditional Sino-gesture of subservience and respect. Vietnamese children learn it at an early age.

I was teaching English to a class of six- and seven-year-olds at five p.m. on a Thursday afternoon. I stood in the classroom under a photograph of Ho

Chi Minh, who gazed down benevolently. Affectionately, adult and child alike refer to him as Bác Hồ, Uncle Ho. To the left of the photo a plaque bore words attributed to him.

The first things are respect and discipline.
The second are knowledge and the Vietnamese language.
The third is love of country.
From these will come successful students.

Hanging on the walls were other quotations ascribed to Bác Hồ. They are intended to inspire and motivate. One of them instructs:

Love country, love Vietnamese.
Learn well, work hard.
Keep solidarity, maintain discipline.
Be simple, faithful, and brave.
Seek good health and cleanliness.
Learn so Vietnam will have glory.

The children see these words every day and, of course, are influenced by them. Skeptics wonder if Bác Hồ ever said all the inspirational things attributed to him.

Pointing at a picture of a lion, I said, "This is a lion," and in unison 20 children repeated my words. When their pronunciation was perfect, I pointed at another picture and asked, "What are these?" The children looked at one scene after another and said, "They are pencils," "They are monkeys," and "They are mammoths." Mammoths, no less. A writing lesson followed the pronunciation exercise with me at the blackboard and the children at their desks. I faltered when I wrote "buffalo" on the blackboard. Did it have one "f" or two? I dreaded being corrected by the children.

The school had been designated a pilot school for the intensive study of English. Students who qualified for the intensive course had eight weekly 35-minute English classes, in addition to normal academic requirements. If the pilot program were deemed a success, it would be expanded to all primary schools in Vietnam, which is what happened.

The classrooms at this school surrounded a large courtyard on three sides. The two-story building was mustard-colored and the rooms were a gray-blue and stained with streaks of yellow and white. Classrooms were brightly decorated but needed paint. Water leaks and time had left their marks. Despite their age, the wooden desks and benches were graffiti-free. They were not marred with scratched initials, rude words, or knife gouges.

After lunch (paid for by the parents), double-hinged desktops were opened to make sleeping platforms for the one-hour siesta. Bigger children slept on the floor, on woven reed mats with schoolbags as pillows.

During class, the children sat in front of me in uniforms that were white above the waist and blue below. Some children were hyperactive, some exhausted. They yawned, stretched, scratched, yelled, and taunted. At one point I saw a seven-year-old boy walking from desktop to desktop, while yet another was under his desk, book in hand, repeating the words "lion," "monkey," and "mammoth" in Vietnamese instead of English. Girls huddling in the back of the room whispered and wrote in their notebooks. Several sat straight-backed, with hands folded on their desks, and earnestly pronounced each English word just so. All of this activity occurred under the ever-watchful eyes of their legendary and revered leader.

"Hello, Uncle Ho."

My appeal to the ultimate teacher always brought order for a few minutes.

A FULL-THROATED WAIL: Vietnamese parents are involved in their children's education. They attend monthly parent-teacher conferences to learn of their child's progress. They are permitted on the school grounds but not in classrooms. As it is the tropics, the windows have bars but no glass. The classroom door remains open. Parents can stand outside and through the glassless windows monitor the teacher and their child. Some call out answers to their little ones, and some censure them from the hallway.

Late one afternoon, I raised my voice at a disruptive young girl. She was interfering with my teaching and her classmates' learning. From the window, a torrent of criticism enveloped the child. Her father had scolded her, and she was terrified. No shrinking violet, she did not quietly weep but burst into a full-throated wail. It was astounding that such a small person could produce such a piercing, continuous sound. She could not be reconciled. Her father glared at her from the window. I ended the class 15 minutes early. At the next class, under the watchful eye of papa, she said she was sorry. I silently vowed not to raise my voice again to any of these little darlings. They stir the heart of this old lieutenant of infantry.

INQUIRING DIGITS: On Saturday mornings six children at a time grouped around me. Seated on folding metal chairs, we faced each other across a low wooden table to practice conversation and learn how to construct sentences. I asked them, "How are you? What is your name? How old are you? How many people are in your family?" I reminded them to look me in the eye when they responded. Culturally, children are not supposed to look directly at an adult. They show respect by looking down.

At six and seven years old, their attention span was short. They forgot where they were and what they were supposed to be doing. They hit their neighbors and rattled off bursts of Vietnamese. Little fingers searched nostrils and, since this is a handkerchief-free country, placed the contents on their clothes or desk. Then those very same inquiring digits promptly reached to play with the hair on my arms. One little girl lifted up her dress by its hem to muffle a great sneeze and then earnestly inspected the material for deposits.

These children were among the best English pupils in their age group at the school. For a fee, they were attending extra lessons in preparation for a proficiency test at the British Consulate. At the last class before the test, I played the role of the Englishman who would administer the exam. In private, I tested each child's speaking, listening, and writing skills. The principal informed the parents that the children must get used to a foreigner testing them; otherwise, they will fail the test.

After they were tested at the consulate, their exam papers were sent to England to be graded. Two months later the scores arrived and deserving students received certificates of proficiency. Parents and students alike prize these certificates. They are necessary for admission to higher-level classes and years later are shown to prospective employers as proof of English competence. In 2007, for this service, the British government charged $40 per child, a princely sum in Vietnam where for many families it is a significant portion of their monthly income. Naturally, because of the cost, poor children cannot take the test.

Public schools are not free. Parents must pay for their children's schooling. Thousands cannot afford the cost and so their offspring do not receive an education. If the children are lucky, they learn free of charge in "love schools" run by religious groups and other charity organizations. Some students do not begin at these schools until they are in their early teens, so classes consist of mixed age groups and abilities. Love schools rely on donations from abroad. Many such facilities are makeshift and shabby. However, dedicated, determined, and caring women staff these schools, and poor students are educated.

In 2004, I taught two classes a week at one such school and was transformed by the joyful and inquisitive students and generous staff. Surprisingly, two of my fourth grade students were 16 years old. The Anh Linh School had begun 12 years earlier in an abandoned pigsty with 19 students who were the children of prostitutes. In 1995 the nuns made a worldwide fundraising appeal to the alumni of their former high school, which had been confiscated by the communists after 1975. Enough funds were received to buy land and construct a walled compound with a small school building and dormitory.

While I was there, a volunteer named Jerri Hirsh was teaching at the school. The nuns found her a room near the compound, where she lived for a year. Upon returning to Minneapolis, Jerri founded Bridges To Learning, a non-profit corporation that raises funds for the school. Over the years, she and her husband, Bob MacMurdo, have raised hundreds of thousands of dollars, which have been used to build modern primary and high school buildings.

Every year 250 children of all faiths are educated for free at Anh Linh School. The curriculum is the same as in the public schools; no religion is taught.

In addition to an education, each student receives breakfast and lunch, a monthly haircut, two new uniforms a year, English language instruction, and a chance to participate in cultural activities. Without Anh Linh and Bridges to Learning, these children would be street kids or worse, with little hope for the future.

TRAINING SESSION: Teachers, predominately women, attend mandatory conferences, lectures, and other instruction to improve their classroom skills. They are conversant with educational theory and seem current with Western educational ideas. I was asked by one principal to lecture on the total physical response method of teaching, which I declined to do for the simple reason that I was not qualified. I had no experience as an educator and I told him so.

On another occasion, Cuong, an official at the Department of Education, asked me to attend a citywide teacher training session. Cuong was 57, bone-thin, and tired-looking. Two white, three-inch-long hairs grew from a dime-sized black mole on the right side of his face; a beauty mark, I was informed. His high forehead, a traditional belief holds, is indicative of superior intelligence.

The classroom was large. Thirty teachers sat in the back. Pen and paper for note taking and bottled water were at their desks. Thirty-five 10- and 11-year-old pupils sat in the front of the classroom and were to receive a 45-minute English lesson. Their teacher distributed a two-page lesson plan to the adult observers and reviewed it with them. She disclosed that the students had studied this lesson about question words three days earlier.

The instruction was in English, which was used to keep order as well. She used songs, writing and conversation exercises, games, and flashcards during the lesson. The students were responsive, and at lesson's end it was clear they understood the meaning and use of the words: who, what, when, why, where, which, how, can, may, and did.

The children were dismissed and the teacher received feedback from her peers. Everyone spoke about her teaching skill and splendid lesson plan. Several teachers took the opportunity to plead with the Board of Education officials for higher teacher salaries and additional money for teaching materials.

Cuong stood and addressed the group. His words were to the effect that Vietnam is using American educational philosophy and teaching techniques and since there is an American in the room, he should be asked to comment about the class and the teacher's performance. Unqualified and unprepared, I stumbled through 10 minutes of praise for the teacher, the children, the lesson plan, and the general state of education in Vietnam. When it was over and the small talk had ended, I edged towards the door but was intercepted by an official who presented me with an envelope containing $7. "We always pay guest speakers," he said. "Otherwise, next time they don't come." Only then was it clear to me that they had planned to have me talk from the moment I had been invited.

NON-VERBAL COMMUNICATION: Many aspects of Vietnamese and English language structure are strikingly different, and thus complicate the learning process. For example, the Vietnamese equivalent of "be" is "là." However, "là" is rarely used to link a subject with its predicative adjective. Many Vietnamese sentences have their own built-in verbs. For example, the words "Nó đói," means "He hungry," but they are understood as "He is hungry."

As I was leaving the training session, several teachers gathered around me and one of them explained that students have trouble learning the English linking verb "to be."

"There is nothing like it in Vietnamese," she said, "but we have the verb 'to were.'" Everyone smiled when she explained that "quơ" is pronounced "were" and means to speak with your hands.

People everywhere use body language to communicate. It is instinctive and doesn't involve conscious thought: clasped hands may indicate anxiety and uncertainty; crossed arms often show negativity and unreceptiveness; a downward gaze and low voice can mean submissiveness; and avoiding eye contact when speaking could indicate the topic is embarrassing or the truth is being shaded.

Gestures convey meaning, emphasis, and emotions, but these movements and meanings tend to be culturally distinct. In Vietnam, it is demeaning to summon a person by extending your arm and moving upturned palm and fingers back towards your body. The proper way is to extend your arm palm-downward and wave your fingers to your palm.

An effective way to make beggars and street vendors leave you alone is to rotate a hand while holding it across your body. No words are necessary. It is efficient and not insulting. Those persons then leave because they realize you are not a tourist. They do not want to waste their time on you. This person knows the culture and is well informed, they reason. If a foreigner does not know this gesture he will be followed and pestered for money.

Although I have studied Vietnamese for many years, I will never know what certain words and gestures mean. One time, Em Thy took me to the electric company to show me how to pay my monthly bill (which in 2004 never exceeded $40). During our walk, she slapped my hand and rebuked me sharply: "Stop that. Don't do that." I had been scratching the top of my right index finger with the pad of my right middle finger. She would not tell me what it meant, but only said, "You don't know what you are doing." Words I still ponder. In time, I learned that curling the middle finger over the index finger refers to the female sexual organs. It is considered a rude gesture. I had been insulting my landlady and the people we passed on the street.

I had expected to wait in a line until it was my turn to pay the electric bill. Instead, I was propelled forward by the push of bodies. Each customer clutched his or her invoice and cash in a raised hand. At the payment window both were snatched randomly by a clerk who counted the money, stamped a receipt, and slid it to a supervisor for approval. No words were exchanged when the clerk handed the receipt to the customer. Those who had paid lowered their head and forced their way through the press of impatient customers. This is also the way one buys a railroad ticket or settles a water bill. At banks and airline offices, though, service is provided in order of arrival, and order prevails.

DEFICIENT FLIRTS: Xuan, a school district chief, invited me to a countryside outing with 70 English teachers who taught grades one to six. A mutual friend conveyed the invitation. He also told me I was expected to give a 30-minute speech on the two-and-a-half hour, one-way bus trip. Fair enough, I thought.

I met Xuan when I arrived at our departure point at 5:30 a.m. He was tall and sturdy for a Vietnamese. This 60-year-old man in a long-sleeved white shirt had a slow but sincere smile. He looked very much the part of an administrator.

We spoke briefly, after which he handed me an envelope. "Thank you for coming, Mr. Martin. Here is $65." I was surprised because I had not been told I would be paid. With trepidation, I wondered what other responsibilities I would have during the trip.

The teachers were dressed casually for their annual outing and appeared in good spirits. At our luncheon, instructors from different primary schools participated in classroom games so they could learn how to use them in their classrooms.

I had prepared a talk on homonyms. What I did not know was that there were three buses. Twice the buses stopped and I was transferred to a new group of expectant, cheerful young men and women—mostly women. Three times that morning I stood before the seated passengers with a microphone in my right hand while my left hand grasped whatever was convenient for stability. On the way to our destination, I was drawn into conversation, at times receiving flirtatious glances and winks, I was sure. After lunch, Xuan asked me to speak on any topic of my choosing for 20 minutes. Not having been given prior notice, I was unprepared. Reluctantly, I took the proffered microphone and with help from the muse of improvisation began by saying that although the Vietnamese had many good characteristics they were not perfect. Silence ruled. I had their attention.

"Vietnamese are deficient flirts."

I continued: "Not only do Vietnamese not know how, when, or where to flirt, they can't even wink properly." The group became animated. The young women agreed that men did not know how to flirt correctly. "What a waste," one said. Under my careful supervision they practiced flirting, and then we had a group wink session. The males responded with unveiled chauvinistic sentiments. It was all in good fun and even the school district chief joined in. My 20-minute presentation stretched to 30. At its conclusion, a lanky woman volunteered in perfect English that it was difficult to become a good English speaker. "Even after learning correct grammar and pronunciation there are many things about the language which puzzle Vietnamese." For example, she asked, "Why is abbreviation such a long word?"

On the return trip, I did not have to come up with new examples of words that sound or are spelled the same as other words but have different meanings. Instead of homonyms, teasing, coy looks, shy glances, touching, staring, mocking, ribbing, and double entendres were explained, discussed, and rehearsed. They were learning a life skill. One young woman asked me the meaning of the words, "Love me, love my dog."

We arrived back in Saigon mid-evening. It had been a 15-hour day. The rigors of the trip and the reality of our age gap combined to make me feel very old. I was tempted to whiten my teeth and blacken my hair.

"My teachers learned a lot of English today," Xuan commented. He invited me to give an oral exam to 30 second-graders the following week. Being a native speaker, he said, I would know the correct sentence structure and pronunciation. Another reason was that parents could not influence a foreigner. If the test giver were Vietnamese, it was possible he would have some connection with a child's family. The results might not be fair. However, I found out there are other ways to influence test results.

I was flattered and in turn curious when Xuan arrived at my house at six a.m. on the test day. I did not expect an escort. In the car, he explained that his niece was the third child I would test. He spoke her name and showed me what it looked like in print. Twice he did this, each time with his eyes locked on mine.

The principal of the school where the test was to be held met our car at the gate and led me to his office. He introduced me to his seven-year-old daughter and declared that she had already received a perfect score on the written part of the test. When her turn came, the teacher who took this child to the testing room informed me once again that she was the principal's daughter.

Both of these men had given me teaching assignments during the school year and I hoped they would continue to. It was clear they wanted me to inflate the test scores for the two girls, but they did not explicitly ask. I would have said no if they had. They tried to compromise me. It was not subtle. However, the intrigue was unnecessary. Both girls received excellent scores on their own merits; the principal's daughter scored 100%, Xuan's niece 90%.

I asked each child four questions. To one eight-year-old I said, "What do you like?"

She questioned back, "Do you mean food or hobby?"

Surprised, I said, "Hobby."

"My hobby," she answered. "Is looking at the stars and the moon. They are beautiful and they make me feel good."

LONG XUYEN: On a Wednesday afternoon, I left by van for Long Xuyen to teach 200 English teachers. The six-hour ride was interesting because of the scenery and because four of my five companions had cell phones. The phones were in use the whole trip, sometimes two at the same time.

My fellow travelers included a Vietnamese director of a British-owned publishing company, his three assistants, and a 52-year-old female teacher. Eight hundred books titled How to Teach English had been sold to the Long

Xuyen Province Education Department. Our job was to instruct 200 Vietnamese English teachers how to use them.

The program began with a welcoming speech, during which the director introduced his team. While talking to the teachers from a podium, his phone rang. Ignoring the audience, he took his cell from his pocket and spoke for 10 minutes. Pinned to the director's chest was a microphone, which picked up his words for all to ponder.

I gave a 45-minute talk on how to read English. During the break I circulated among the teachers, asking several of them if they had understood me. They answered more or less the same: "Yes, about 70%. You spoke slowly and clearly but I didn't understand all your words." One of them observed, "You must remember, Mr. Martin, we are teachers from the countryside. We don't know as much English as teachers from Saigon. If we did we could have gotten jobs there or in Hanoi." A male teacher volunteered, "Why do the children of Long Xuyen have to learn English?" He continued, "There are no foreigners living here, and anyway, all of the children will grow up to be farmers or farmers' wives."

Long Xuyen is the name of a province and its largest city. The province, with a population of two million, is the rice bowl of Vietnam. Beautiful, bright green rice fields stretch to the horizon on either side of narrow, poorly maintained roads. I knew these were the same fields I had trudged across in 1963 while looking for the shifty Viet Cong. This time my mission was quite different.

After lunch on Thursday, the director told me we were going to spend the night in Long Xuyen City and then go to a Cambodian border town to see a famous temple. The next morning we sped to Chau Doc, a three-hour drive. The shrine was built in honor of a spirit woman (Bà Chúa Xứ, or The Lady of the Realm) who lived on Sam Mountain overlooking the town. She protected the people with supernatural powers and would grant wishes and change bad luck to good if one left an offering, preferably a suckling piglet. When we arrived, we found one such offering on a table in front of the altar.

Next to it was a massive, four-foot-high iron safe. A huge padlock secured the door. A slot for cash donations had been cut into the top. My companions (all Buddhists) prayed, burnt incense, and offered donations. On the altar towered an enormous statue of The Lady of the Realm.

At the temple, caged songbirds were on sale for a dollar each. The purchaser would release a bird to fly away. The bird would carry the buyer's prayers and wishes to The Lady of The Realm, and she would reward the person's act of kindness.

"Is this a Buddhist temple?" I asked.

"No," I was told, "but the story about Bà Chúa Xứ might be true so we honor her." One million people a year come to pray at this shrine.

Scholars believe the Lady's statue is an ancient artifact, brought by boat from Cambodia and placed on the Mountain. It's theorized the statue is actually a male figure that the Khmer in ancient times placed on the Mountain. Unknown is why the Vietnamese so long ago moved the statue into the temple and painted it as a woman in silk dress with jewelry. One wonders why there is disagreement about the statue's sex. Are there no anatomical clues?

We stopped at a border free-trade zone to get bargains. While I was being told about the free-trade zone, my companions all laughed and one of the assistants said, "Smuggled goods."

A woman was selling what looked like industrial bras. You know what I mean? She stood in front of a table of 50 carefully displayed multicolored ones. The woman teacher with us inspected several before picking one that she tried on over her blouse. She turned this way and that and we told her it looked good. However, she was cautioned by the director not to be provocative.

During the trip, we had four restaurant meals. They were delicious. I had forgotten how good Vietnamese food could be. The meals were far better than any Vietnamese food I'd had in Saigon during the preceding six years.

By my reckoning, I spent 18 hours in the car with these people. I can speak a little Vietnamese and can understand somewhat more, so most of the time I looked at the countryside while they spoke to one other over loud radio music and noisy cell phone conversations. At times, I heard them speak my name to get what they wanted. "Martin has to go to the toilet." "Martin needs coffee." "Martin is hungry."

"Martin has to go to the toilet" was said more than once. At those times the car would pull over and several passengers would rush out to relieve themselves, but first a fee had to be negotiated with the owner of a nearby house. For six cents each, we were allowed to walk through the ground floor of someone's home to the squat toilet at the back of the house.

From time to time they practiced their English. Sometimes I was asked the meaning of idioms. "What does 'knocked up' mean?" one woman asked. Buying time, I said in England it means to call someone on the telephone or to knock on someone's door. "No, no, what does it mean in American English? I saw these words in a story on the Internet; a man wrote it from California. What does it mean?" She insisted. I explained that it meant to make a woman pregnant, or to be pregnant. My example was "Martin knocked up Joan." Laughter followed as the woman translated this into Vietnamese.

Public manners in Vietnam are atrocious, but in private Vietnamese are polite. The director and his assistants were very kind to me, deferential, and solicitous. "Are you comfortable? Are you tired? Do you want water? Are you hungry?" I was an old American man who they were looking after.

The car had interior, stick-on window screens to shield us from the sun. As the car twisted, turned, and changed direction, the screens were adjusted. At one point the sun shone directly into the front seat. The director, who was sitting in the front passenger seat, placed the screen on the right side of the windshield. The driver did not have a full view to the front, but the boss was comfortable.

We arrived in Saigon at one p.m. on a Friday. The car pulled into the driveway of the director's office. As we were in the driveway, I opened the car door without looking behind me. A passing motorbike crashed into the door, and the driver, who had taken a short cut, fell to the ground. His load of stones spilled out. I instinctively started in the direction of the prostate driver but was intercepted by the boss and steered away. Everyone ignored the fallen man, who was moaning. "He pretend," said the woman teacher. "Stay away. He want money."

At the office, I was paid my wages of $30 and given two bottles of wine as a bonus. The motorbike driver was standing by his motorbike as we left the office. He was repackaging his load of crushed stone into plastic bags.

REFEREE: Several years ago, Vietnam decided to change from teaching students British English to teaching them American English. This required revising textbooks and other teaching materials, and retraining every Vietnamese English teacher. Students are now taught American pronunciation and spelling. Good-bye, cheerio!

Teaching materials typically include cassette tapes and DVDs featuring native English speakers reading dialogue from the revised textbooks. I had been recruited for the textbook English Eight. Once finished, my voice and image would be added to an inventory of other native speakers' recordings of the exact same reading. I was told that Hanoi would decide from among all the recordings which voices and images would be used for the revised teaching materials.

Five minutes after arriving at the recording studio, and without practice, I began reading the script. I stumbled over words and forgot whole sentences, but eventually I got it right. One passage was about Antipater of Sidon who, as everyone surely knows, was an ancient Greek writer and poet. He is famous for his list and observations of the Seven Wonders of the World. Not knowing how to pronounce his name, I consulted a dictionary of proper nouns for guidance before recording.

Two weeks later I received a call from a man at the Education Ministry in Hanoi. He did not speak English well. Several times, I asked him to repeat himself. He wanted to know why I had said "eleven hundred" for the number 1,100 when another native English speaker had said "one thousand one hundred." He also questioned my pronunciation of Antipater of Sidon. An American had enunciated it differently on her recording. "Which one is correct?" he mumbled.

As with most matters dealing with education, the English textbook revision project, right down to pronunciation and usage, was controlled from Hanoi. Although the taping of the revised textbook was being done in a Saigon recording studio, a bureaucrat from Hanoi would review all decisions. He was the English referee. I was on pins and needles, fearful of the worst, until I received the wonderful news that the referee had twice ruled in my favor.

In 2010, John and Eileen, our six-year-old twins, were recruited to record CDs of second and third grade English textbooks for use in primary schools throughout Vietnam. A car from the Department of Education drove us to the soundproof recording studio. This was the twins' first job. Understandably, they were unsure and apprehensive, but after a while they settled in and enjoyed themselves. Soon they were acting out and being rambunctious. The twins used hand gestures to emphasize the sentences they were recording. Pantomime added clarity to the words they read. To the boss's dismay, they added humorous remarks not contained in the textbooks. Department employees gathered to watch, laugh, and clap. We returned home by car. John and Eileen had each earned $30 for three hours of work.

One month later they were invited back for a second session, and a second payday. In both instances the CDs could not be released until approved by the Education Ministry.

BE CAREFUL, MARTIN: The books I used for teaching were usually published in England, then translated into Vietnamese and finally into American English. The multiple conversions caused numerous typos and obvious mistakes. My favorite was the explanation of the expression "rather you than me." Its meaning was described in both American English and Vietnamese as "I prefer to be you, I wish I were you."

On Mondays and Saturdays I taught English to six nuns in their walled convent. Classes were held from two p.m. to five p.m. and seven p.m. to nine p.m. In between, 30 nuns and I attended Mass and then had dinner. They enjoyed having a man in their midst and fussed over me. They served me special meals, exotic fruits, and drinks.

The sisters insisted I use salt on all my food. They said that it keeps one healthy. The Vietnamese put salt on fruit, bread, fish, and everything else they eat. One nun explained, "Vietnamese don't have many stomach problems because we use a lot of salt and Westerners have stomach problems because they don't use enough salt. Salt kills germs."

At each meal, the women told me about themselves, their jobs, and their concern for the unfortunate. They worked with the blind, AIDS patients, drug addicts, the poor and hungry, street children, lepers, and the sick. The nuns did not travel in pairs, nor did they wear traditional habits in public. They rode motorbikes to their jobs. They were bright, inquisitive, dedicated, and fun. I taught them pronunciation and usage. They tried to teach me English grammar. It was maddening to hear them sweetly say, "No, Martin, no, Martin, you are mistaken. The rule in the book is…"

During the sessions we also covered vocabulary and reading comprehension. One lesson included the phrases "as is," "not a leg to stand on," and "it will sort itself out." I used pantomime to get the meanings across and instruct. To show me they understood, the nuns repeated my words and imitated my movements.

Twice a week I held lessons in my home for people with full-time jobs or who attended university. Sometimes I was not where I was supposed to be and sometimes students showed up at the wrong time or not at all. Most times, I did not know whose mistake it was. The confusion was permanent and memorable. The following notes were left at my door.

Teacher!

This morning I go to your house, you have gone. At 8 o'clock, your house lock. I leave home 7:30 a.m., I lost way. About 30 minutes I find out your house. I think that you are very busy. You arrange schedule for your job and you call me.

8:00 a.m. Saturday. Student Tran Mai.

Dear Sir,

I'm Thu-Huong, your pupil. I came to your house this morning to visit you. But you not home. I have some eggs and fruits for you. Today I really recover from flu. So I'd like you help me study English again. But I busy every night except Sunday. How do you think of this? I will call you to ask for your schedule. I very grateful you help.

Yours sincerely
Thu

One adult student said she would take me shopping and, to my surprise, quickly listed what I needed: dishes, glasses, cutlery, pillows, sheets, soap, toilet paper, towels, and pots. When I explained that I had already asked my landlady to buy them, she told me that I should not let my landlady do too much for me.

"Your landlady come in your house every day to clean. She look in your bags and read your papers. She know everything about you and she try to control your life. Be careful, Martin."

I assured her that I would not let anyone control me. She volunteered, "One day soon I will come to help you rearrange the furniture. It is not so nice now. And I will take you to buy a big potted plant for the living room. You need someone to take care of you."

Ten

ADULT STUDENTS

Teach me one word, you are my teacher.
Teach me half a word, you are still my teacher.
-A Vietnamese saying

Everyone in Vietnam showed me respect and courtesy. The nuns, university students, seminarians, and street children offered me water or fruit juice during each class. "You have lived longer than us," they would say. "You have more experience and you know more than we do. Please give us your advice." One university student said, "Mr. Martin, show us your wisdom."

It was very different in 1963. Back then, the Vietnamese I worked with patronized and ignored me. Understandably, the 45-year-old commander of the infantry battalion I was assigned to had no interest in suggestions from his inexperienced, 23-year-old American advisor. He had been a soldier since 1940, fighting the Viet Minh, the Japanese, and then the Viet Cong. He was a captain and I was a 1st lieutenant. He had seen and done things I could not imagine. Pride and ego on both sides got in the way of a useful working relationship.

The best that I can say about my tour as a combat advisor is that I did not embarrass my country, or my family. In reality, I was only the captain's aide, expediting supplies and arranging for air evacuation of the wounded. I directed air strikes; all the supplies and gunships were American. At times, by choice, I was another rifleman, but a rifleman better trained and more aggressive than the South Vietnamese soldiers were. I came to know and like them, but I did not respect their soldiering ability; they were poorly led and trained. The typical ARVN soldier was unmotivated and cavalier, it seemed.

*****

SHOW ME YOUR WISDOM: Judging by the folktale one of my students told me, wisdom encompasses cunning. The story explains why tigers have stripes and water buffalo have no top front teeth. Not incidentally, the tale conveys lessons about the limits of strength and the grave consequences resulting from attempts to undermine authority and the established order.

A tiger came upon a farmer and a water buffalo. Either one would make a nice meal, he thought. However, before dining he wanted to learn the farmer's secret. If the tiger could make animals do his bidding, he would be well fed in the future without having to hunt.

"Why do you let this weak man make you work for him?" the tiger asked the buffalo. "He is small and you can knock him down and get away."

"No, I can't," replied the buffalo, "because the man has wisdom."

"Show me your wisdom," said the tiger to the farmer, but the man replied, "I have left my wisdom at home today." The farmer, afraid that his helper would be eaten, refused to retrieve his wisdom until the tiger agreed to be tied to a nearby tree. When the tiger consented, the man left for home and the water buffalo shook his head in the dirt from side to side and laughed. In fact, he shook his head so hard that the earth knocked his top front teeth out.

"You have seen his wisdom, it is in his head," shouted the buffalo.

The farmer returned with hay for fuel and set the tiger on fire as a warning to leave the buffalo and him alone. The tiger's black stripes are from the flames. They serve as a reminder to the tiger and those who see them.

THE LADY HAS EGGS: On Friday evenings I taught 14 seminarians. Most were recent university graduates who had studied English for years. We practiced conversation for 90 minutes and then had dinner in the seminary dining room. Our topics included: Why does God allow the gap between rich and poor? Why is there suffering in the world? Why do bad men succeed? Do natural disasters have a purpose? Another subject was the morality of the American War in Vietnam. I told them what I thought about these things when I was asked.

During a discussion of free will I gravely intoned, "The line between right and wrong is not always visible." One of them responded, "Yes, Mr. Martin, we know, but we must keep looking for it."

They were sincere and intelligent. We learned from one another. I watched them struggle to put their thoughts into English, most times with success.

Speaking of education, they complained that Vietnamese teachers require students to memorize everything. Questions are discouraged, and ideas and opinions are unsolicited. Intellectual curiosity is not fostered. Exam answers must repeat verbatim the words of the teacher. An essay question that is not answered paragraph-by-paragraph and word-by-word exactly as it appears in the textbook or as recited by the teacher during class will get a poor grade.

One student was to be ordained as a Catholic priest. He invited me to attend the ceremony and the party to follow. When I arrived at the church door, a deacon escorted me to my seat. I was surprised when I was seated in the back of the church and irritated at myself for caring where I sat. Perhaps the constant politeness and respect shown to this old foreigner had created a sense of self-importance, or perhaps I came to Vietnam that way.

Minutes after being seated, I recognized a woman as she sat down in front of me. She was Quynh, one of my students from the pharmacy at a local hospital. A few days before, I had shown her my written invitation. She had translated it for me so that I would not go to the wrong address, or arrive on the wrong date or at the wrong time. I was surprised to see her at the rite because she had not told me that she, too, had been invited.

The church filled quickly, and just before the ceremony began it dawned on me why I was seated in the back of the church. I was the tallest person there and the only Westerner; most people were four inches shorter. The short invitees were seated up front. I would have blocked their view. I laughed at my earlier conceit.

My escort collected me at the conclusion of the ceremony. He took my right elbow and led me to the banquet hall. On my left walked Quynh, close but not touching. The deacon and I exchanged glances. He had not been told that I was bringing a guest, and my raised eyebrows showed him that I was surprised by Quynh's presence as well. He and I quickened our pace and so did she. We turned left and right and left again, and so did she. There was no discouraging her. Quynh sat next to me at the table. Across from us was the priest in charge of the seminary. He had organized the event and approved the list of invitees. It was obvious that Quynh had not been invited. She had crashed the party based on my invitation.

As food was being served, a cassock-clad seminarian arrived at the table and, not very discreetly, presented Quynh with a formal written invitation, which she quickly pursed away.

I related by email this story to my liberated sister Una. She responded, "The pharmacist lady has eggs."

AN OLD JOKE: Words a man does not want to hear when he is standing at a urinal are "I love you."

In Vietnam, people of all ages diligently pursue opportunities to practice speaking English. Westerners are stopped, interrupted, and followed by eager learners in hope of a conversation with a native English speaker. One must walk around them because they block one's way. It can be annoying and, depending on the circumstances, exasperating.

One evening a man at an adjoining table of raucous men followed me to the toilet, lurching as he hurried to walk beside me. The bathroom was crowded. I waited my turn. While relieving myself, the drunk leaned his chin on my shoulder and whispered into my ear, "What's the weather like? Is it cloudy? Is it sunny? Is it windy?" These were questions straight from an English lesson book. Angrily, I expressed my displeasure with his interruption and shrugged him off my shoulder. "I learn English," he shouted. Back at my table, my lovely companion Thao laughed at my tale and told me, "Not to worry, Martin, he only want English."

I'M JUST A LITTLE BROWN: Once a week for 11 months I taught eight graduate students, one male and seven female, at their university. They selected conversation topics including: the Cuba-U.S. problem, how to keep a boyfriend, tension between family and career, elections in America, HIV/AIDS, love and marriage, marriage and money, the Queen Mother, problems associated with marriage to a foreigner, Israel, Palestine, and drug addiction.

They asked me many direct and penetrating questions about the United States. I corrected their pronunciation and grammar and helped them express their opinions. The students were intelligent, spirited, and fun. We departed each class on good terms, I thought.

Some topics were politically sensitive. Students quickly corrected one another when statements were thought to be out of step with Party teachings. I was careful. My comments were balanced. At every opportunity I spoke of the similarities between our countries; they spoke of the differences. Their knowledge came from schoolbooks, movies, and television. Some of their ideas about America were right on, but some were fanciful:

- A man can bring home a woman he meets in a bar and sleep with her and his wife in the same bed.
- Women want to be sexy.
- The police will make you pay $50 if you throw paper on the ground.
- Americans don't wear clothes in the ocean.
- Everyone has a gun for shooting the police.
- Women marry and divorce many times.
- Women have two boyfriends at the same time.
- Women go out at night alone.
- Women have low morals.

Their comments revealed the puritanical streak so prevalent in Vietnamese society and the high moral standards by which women are judged.

The Education Ministry requires every high school girl to wear a white áo dài to school. It is a tight-fitting, translucent, two-piece silk costume. A high-neck blouse has front and back panels that start at the waist and reach to the ankles. The pants are wide at the bottom. As young women travel by bicycle, motorbike, or on foot, their áo dài's billow in their wakes, unless for safety they sit on the back panel: otherwise it might get caught in the spokes of the rear wheel. Glittering, black, elbow-length tresses decorate slender backs. These lovely creatures impart a sense of serenity to the bedlam of Saigon street life. Their virginal presence is a daily reminder of the virtue of Vietnamese women. Pure they may be, but Vietnamese parents acknowledge the unpredictability and volatility of these young women: "Living with a teenage girl is like having a bomb in the house."

It took me several lessons to understand that the female graduate students all had powerful, well-connected patrons who had secured for them part-time university positions that required little actual work. Five were daughters of party members. One was the daughter of a former Viet Cong who was now a police colonel. The remaining woman was the only child of a wealthy Chinese family.

The lone man was very different. He was a stout, 40-year-old rice trader who owned three houses and two trucks. At night he worked as a telephone sex and marriage consultant for the City of Saigon. During every class discussion, whatever the topic, he interjected salacious details from his previous night's work. He knew many coarse English words. The young women were constantly embarrassed by his stories and made uncomfortable by his language. So was I. They bridled at his comments and not so subtle innuendos. Finally, the colonel's daughter turned on him in class one day and said she did not want to hear that kind of talk anymore.

"I've had enough of you," she said. She was tired of his comments and would tell her father if he did it again. All the women agreed. One later told me, "She can talk angry, her father is big."

In one lesson I was asked by a 22-year-old daughter of a party member from Hanoi, "Why are Blacks not liked in America, and why do Americans say that Asians have yellow skin? Look, Mr. Martin, I'm not yellow. I'm just a little brown."

I admitted that racism was a problem in the United States and had been since before 1776. We now have laws that punish people and companies if they do not treat people of different races the same. I told them we are trying to solve the problem, but laws cannot change what is in people's hearts. On both sides it is a permanent problem.

All true, but incomplete and lame. However, racism is no stranger to the Vietnamese. In fact, racism is prevalent in Asia, especially among the Chinese and those peoples (such as the Vietnamese) who have been colonized by the Chinese or otherwise forced to live in the shadow of Chinese cultural influence. Race and skin color are factors in business and social arrangements. Women warn each other to cover their arms and face when they go outside. "You get too dark, be careful. Men no want you."

This same intelligent and beautiful daughter of the North asked me other emotionally charged questions.

"Why did America come here to kill women and children? Why did you bomb us and do such horrible things? And you, Mr. Martin, why did you come here as a soldier? Why?"

The sex-obsessed man who she had chastened before interjected that these questions were embarrassing me and suggested discussing other things. However, I wanted to answer.

"My country thought it was right to help the South Vietnamese government fight the communists," I said. "I did, too. We did not understand it was a war motivated by nationalism and a desire to be free of foreign rule. We made a mistake. We were wrong. When the American people became aware of the mistake, they forced their government to withdraw the U.S. Army from Vietnam."

I did not try to explain America's 50-year global struggle with Soviet communism or the domino theory, which held that if Vietnam fell to communism then the rest of Southeast Asia would be forced to adopt our enemy's ideology.

She made no reply to my words. Although quiet, I sensed she was still upset. People from the South reacted differently when they learned I had been a soldier in Vietnam. They opened up about their relatives who had been in the ARVN or who had been interpreters for the Americans. Usually they spoke derogatorily of Northern rule and gave examples of its harshness, incompetence, and corruption.

In the course of a talk about HIV/AIDS, one young woman maintained there were no gay men in Vietnam. Using unclean needles for drugs was the cause of the disease. "Anyway," she continued, "gay men just kiss, so how can they get HIV/AIDS?"

The male student and I exchanged glances, but we said nothing. It would have been inappropriate for me to explain, and the colonel's daughter had already warned him.

FAKE MONKS: Although religion has been an important part of Vietnamese culture for centuries, these students were communists, and not interested in discussing God or creeds. They seemed to have no interest in abstract, pious ideas. For them such things were the monks' concerns. Nevertheless, the students took part in a discussion about monks and provided the following insights:

- Some are good and some are bad.
- At the age of 10 a boy can begin living and studying in a monastery.
- A monk can leave the monastery at any time and return to civilian life.
- He does not take lifelong vows, but agrees to follow certain rules of Buddha, which include abstinence from sex and alcohol, and no food before daylight or after dark.

- A monk must study, pray, and meditate, examine his life, and confess infractions of the rules to other monks.
- A monk's possessions consist of one robe, a piece of cloth to sit on and another to strain drinking water so as not to swallow insects (thus killing them), and a washcloth, towel, blanket, and iron alms bowl.
- He must avoid touching women.
- Most monks are vegetarians. They can eat meat, but they cannot kill what they eat; someone else must kill the animal.

Traditionally, in the morning, monks walk through the streets holding their iron alms bowl in an upturned palm. They do not ask for food; they beg silently. People who give will be blessed in this life and the next. Always before noon, the monks return to their temple to share the donated food.

After 1975, monks were prohibited from begging for food in public. The communist government did not consider the centuries-old practice compatible with an egalitarian worker's paradise. Today, saffron-robed men never making eye contact solicit alms. One student told me that they were false monks because real ones would not defy the authorities. Another said, "Vietnam is modern now, monks can beg." They explained: if a monk is fat, he is probably an imposter; if a man in monk's robes is begging after noon, he is not a real monk; if he promptly eats food put in his bowl instead of returning to his temple with it, he is a fake.

Another topic of conversation was hypnotism. Is it possible to control another person in this way, and what techniques are successful? Speaking of the hypnotist a student explained, "He talk slow. He put mirror in your face. A ghost help him." A young girl showed the class a garlic bulb she kept in her handbag to prevent evil men from hypnotizing her and doing bad things.

One day the rice trader explained to me why he had been absent from class. One of his trucks had been involved in an accident with a motorbike, which resulted in the death of a 30-year-old father of three. The truck driver had not been at fault. Witnesses told the police that the victim had swerved in front of the truck. The truck, however, had been impounded and the driver jailed. The police informed the rice trader that he must pay money before either would be released.

He had missed class the previous week because he was at the police station negotiating with the dead man's family. The police mediated a settlement that required him to pay $3,000 to the family in return for his truck and driver. He told the class he did not like paying the money because the death had not been his driver's fault, but he knew it was fair and the right thing to do because now the family had no one to earn money.

PART OF A WOMAN'S BODY: The Vietnamese say their country will last as long as there is a Vietnamese language. It is a rich language with northern, southern, and central accents. The dialects identify factions. They set people apart.

In the 17th century, in order to translate the Bible and other religious tracts, Portuguese and Italian missionaries devised a Roman alphabet for the Vietnamese language. Previously, writing was done with modified Chinese characters (Chữ Quốc Ngữ). Alexander de Rhodes, S.J., was another major contributor to the romanization of Vietnamese writing. He built on the work of the earlier missionaries and altered the Roman alphabet to accommodate the five tones of the Vietnamese language. Except for names, Vietnamese words in this book have diacritic marks to show tone and pronunciation. Getting the tones and diction right is what makes learning the language so difficult for Westerners.

Some writers maintain Rhodes was French; however, he was born in Avignon, which was then part of the Vatican, and he was a Vatican citizen. He was schooled in Rome, and after returning from Vietnam in 1651 he published in Rome the first Annamese-Portuguese-Latin dictionary and the first romanized Vietnamese catechism.

In Vietnamese there are many different ways of writing the letters a, e, o, d, and u. For example, "a" can be written 15 different ways depending on the placement of diacritical marks. Four Roman letters are not part of the Vietnamese alphabet: j, f, w, and z (though the pronunciation of the latter two can be heard in speech.)

Vietnamese is a monosyllabic language. Arrangements of letters have only one syllable, but words can consist of two letter groups. Sai Gon is an example, and so is Viet Nam.

Vietnamese words are no more than six letters long, except for nghiêng (incline, lean, tilt), the sole exception. The same arrangement of letters has different meanings depending on tone. Ma can mean ghost (ma), cheek (má), mother (má), but (mà), tomb (mả), horse (mã), and rice seedling (mạ).

There are no verb conjugations from singular to plural or from present to past tense. Tense is conveyed by words indicating future, present, or past: sắp or sẽ for future tense, đang for present, and đã for past.

One mark of a Vietnamese who is a fluent English speaker is the correct pronunciation of plural nouns. Vietnamese words do not end in "s."

In Vietnamese, a word's position in a sentence determines its meaning. For example, tôi can mean I, me, my, or mine.

Western students of the language are easily frustrated. They cannot master the tones and are discouraged to find out that the words Nó đến sao không bảo? (He came. Why didn't you tell him?) can be marked and arranged, according to NYU Professor James Lop, to produce 120 different meanings. I have met few Westerners who have mastered the language.

Since Vietnamese is monosyllabic and tonal, it is easy for a foreigner to say mistakenly something hilarious, impolite, crude, or offensive. I developed a good sense of when I had just said something terribly inappropriate. Consequently, the more words I thought I had learned, the less confident I was speaking Vietnamese.

In Vietnam animals have associated numbers and names derived from a Chinese gambling game called Tài Xỉu (big and small numbers). The billy goat, renowned for its sexual appetite, has the number 35. A man who stays out late drinking and chasing women is also called ba mươi lăm (35). His friends laugh, joke, and slap him on the back, for to be called ba mươi lăm is a badge of manhood. A woman who moves from man to man is called many things. Colloquially, prostitutes are "chicken girls," or "taxi girls," or "butterflies."

The male and female genitals are designated by various words, such as chim, which means "bird" as well as "penis." "Gun" (súng luc) can signify penis, too. The word for butterfly (bướm) also means vulva. In the company of locals, I learned to be prepared for laughter and humorous speculation when speaking in Vietnamese or English about goats, birds, butterflies, or guns.

On one occasion, a seminarian laughed at my Vietnamese and said, "No, no, Martin, don't say that word. It means a part of a woman's body." The blind students I taught would chortle and repeat a crude word I had said as if to memorize it. My students from the university giggled, smiled, and joked when I used a tone that changed a word's meaning into something rude. The nuns would look at one another and roll their eyes.

WET NURSE: The Vietnamese also make mistakes speaking English. One of my university students brought a kilo of mangosteens to class. While we peeled the purple rind and ate its sweet, white fleshy fruit, they talked at length about Vietnamese foods they considered exotic. The students took turns describing how to prepare different items (e.g., duck blood cake, boiled dog fetuses, coconut worms, rats, and insects) for consumption.

Just before ending the session, a young woman looked me in the eye and asked, "Have you ever tried a wet nurse?"

I wondered about the question and answered, "No."

"You should," she said. "They're full of milk."

When I said that I did not understand, she consulted her Vietnamese-English dictionary. The first meaning was "a woman who suckles a baby not her own." The second was "milk apple" (vú sữa). The students huddled together and then their spokesman, the sole male, said, "She means milk apple, not wet nurse." Everyone smiled and the class ended. A "milk apple" is a local fruit that is apple-shaped and full of a milky, sweet liquid. The woman promised to bring the fruit to our next class.

ANXIETIES: At another session, the topic they chose was "my biggest fear and what to do about it." They were frank and open in expressing their feelings, and I found it surprising and a little sweet. The man in the class calmly described how he is afraid of ghosts—visitors from the spirit world—and how they come at night in different shapes and colors. When he locks the door and shuts the lights off, they always go away. One girl said he should not worry because ghosts are not real, but he said they are for him.

Other fears mentioned were living alone; not getting married; getting attacked in the night and being hurt; having poor health; and being unemployed.

A female student described symptoms of her biggest fear—depression. "For a few days each month I am sad and feel poorly in my mind. I cannot do anything and I stay in my room. My parents say I must see a doctor and I am going to." When I asked her how she got better each month, she said, "I get on my motorbike and ride around the streets and then I go shopping." The other women agreed, saying that was how they got rid of the same problem. I told them American women do that as well. At this point, the marriage consultant began to speak, but the colonel's daughter silenced him with a withering look.

HER FIRST LOVER: Sometimes, as a teaching tool, I asked my students to bring Vietnamese proverbs, idioms, and poems to class for analysis. Studying them was instructive and fun. My students translated the following:

Plum now asks Peach
Loving garden has anyone ever entered?
Peach said, I'm pleased to reply
Loving garden hasn't received a footprint yet.

These lines are an example of a type of poem favored by the Vietnamese. The real meaning is hidden and this reflects the cultural reluctance to express directly one's wants and feelings. The girl (Peach) affirms that this is the first time she has fallen in love. The boy (Plum) is her first lover.

Below is another example, again about love: love is not always reciprocated; sometimes you just pine away.

Did boat miss harbor when returning?
The harbor waits patiently for the boat.

These are called six-eight verses because in the Vietnamese language the lines alternate between six and eight words. Traditional poems are either five-seven or six-eight. In translation, these traditional structures are sometimes lost.

The poet, like the teacher, is revered. Phong, my father-in-law, gave his grandchildren, John and Eileen, the following six-eight poem which he penned in Vietnamese on the occasion of their first birthday, Christmas Eve, 2005.

John and Eileen,
our grandson and granddaughter,
With an American father and a Vietnamese mother,
You should never forget your roots.
We are celebrating your births
By cesarean section on Christmas Day
Exactly one year ago.
Your greater maternal family sincerely wishes
You, Phuc and Thao My, peace and good health
And love between brother and sister to increase day by day,
Success in your schoolwork, intelligence,
Success in your careers, great man and woman in the future.
How did your previous lives work so that
You were born as twins?
As brother and sister in this life,
You should always keep in mind filial piety to your parents
And harmony between you two.

A SOMBER-LOOKING MAN: A somber-looking man of about 55 attended a Friday class. He was introduced to me as Mr. Nam. He spoke no English (for the English conversation class!). The young women had selected topics about love, career, marriage, and boyfriends. It was an amusing 90 minutes. They were outrageous and so was I. The man, in contrast, sat stone-faced. I suspected he was from the government, sent to observe. I never saw Mr. Nam again, nor did I learn who he was.

Miss Hoa, my contact and a vice-director at the university, called me when I got home. She asked if any of the students had told me they were upset about the class. Immediately, I thought about the somber man and wondered if I was in some kind of trouble. What had I said? I responded that none of the students had said they were upset. She replied that the students who did not attend that Friday's class were upset that they had missed it. They were supposed to tell me so.

The university program includes a compulsory military component. Each student receives one month of training from army instructors. They learn close order drill, marching, rank identification, and how to assemble and disassemble weapons. Students are taught how to aim and shoot, but there is no target practice. They never fire the weapons; that would be expensive. The training instills patriotism and fosters understanding and respect for the military in young men and women who will be the country's future leaders.

I discontinued the classes when twice in succession I arrived at the university and there were no students. No one had called to tell me our classes were cancelled. The students were at meetings, the receptionist told me. I offered to hold the class at my house in the future, but declined to travel to the school again when they asked me to. I do not know why the classes ended this way. Perhaps I offended someone. Alternatively, maybe the reason was as simple as not giving value to what they received for free.

GUMSHOES AND MANTRAPS: The young nun winked at me as she translated what the older nun had said: "It's a new feast day, the International Day of Women." The 30 nuns and I celebrated the day with a special lunch. They stood and applauded when I was introduced. The applause was repeated each time the Mother Superior told the other nuns what she had learned about me. "He's married." "He has two children." "He's a lawyer." "He's here for a year."

When it was time to leave I asked them to call a taxi, but a nun said, "No, it is too expensive. You should return by xe ôm." It is cheaper and more interesting, she promised, and I would be safe with the driver they called. The Mother Superior asked if I had small bills to pay for my return trip. She gasped and took the wad of đồng I pulled from my pocket, counted out the equivalent of $1, and told me to put it in my shirt pocket. "Use the shirt pocket money to pay the driver and put the rest out of sight, deep in your pants pocket."

On the way home a lady of the evening pulled alongside our motorbike, patted the empty rear seat of her Honda, and invited me to join her. My driver indignantly shooed her away saying I had just come from the nuns' house and was not interested in her business.

I attended a Saturday evening Mass at the convent. The priest gave a lengthy, spirited sermon I could not understand. Later that evening he took me by motorcycle to my house. "It was a waste for you not to have understood my sermon," he said as we started out. I, of course, agreed. He then proceeded to repeat the sermon in English as we rode through the city, a 20-minute ride.

I enjoyed teaching the nuns. They were innocent (really), humorous, and disarming. While reading a passage describing a shark attack, one of the nuns stopped and asked, "Why do gumshoes fall into mantraps? And what is a gumshoe?" These words were not in the article. Where to start?

She had seen something on TV about gumshoes and mantraps. Although she did not understand completely, she knew that a mantrap was a way that a woman attracted a man. A smile crossed her face when I explained that a gumshoe was a policeman or an investigator. Not satisfied, she pressed for the word's derivation. How had gum and shoe come to mean policeman, she inquired.

I attended a Mass and ceremony at the convent. Nuns study and pray for years before they promise themselves to God. Four of the nuns in my class took final vows of chastity, poverty, and obedience during the Mass.

The vow taking was formal. Each of the four stood in turn, prostrated themselves, spoke the words, and then signed a statement confirming their vows. Symbolizing marriage to God, the Bishop placed a silver ring on the fourth finger of each woman's right hand. Parents and other relatives cried, applauded, and sang. The event was warm and emotional and I shared in their feelings.

Immediately following the Mass, the convent served a formal lunch for 200 persons. It was a traditional Vietnamese wedding feast with multiple courses and entertainment. It even had singing nuns. I was seated at a table of elderly nuns and priests, and was the only one who turned down the offered beer. It was 10:30 a.m. Each of the religious drank exactly one can of beer during the meal.

In 1963, it was difficult for me to go to church. There were no chaplains of any faith with the battalion. To attend a rural church (if I could locate one) without a heavily armed escort would not have been prudent.

Persons solely of the same belief inhabited many delta villages. There were Cao Đài, Hòa Hảo—both are indigenous religions—and Catholic, Buddhist, and Viet Cong villages. If the battalion did not know a village's allegiance before entering it, the tenor of our reception quickly informed.

HER BROTHER'S JOB: Hien's father qualified under an American program that allowed Vietnamese who had been imprisoned at least three years in a reeducation camp to immigrate to the United States. He had spent eight years in prison. Together with his wife and 12 of their children, he departed for sunny California in 1991. At the age of 19, Hien, his youngest child, was left behind to live in the family house. The government would confiscate it if the entire family left the country, and the parents wanted to keep their house in case they ever came back to Vietnam. Today, Hien has a good job as an assistant pharmacist in a clinic that caters to foreigners. She became one of my English students, but she was not my student for long.

I had been teaching Hien, another pharmacist, and a woman doctor twice a week. When the physician left Vietnam for a position in India, another doctor joined Hien's class.

I sensed something was wrong when the new doctor arrived for the first session. Hien was uncharacteristically quiet and reserved. I assumed the problem was that I had put the new doctor in her class without consulting her.

That evening Hien phoned to say she could not be my student any more. It turned out that the new doctor's brother, a Northern man, was the administrator of the hospital where Hien worked, and she was studying English on hospital time without permission. She was afraid the doctor would inform her brother and she would lose her job. Kindly, Hien offered that she would not have made the connection between the new physician and the hospital administrator even if I had notified her in advance. Only when the doctor told Hien what her brother's job was did she realize her peril. I was saddened by the outcome because she was a serious student and I liked her. A week later, I received a pleasant letter from her. (See Note 3.)

After receiving her letter, though, I did not hear from Hien for several months. She was refused a visa to see her hospitalized father in California. The U.S. Consulate did not believe she would voluntarily return to Vietnam when it expired. Hien was angry at America and did not want to see me again because she feared she would be rude to me. In time, she called to apologize and explain why she had been avoiding me.

Eleven

PHILOSOPHY, SUPERSTITION, AND THE EXISTENCE OF THE DEAD

Philosophy will clip an angel's wings.
-John Keats

The Vietnamese believe that people who live a simple, natural, and honest life will find harmony if the natural order of things is in balance. In the Chinese tradition, this balance is achieved when the yin force is equal to the yang force. These primary principles are comparable to gravity in that they have existed for all time and are an essential part of the universe's organization. The five basic elements—metal, wood, water, fire, and earth—are changed by the interaction of yin and yang. These forces of symmetry and discord join as well as separate the elements to form and maintain all aspects of the universe and life. Harmony is lost when one force gains supremacy over the others. Rulers then lose the Mandate from Heaven—the right to rule—and are overthrown. Wars are fought, harvests fail, relationships dissolve, and sickness strikes when the pendulum swings too far towards yin or yang.

Cultural roles are derived from social status, rank, and gender. Yin is female, cooperative, egalitarian, and impulsive. Yang is male, authoritative, assertive, domineering, and competitive.

Food can be hot yang or cold yin. Mango, durian, and jackfruit are hot. Dog, water buffalo, and chicken are cold, and so are most vegetables. One will sicken if yang and yin food intake are not in balance. A marriage will be happy if one party is yang and the other is yin. It will be unhappy if both are of the same natural force. All things are best when balanced.

Long ago, Greek philosophers proposed similar basic truths—there are four indestructible elements from which all things are made. These substances are earth, air, fire, and water, which, when acted on by the general forces of harmony and strife, join and separate to form all matter.

Given the barriers to travel and communication in antiquity, it is curious that the ancient Chinese and Greek theories of cause and effect are similar.

*****

THE THREE WAYS: Confucianism, Taoism, and Buddhism are considered The Three Ways to individual and community happiness and accord. These time-honored beliefs provide the foundation for a system of relationships that, even today, profoundly influence Vietnamese society. They are not religions in the Western sense because they do not believe in an external, all-powerful God who is the creator, guardian, and ruler of the world and all its life. Instead, they recognize the existence and supremacy of spiritual and moral law, virtuous conduct, and cultivation of the person. The Three Ways encourage consonance with others and with nature, and a tolerance of different beliefs.

Buddhists believe that all living things (humans, animals, insects, and plants) will be reborn in some form, somewhere, for a limited period. Selfishness and ignorance are the causes of rebirth because unsatisfied desire leads man to seek a life extension. When ignorance is destroyed, desire is extinguished. To destroy ignorance one must attain truth, which only occurs when one empties oneself of all needs. Emptiness is the ultimate truth. With it, the self does not exist. Intelligence, wisdom, and altruism follow from emptiness. Having attained truth and enlightenment one realizes that rebirth is worthless.

Buddhism teaches that men and women are equal and both are able to reach truth. Notwithstanding, many believe that it is impossible to arrive there from a female body. Therefore, women must be reborn as a male if they hope to empty themselves of all needs.

A person must live a good life, stockpiling merits along the way; otherwise, rebirths will not improve on the present.

Renewal is not always immediate upon death. One can exist in the spirit world until a suitable new earthly life is found.

Hardly any Vietnamese are concerned with these elusive metaphysical notions, but in their daily lives they follow the form and practices of the religion in much the same way as the adherents of all religions do.

SUPERSTITIONS AND FABLES: Superstitions and myths are common in agricultural societies like Vietnam. Recall the goat-footed, half-human sirens—from the phantom-ridden magic and enchanted woodlands of Celtic, Greek, and Chinese antiquity—which competed with man for mates, space, and existence.

Rural Vietnamese who live close to nature and its apparent mysteries are more likely to respect superstitions, of which there are hundreds. Some beliefs encourage good hygiene, some are based on old legends, and many have no rational explanation. Educated Vietnamese look upon them as silly, but many still respect and follow them.

Mushrooms are grown in dark rooms, away from the light. Otherwise, they will break open and sell for less in the market. A bowl of rice and water left in a corner will turn to rice wine in two days. Mashed bananas will turn to vinegar if placed in a bowl with a special worm. The worm must be fed rice; the more rice it eats the stronger the vinegar will be. However, if a menstruating woman walks by, the mushrooms will crack open in the dark room, the rice will not produce alcohol, and the worm will die in the bowl.

Young teenage girls have magical strength; they can do anything.

If one picks the first fruit of a tree, the tree will never bear fruit again.

If a pregnant woman walks by a buffalo tied to a rope, gestation will be longer than normal. Thus, a woman whose pregnancy reaches beyond nine months is called "buffalo pregnant." She will promptly deliver her child if she cooks and eats rice begged from her neighbors.

An expectant mother should not attempt to negotiate in the market after agreeing to a price. To do so might result in her baby having extra toes.

A woman's pores open during labor, causing her harmony to be disturbed. To prevent sickness, precautions are taken; a tray of hot coals is kept under the mother's bed for 30 days to ward off the damp and chill that might otherwise enter her enlarged pores.

A woman and her newborn baby stay in bed until the infant's bellybutton heals. The scab that falls from the healed navel should be fed to the baby to obtain high intelligence. In the case of twins, lasting love occurs when each consumes the other's scab.

A newborn is weak and vulnerable and must be kept away from light and people until it has established harmony with yin and yang. After a seclusion of 30 days, family and neighbors are invited to view the baby and celebrate its arrival. In addition, a new mother should wait 30 days before washing her hair. Otherwise, she will have headaches when she is old.

Speaking of hair, a Vietnamese grandmother told me: "A newborn's blood hair is thin and not pretty." At three months and ten days old, a baby's birth hair is shaved. If done earlier the little one might die from a cold. In this way, the infant is given a new start in life, and, if the spirits cooperate, the second hair will grow quickly and be glossy black.

If a child does not eat all its food, the mother must finish it. Otherwise, her child will not have enough to eat in the future.

A stray cat, a dead bird, or a turtle in one's house is bad luck, and could result in something harmful happening. One afternoon, my young daughter brought a small turtle home; she'd found it in a church fountain. Thao insisted Eileen take it back but the church was closed. That evening I was cheated at a store; I was given the wrong change. The turtle was blamed.

Phong, the old soldier, believes that since no one knows if superstitions are true, it is best to follow them as long as the cost is small and no harm is done.

THE SPIRIT WORLD: Western and Vietnamese traditions concerning death and the afterlife are significantly different. In the West, there is death and either a heavenly reward or a hellish punishment depending on how one has lived. The Vietnamese believe in the existence and reality of death and of the dead: this fact is a central theme of their heritage and traditions.

Belief in the hereafter, ancestor worship, and astrology are all part of Vietnamese culture. They predate but are not considered inconsistent with the teachings of The Three Ways. In fact, the origins of these beliefs came before organized religions. Ancestor worship is so deeply rooted in the culture of Vietnam that it has survived the influence of Western civilization and the spread of Buddhism. The hierarchies of Buddhism and Catholicism have had to find ways to accommodate these timeworn tenets. Catholics compare the spirits to saints and explain ancestor shrines and prayers as communion with them.

Confucianism is not antagonistic to ancestor worship. In The Doctrine of the Mean, Confucius instructs his disciples that:

It is the highest filial piety for offspring
to serve the dead as they would serve the living,
and to serve the departed as they would serve the present.

These words seem to call for ancestor reverence and respect, not fear and appeasement. However, in the tradition of Vietnam there are good ghosts and bad ones; they must be placated, or harm and ruin will come. Spirits have human traits. They can be jealous, vengeful, and compassionate. They are also forgetful and can be tricked. Departed ancestors need love and attention; happy spirits will bless their family and warn them of danger in their dreams.

Phantoms exist in both living and dead things. Deceased persons dwell in the spirit world and eventually return to earth reincarnated. What one returns as depends on how one conducted oneself in one's prior life. If you lived a bad life, you might come back as a tree, a dog, or a useless thing. Children are warned that if they are bad they will return as a woman in their next life. This warning reflects the reality that most women (everywhere) have a harder, more difficult life than men, and not, of course, that they are a lower life form or a useless thing. Oh, no, certainly not.

A SPIRIT EMBRACE: Saigon is changing. However, many things remain the same.

My friend Charlie, a Scotsman, is gone. He was out one night with his buddies celebrating his new teeth and lucrative eBay sales. They would not let him drive his motorbike home, a bit woozy he was. Instead, his friends sent him by taxi. Safely home, Charlie fell off his third-story balcony, landed on his head, and died instantly.

His wake was held two nights later at the Voodoo Bar, a 5-meter-wide, 30-meter-long drinking spa. Fifty old, sweaty, unrepentant, desperate, Western expats came to send Charlie off. Thirty beautiful, black-haired, silver high-heeled, red mini-skirted, black haltered, calculating, highly confident, 18- to 25-year-old Vietnamese women helped those saddened men through their grief. There were winners and losers that night, but mostly the expats lost.

Charlie was toasted and roasted. As the evening progressed, stories were shared and Charlie became heroic. Tears were shed. The hostesses contributed their memories as well. One lovely woman allowed that Charlie had visited her at one a.m. the night before the wake. "That the time he came see me when he on earth." She paused, looking for the right words, and said, "Charlie is yummy spirit."

Charlie made his living by selling Zippo lighters on eBay. He had agents scouring the countryside for the thousands of Zippos left by U.S. soldiers. They are engraved with helicopters, gunboats, parachutes, peace symbols, and inscriptions (some profane) about sex, drugs, enemy killings, and home. Some he bought from a Vietnamese knock-off artist—but, Charlie insisted, "Only if demand exceeded supply." He also told me, "I sell all over the world to collectors. I give them what they want."

Indeed, if the Zippo Charlie was to offer on eBay lacked an inscription, he had the artist scratch on the metal case sayings like, "God and love are mysteries," "Love is 4 soldiers," "Duty, Duty, and Duty," "Air Cav 4ever," "Sex=War," and "Death in a rice paddy." He was proud that one of his lighters had sold for $90. On the morning of his departure, he had purchased new teeth and had sold $200 worth of Zippos to a collector in Saudi Arabia.

The owners of the Voodoo Bar and the mourners deemed the wake a huge success, so it was scheduled again for the next night. Every society has its own funeral rites. Obviously, I was there only as an anthropologist, to observe and record this Western/Vietnamese cultural exchange.

BURIAL: Burial practices are rooted in the folk religion of Vietnam. Customs and ceremonies vary depending on a family's religion, education, and lifestyle, but all burials accommodate the requirements of both the departed and the living. I use the word departed because in Vietnam the deceased is not considered dead. They are all around, just not visible.

When in the spirit world, one has the same needs as those on earth. Bodies are buried with items or pictures of items that will be necessary in the afterlife. Images of cars, houses, food, loved ones, clothes, and U.S. dollars are placed in the coffin.

To leave this world among family is a cherished ideal, so when that time nears, family members are summoned home. The goal is to help the person leave for the spirit world with a happy heart and no ill feelings toward the living. Apologies for life's errors and inconsiderate behavior are made. Prayers for a better life in the next incarnation are chanted. Incense smoke, which purifies by driving out bad spirits, fills the bedroom with fragrance.

On one's passing the civil authorities are notified, a coffin is purchased, monks are summoned, and a fortune-teller is consulted. The clairvoyant selects the day and time to move the corpse from the house, and also the appropriate date and time for burial. If the family rejects the seer's advice, the loved one may never find peace and his ghost may be left to wander, unhappy and revengeful. Worse, it may stay in the house and not be reincarnated. As for the errant family, they will lose their money suddenly and never be able to hold their heads up like rich people.

The coffin weighs more in the house than it does outside because the spirit does not want to leave home. Monks must pray to drive the lurking spirit from the house. It takes fewer men to carry the casket once it is outside. At that point the coffin must be turned so the head faces the house and the departed can say good-bye.

Cremation is not uncommon. The ashes are buried in the ancestors' graveyard. Cremation is "too hot" for most, though, and they ask to be buried instead. Traditionally, interment is a two-step process. The body is first buried in wet soil to foster decomposition. A year later, the oldest son re-inters the bones in the family graveyard.

One's death day is more important than one's birthday. Memorial ceremonies are held after 30 days, one year, and three years, and periodically thereafter until, supposedly, the 100th year after death. A family's oldest son is responsible for his ancestors' graves, but as generations pass, only time, the great watchman, monitors them.

Trips to the cemetery are steeped in ritual. Different colored headbands indicate the status of family members. A white headband and bamboo staff identifies the husband or eldest son, who walks in front of the casket. As a sign of submission to her husband and to scare away bad spirits, a hooded widow walks backward behind the coffin.

Distinctive gold and green funeral hearses, custom decorated, carry the body to the cemetery. Wailing mourners clothed in white—sometimes family members, sometimes professionals—trail the hearse. Other times, tape-recorded laments are broadcast from oversized speakers on top of the hearse.

Grave location is determined by the family's ability and willingness to pay. If they are poor, then the grave will be in a bad place and the spirit will be sad. The Vietnamese say that in death, as in life, the rich live fronting the sunny street and the poor live in the dark, dirty alley. Family members leaving the country are expected to visit ancestors' graves to say good-bye.

Wakes are held at home or at mourning parlors, which are a fixture of city sidewalks. The grieving family and friends console one another over green tea and baked watermelon seeds at long tables under awnings, which stretch from building to curb. Monks and relatives pray at makeshift altars while the spirit is given a thunderous sendoff with shrieks, funeral music, and rhythmic drumming.

I once asked a neighbor why she was jumping over a small paper fire in her doorway. She responded that if you were not careful after attending a funeral the spirit will follow you home. It will enter your house and refuse to leave. To prevent this, mourners must build a small fire at their doorstep and jump over it five times.

Over coffee one morning, Lanh, an educator and my friend, told me he had cancer and would be operated on the next day. He died four months later; radiation treatments and another operation were to no avail. His wife called me at six a.m. to tell me of his death and that I should come to the house before eight that morning if I wanted to see his face one last time. He was on the ground floor, laid out in a coffin, dressed in a traditional costume of red and gold silk and a large white headdress. At eight sharp the casket was closed, but not before his eldest son placed a knife on Lanh's chest to keep evil spirits away. He was covered with black tea leaves to mask the smell of the decomposing corpse because Saigon is in the tropics and he was mourned at home. Friends visited, monks chanted, women wailed, and musicians produced loud, discordant music. For three days he lived with his family in their three-meter-wide house. On the fourth day of his death, at six a.m., he was taken from the house to the cemetery. Upon exiting the front door, the pallbearers turned the coffin so Lanh's head faced the house and they bowed three times. The body was carried to a splendidly decorated, 10-foot-high, open-sided, motorized hearse. Family members dressed all in white and, wearing hoods or headbands that designated family status, sat on each side of the casket. Lanh's wife lit a small fire at the doorstep to prevent his spirit from re-entering the house.

A woman mourns her husband for three years, but a man mourns his wife for only one. "Men and women are different," I was told. "Women are used to waiting. Men can't wait three years for a woman."

As an act of mercy, people release caged birds sold by street vendors. They receive spiritual merits because they have freed a spirit to visit his family. Outside Lanh's house, I stopped a peddler and paid to liberate an imprisoned bird. The $1 cost was low and I was elated.

LIAR: Vietnamese names begin with the family-dynasty name and end with the given name. Three- and four-word names are the norm. There are 11 common family names. Nguyen was the name of the imperial family that ruled Central Vietnam for 150 years. As a mark of loyalty, children born during that regime bore the name. As a result, Nguyen is the family name of over 60% of the population.

Males often have Van as a middle name, which portends success in the state exams. The middle name of many females is Thi. It is a Sino-Vietnamese word meaning "market." There are different explanations for why it is part of a woman's name: a woman must be savvy at the market; or perhaps it's because women are talkative like a market. Alternatively, it expresses a wish for many children, or that the baby girl will grow up to be a good daughter, wife, and mother, or that the child will think of her family before all else. Thi is also the name of a non-edible fruit that fills a room with a sweet fragrance, like a perfumed woman.

A baby is never named after a relative, living or dead, because this might anger the spirit of the person and cause the baby difficulties. The ghost, responding to the sound of its name, might enter the house when the baby is called and bring harm to the child. To confuse the spirits, a person's given name is often kept secret. He or she is called by a false name, which may be a number corresponding to their birth order in the family. To baffle the evil spirits, the firstborn is sometimes called "two" or "second." The parents believe that "one" and "first" are reserved for the emperor.

Generally, Westerners do not know the meaning of their given names. One must go to the books to be informed. In contrast, Vietnamese parents give their children names associated with nature or character traits, the meanings of which are obvious.

A famous fable and song portrays a poor boy named Cuoi who tends a landlord's buffalo. Cuoi is constantly in trouble because he tells lies, which at first fool everyone. In time, however, no one believes what he says, so he flies to the moon where he lives the rest of his life under the branches of a banyan tree. Cuoi is the folktale explanation for what sometimes looks like a man on the moon sitting under a tree. "To tell a lie like Cuoi" is a well-known phrase. Surprisingly, some parents name a son Cuoi.

It is my experience that Vietnamese do not give their name when they place a telephone call, nor do they usually introduce the people they are with at meetings or when they encounter friends and acquaintances. Why are identities not offered, one must ask. This practice may be derived from name superstitions, or perhaps it shows caution stemming from centuries of conflict and persecution.

LUNAR DATES: The Vietnamese simultaneously follow both the Gregorian (solar) and the lunar calendars. It can be a source of confusion for Westerners. The Gregorian calendar, introduced to the Vietnamese by the French, is used for business and government affairs and by most city people. Rural people are more likely to follow the lunar calendar, which came from China thousands of years ago and is based on the regularly changing phases of the moon. It is the timekeeper of traditional culture.

Printed calendars hang from walls in homes and businesses. They provide both the Gregorian and lunar dates in the same box under the day of the week. The dates for the second Sunday in December 2005 are December 12 on the Gregorian calendar and November 1 on the lunar calendar. To avoid confusion, the Vietnamese say the word "up" or "down" after the date. "December 12 up" means December 12 of the Gregorian calendar. The Gregorian date appears in the upper part of the box while in the lower part is the lunar date. "November 1 down" means November 1 of the lunar calendar.

There are 355 days in a lunar year, which is comprised of 12 months with 29-30 days. Every third year one month is added to adjust for the inaccuracy of the lunar calendar and to synchronize the lunar and solar years. The 13th month shares the name of the month that succeeds it. For example, successive Februaries occurred in 2004. Buddhist holy days and festivals that occurred in the first February of 2004 were celebrated in the second February as well. A lunar month and a Gregorian month may also have a different number of days. The lunar month is one month behind the Gregorian month, except in years with 13 months. For example, January of the lunar year is the Gregorian month of February.

The lunar calendar is based on separate 10- and 12-year cycles—interlocking cycles lasting 60 years. I was born in 1938, the year Mậu Dần (Year of the Tiger). Sixty years later, in 1998, the year Mậu Dần returned.

Each year in the 12-year rotation is named for one of the 12 animals of the zodiac. Each animal also claims two hours of each day. Separately, a set of 10 celestial signs consecutively modifies the traits of the animals. One's personality, character, and fate are influenced by the interaction of the relevant zodiac animal and celestial signs at the moment of birth. Since I am a tiger, I am quick to anger, indecisive, flexible, and accommodating—all true. I am king of the jungle and nocturnal. During the Hours of the Tiger (three to five a.m.), I return to my lair. The stars reveal that I am talented and suited for a high position. True.

Important days in the lunar month are the first and 15th. On these days joss (incense) sticks, printed prayers, and photographs of material things such as money, motorbikes, and food are burned day and night at thousands of curbside fires throughout Saigon. Smoke from these offerings transports prayers and material goods to the spirit world, satisfying the ancestors' needs.

Dates that add up to five are considered unlucky. Thus, the 5th, 14th, and 23rd of the lunar calendar are dates when one should avoid dangerous situations and stay close to home. Likewise, the number three is unlucky as well as two-digit numbers ending in three, such as 13. A photograph of three persons should not be taken. It is believed that all three would face a bad future.

CHILDREN'S DAY: The Mid-Autumn Festival, also known as Children's Day, is held on September 15 (the 15th day of the eighth lunar month). Throughout Vietnam, from city to village, people gather to celebrate. Children and adults don masks, beat drums, tote star-shaped lanterns, compete in contests, and are entertained by the Lion Dance. Masked and costumed actors perform the dance, recreating a mythical battle involving a courageous woodcutter and a savage lion. The lion is angry over the disappearance of the moon's reflection in a woodland stream and threatens a nearby village. The woodcutter kills the lion and saves the villagers. In the festival, the lion and woodcutter dance from sidewalk to street to alley, lunging, rearing back, and retreating. The audience of masked, laughing children and delighted adults surge after them, moving together like a school of fish.

The festival celebrates autumn and, significantly, the full moon. The moon is perceived as yang and is balanced by the earth, which is yin. The light rain that falls at this time of year is explained by the tale of the celestial boy and girl whose parents have denied them permission to marry. All year the Jade Emperor keeps them separated in different parts of heaven, but on Mid-Autumn Day they are allowed to meet in the middle of the Milky Way. Their tears of joy cause the soft, misty rain prevalent in that season.

Mooncakes are a traditional Mid-Autumn delicacy. One morning several days before the festival, Em Thy and her friends borrowed my kitchen to make mooncakes. At nine a.m. four women arrived at my door. Minutes later an electric oven arrived by bicycle. The women spent the next three hours chopping, kneading, mixing, and baking. They talked a bit, too. The Vietnamese say, "Two women have a conversation; three are a market."

"Two women and a duck are a market" is another saying that recognizes the verbal prowess of Vietnamese women.

Most mooncakes are sweet and fatty and smell of herbs. There are many recipes. My landlady's were made from pork fat, ginger, lemon, squash jam, lotus and sesame seeds, watermelon, roast chicken, Chinese sausage, salt, egg yolk, white sugar, sticky rice powder, washed out wheat flour, red sugar, three different kinds of rice, and "special liquid." They are an acquired taste, a bit like a dreadful English fruitcake.

Students were in my living room during part of the morning and were patient and understanding of the noise and interruptions. The sweet fragrance of freshly baked goods was their compensation.

FOUR MORE SONS: Fortunetelling most likely began soon after humans learned to speak. It has enjoyed an extraordinary longevity. Curiosity about the past and the future is an element of self-awareness, which probably is unique to humanity. Those who claim the ability to foretell the future have sometimes been revered, sometimes feared, but always fortune-tellers have had a special place in society. Throughout history they have been consulted about every aspect of life and their advice has been weighed, reflected on, and frequently followed. Those who want simple answers will find fortunetellers rewarding.

Today in the West, nearly everyone considers prophesying a form of entertainment, something to savor and tell friends about. Predictions are general and subject to conditions, and if some come true, so much the better. Overall, it does not play a part in the lives of Westerners. Most do not rely on astral positions or influence to choose a course of action in their lives. Such ideas are not deemed intellectually respectable.

In Vietnam, the acceptance of fortunetelling is more complex. Although condemned by both the Communist Party and the Catholic Church, all segments of Vietnamese society to some degree embrace it. Many Vietnamese believe that a skillful psychic can accurately reveal both a man's past and his destiny. Major decisions are based on a fortuneteller's advice. For example, seers are frequently asked to approve or disapprove of a marriage partner, a wedding or burial date, the purchase of a house, the location of a kitchen, front door, or bedroom, and the opening day for a business. The fortuneteller will predict if a business venture is to be successful, when a person will die, and how many children one will have, their sex, and if they will be successful and respectful.

In an American history class I taught, I expressed an interest in having my fortune told. Vi, a student, inquired if I would like an appointment with a fortuneteller; her favorite, she claimed. I promptly agreed.

When we arrived, Vi parked her motorbike in front of a small house on an unpaved street in one of Saigon's poor, distant suburbs. Inside, we were seated on bamboo mats on the dining room floor. Pillows and light blankets were strewn along the walls. At night the space served as a bedroom. With our arrival, the family of seven moved to the kitchen to finish their lunch. Stairs in the small kitchen led to the parents' bedroom. In the space under the stairs was another pillow and blanket. It was not possible to open the bathroom door and the refrigerator door at the same time. The bathroom had a seatless commode, and no sink or window.

A woman, all skin and bones, joined us on the floor while brushing her long black hair over her right shoulder. This was the mother and my fortuneteller, I realized. For $3 she read my palm and consulted playing cards to predict my future. She told my horoscope. Her manner was stern, appraising; her seriousness lent credibility to her words.

It is a good job. She works at home and pays no taxes. Her neighbors hold her in high regard.

Astrological charts have been used for centuries both to predict future events and reveal the past. A certain mathematical proficiency is considered essential. The soothsayer applies one's date and time of birth to the charts and, of a sudden, knows your past and future. Oh, I wonder how many people know the exact hour, minute, and second of their birth. I fudged the time, as do most people. Unquestionably, this explains why the results are not 100% accurate.

We talked for a while about my likes and dislikes. She asked about my family, my job, and my life. I have read that fortunetellers are accomplished students of human nature and are able to pick up clues about the client's past.

During these preparations, other patrons arrived and seated themselves on the mats. Everyone faced the seer. She consulted books and drew my chart, which showed how the movement of the stars and planets influenced my character and life. Blue and red lines delineated 13 rectangular boxes transected by black arrows. Each box contained words and numbers and showed the result of applying my date and time of birth to a particular alignment of the heavenly bodies. The chart, as she interpreted it, revealed information about my past, present, and future. Some of what she told me was a recasting of my words from our initial conversation. She explained what the words, numbers, and arrows meant; Vi transcribed verbatim in Vietnamese.

The fortuneteller took my hand and spoke to me in a husky voice. She had the spirit in her heart. She told me that in my last life I had been a man and, because I had been good in that life, I had come back as a man again. Alas, she could not tell me who I had been in my prior life.

The other customers, who were huddled on the mat around me, made sounds of joy or condolence when appropriate. Later, Vi translated her handwritten account into English. (See Note 4.)

The experience was theater and entertaining, especially the fortuneteller's prediction that I would father four more sons. She was confused about that; in my 66th year, on December 24, 2004, Thao gave birth to a boy and a girl. Much of what the fortuneteller got right was clever guesswork based on what I had told her at the beginning of the session.

Many Vietnamese believe in the power of the clairvoyant, and even skeptics and nonbelievers frequent them.

Twelve

TRADITIONS AND VALUES

The reverence due to a tradition increases from generation to generation. The tradition finally becomes holy and inspires awe.
-Friedrich Nietzsche

For 2,000 years, Confucian teachings have influenced the lives of people in China, Korea, Japan, and Vietnam. It is part of Vietnam's ubiquitous Chinese cultural legacy. Over time, a system of philosophy and humanism developed into a lattice for both rulers and subjects. Confucianism is marked by social class, growth of virtues, and opposition to injustice and tyranny.

In keeping with these concepts, high esteem for authority is central to Vietnamese culture. It fosters stability. Strife is avoided by testing ideas and acts against set values and rules. By obeying one's king, teacher, and father, anarchy and social confusion is avoided. An age-old Vietnamese maxim declares:

If the king says die and you don't, you are disloyal.
If your teacher says study and you don't, you are ruined.
If your father says die and you don't, you are a bad son.

The perfect family seeks respectful dealings and loyalty among its members. The non-family relationships necessary for balance in Confucian society are ruler-subject, teacher-student, and friend-friend. The top person in such pairings must be fair, helpful and considerate. In the family, the parent, husband, elder brother, and ruler must treat the child, wife, younger brother, and subject with kindness and solicitude. In return, the lower-ranked must be obedient to the superior, but only if the higher-up actually is kind-hearted and caring. The king and the mandarin are considered parents of the people. They must give to, and not take from, the people. A ruler who is not beneficent, who disregards the moral order of the universe and thus loses the Mandate From Heaven, can be replaced by force.

*****

WOMEN'S STATUS: The status of women in Vietnam derives from the teaching of Confucius and his followers. As in many other Asian countries, gender and age determine status in Vietnam, particularly within the family. An old man told me, "Men rule and woman obey" and "You only fully become a man once your father has died."

Although Vietnam is a communist country where everyone is ostensibly equal, it remains a male dominated and hierarchical society. Although ideology is one thing, the reality of women's lives is another.

Women have an inferior position to men regardless of their character or qualifications and are subject to the Three Obediences: obedience to her father until married; obedience to her husband after she leaves her father's house; and obedience to her eldest son should she be widowed. She and her family will benefit or suffer depending on her compliance. Although women defer to men, they still wield great influence. Vietnamese women are strong, powerful creatures, indeed, especially when it comes to family matters. They are considered the "family warrior." However, a man married to an opinionated, outspoken woman is pitied; he has "a lion in the house."

The sayings below are attributable to the disciples of Confucianism. It is fair to say that the Confucian take on woman and her worth is controversial today:

- Woman's greatest duty is to produce a son.
- A woman ruler is like a hen crowing.
- Disorder is not sent down by Heaven; it is produced by woman.
- A woman should look on her husband as if he were Heaven itself and never weary of thinking how she may yield to him.
- We should not be familiar with the lower orders or women.
- Those who cannot be taught cannot be instructed. These are women and eunuchs.
- A woman's duty is not to control or take charge.
- The woman with no talent is the one with merit.
- Women are to be led and to follow orders.

How wrongheaded could the disciples be! Obviously, they were neither observant nor perceptive.

Women in the United States do not fit the Confucian mold. It is common knowledge they are generous, rational, hyper-intelligent, and loyal. None are selfish, dull-witted, self-absorbed, or unfaithful. Oh, no!

Em Thy told me that the Vietnamese believe America is heaven for women and Vietnam is heaven for men.

In this feminist period of American history, a lot of ink has been spilled trying to separate Confucius from the views of his followers. Learned folk have diced and parsed his words and ideas ad nauseam to demonstrate that he too was not a sexist.

Confucianism is rightfully condemned for teaching that women's subservience to men is natural and proper. Nonetheless, it is important to note that Vietnamese thought and action occur under the shadow of this notion. Women count for less than men do.

Vietnamese men say, "Women are beautiful, but very dangerous." Notwithstanding, women are expected to possess four essential virtues: skill with hands, agreeable appearance, prudence, and exemplary conduct. Surprisingly, this ideal is not always achieved!

Often, men speak scornfully of women. "Women are roses with many thorns." "It is better to have a stupid wife than to have warped chopsticks." "Speaking to a woman is like talking to a duck in thunder." "The two most difficult things for a man are to dig up bamboo roots that have grown into his garden and to find a good woman."

Due to the demographic imbalance caused by war, many older women are unmarried. It is considered a tragedy to be unwed and childless. The saying "A house without children is like a cage without birds" expresses this sorrow. Childless women wonder who will care for them in their old age.

During a discussion of family values and women's status, a student commented that in an American family it seemed like the children come first, the wife second, then the dog, and finally the father. Based on the content of our cultural exports, it is an understandable belief.

In the United States we foster individualism and take great pride in raising our children to be independent. Nonetheless, as we age we wonder where they have gone. The cost/benefit of this individual freedom is supposedly self-reliance, but I wonder if this is true today given the multitude of government benefits available to all.

It is very different in Vietnam where dependence on extended family is the norm and individual freedom is not a priority. A family member's primary responsibility is to advance the family as a group, socially and economically, and to bring honor to the family name. The child exists to benefit the family. A traditional warning instructs, "Be nice to everyone but trust only your family."

For Westerners it is difficult to grasp the importance the Vietnamese attach to their family. In the United States we think the family's primary purpose is to advance the happiness and prosperity of individual members; the family exists to benefit the child.

AWFUL DECISIONS: The killing of infant girls is reported to be a common practice in India and China. Family members carry out the gruesome task. The practice is so widespread that it has resulted in a gender imbalance. Chinese men who cannot find a woman to marry go to Thailand, Indonesia, or Vietnam for one. According to Vietnamese newspapers and my students, the Chinese employ Vietnamese agents to search for beautiful young women from poor families. For $25,000 the family forces the daughter to marry the foreign man. Impoverishment forces awful decisions on these people; they do what they ought not to do. Poverty is a powerful anesthetic. Traditional values of obedience, loyalty, and sacrifice ensure the woman's cooperation.

Upon arrival at her husband's house in China, her passport is taken from her and she is treated as a servant. In some cases, she becomes the general wife for the male members of the family.

THE FAMILY WARRIOR: When it comes to sex and loyalty Vietnamese men are not any different from men everywhere. However, Vietnamese culture permits men to act on their fantasies. The low status of women under Confucianism entitles men. It is not uncommon for a man to have two families. He splits his time between his legal wife and his "warm wife." The "warm wife" is prized, men say, because she is incredibly affectionate, easier to get along with, and does not require foreplay. Most likely these attributes spring from her lack of legal rights. Women accept the arrangement for economic and cultural reasons.

Minh was loud, abrupt, handsome, wealthy, and famous. At 39, he was the owner of a successful textile company. He had two children by his legal wife and would soon have another—but by his first "warm wife."

Minh selected Lan, a 27-year-old employee of his company, to be his second "warm wife." She refused and quit her job when he persisted. Unwilling to give up, however, he started following her to and from her new job. He trailed her to church and to the market. He called her day and night. He began threatening to hurt her boyfriend.

Lan lived with her teenage brothers in a house her parents had given her. Her only sister, Huan, was 35, a Catholic nun, and my English student. Lan asked her elder sister to help her, and Sister Huan asked me for my advice.

Sister Huan telephoned Minh. "Forget Lan, she doesn't like you. You cannot have her. You already have two wives."

"I will hurt your brothers and burn their house down if Lan refuses to be my wife," he responded.

Sister Huan complained to the police, who then arranged a meeting with Minh's legal wife. Neither Lan nor Minh were invited. The police and the unconcerned wife downplayed Minh's threats and concluded the meeting by declaring to Sister Huan that there was no problem.

The stalking continued, and then the police began investigating to determine if Lan legally owned her house and if her brothers were lawfully living in Saigon. The focus of police interest had shifted from the famous predator to his prey. Minh had made the police his friends.

Minh phoned Sister Huan at her convent, insisting on her cooperation and threatening her if she refused to give it. He proposed meeting in a restaurant to discuss the problem. She countered with an offer to meet her at her convent at 7:30 p.m.

"Don't meet with him alone," I warned her.

"I will be in the room with him, but the room has no door and nuns will be listening."

Minh arrived alone and on time.

"Right away when he come, he ask why we meet," she told me afterwards. "I tell him leave my little sister alone. She not for you. He begin shouting. Nuns look in room. He go away."

I grin from ear to ear every time I visualize that meeting.

Sister Huan worried not only about what Minh might do, but also about the police. She said that since she could not fight him she would create problems for him instead. She decided to see Minh's parents and explain the situation to them. They were embarrassed by what she said and agreed to tell him to leave Lan alone.

Culturally, Minh was obligated to obey his parents and he did. Although Minh was a bad man, on that occasion he was a good son. The harassment ended.

Using a proverb, Sister Huan predicted a bad end for Minh: "A pig doesn't want to be fat and a man doesn't want to be famous."

JOB INTERVIEW: Unmarried Vietnamese are expected to accept their father's decisions about important matters. A man I hardly knew asked me to accompany his 26-year-old daughter, Huyen, to a job interview for a position as a cook with a Malaysian family. He was afraid that in Malaysia his daughter might be sold to "bad men." The presence of an elderly Western man at the meeting was intended to impress the interviewer and give him second thoughts if he had bad intentions.

The interview took place in a Saigon hotel early one morning. The prospective employer was well dressed, articulate, and intelligent. He handled my presence well and after inquiring who I was and why I was at the interview, said it showed that the young woman came from a good family.

The man ran the Vietnamese subsidiary of a large Malaysian industrial company. He and his wife were directors of the parent company and his father-in-law was the president and chairman. He gave me a copy of the company's annual report, which confirmed the foregoing. His wife and pre-teen sons liked Vietnamese food but none of the seven staff that cared for his family in Malaysia could cook it. He wanted to please them and that was why he was interviewing in Saigon. Obviously, he was a wealthy man.

Huyen's cooking credentials were impressive and she was a pleasant person. She was offered a good salary, her own room, Sundays off, an annual three-week vacation, and a round-trip airline ticket. Huyen wanted the job but told the man she needed her father's approval. He said he understood and would call her in two days. After receiving a full report on the interview, Huyen's father asked me if the Malaysian was a good man. "I don't know," I answered, "but he is not in the business of selling women."

In the end, Huyen's father refused to give his approval, so she turned the job down. If she had acted contrary to his wishes, she would have invited unending criticism from her family. Huyen wanted to cook for this man's family and she wanted to travel, but she could ignore neither her father's wishes nor traditional Vietnamese values.

MARRIAGE: Traditions combine age-old truths and principles and give insight into the culture of a people. Over time, the ancients developed practices and rituals that they believed would, if followed, encourage behavior beneficial to family and society. In Vietnam, family is the most important part of a person's life. Through the years, kinsfolk stay together, protecting and caring for one another. Three generations commonly live in the same house. They pray to and revere their ancestors, and do whatever is necessary to protect the family's future. Relatives are obligated one to the other, first and foremost.

The Vietnamese view marriage as the origin of all happiness and therefore as the most important decision in life. In addition, marriage perpetuates the honor and respect that one's ancestors are entitled to. To die without a son to care for the family grave is a great misfortune.

Parental approval of a marriage partner is a tradition that has developed to ensure family happiness and stability, but it also gives parents extraordinary control over their children's choices and happiness. Parents are obligated to guard against harmful alliances. Their decision is based on impressions and information gleaned from meetings with, and investigations of, the intended partner and his or her family. It is believed the experience and wisdom of the old is more likely to judge correctly the merits of a prospective marriage partner than the passion of the young. Contrary to what happens in the United States, marriage is a decision too important to be left to the inexperienced.

In the past, to marry without parental consent resulted in being banned from the family home. Even today, parental blessing is sought, and it is not a mere formality like in America where, sometimes, the man asks the woman's father for her hand. If both sets of parents give their permission then the fortuneteller must determine if the birth dates of the couple and the alignment of the stars will allow for a happy and lasting union. If the oracle predicts a happy alliance, he then advises which wedding date would be luckiest. However, unreasonable demands, hurt feelings and strong-willed participants can undermine the consent process.

The 28-year-old son of my friends asked his parents for permission to marry a 26-year-old neighbor. As is customary, the couple would live with the groom's parents. After a meeting to discuss the merits of their children's marriage, both sets of parents gave their consent. Days later the girl told her mother-in-law to-be that she was pregnant. In Vietnam a pregnant bride is bad luck; the marriage would be unlucky. The boy's mother withdrew her approval but said she would consent to the marriage if the girl agreed to always use the back door (never the front door) and to not pray at the family shrine. The young woman refused this humiliating condition and said she would kill the fetus. She reasoned that her threat would change the mother's mind, the marriage would go forward and she would be able to use the front door and worship at the shrine. The mother warned that there would be no marriage if her grandchild were killed. The young woman had an abortion days latter. The marriage was called off.

Pre-wedding activities are based on custom and require focused direction. The future in-laws visit, gifts are given, and wedding arrangements are negotiated. Both sides must be on their best behavior, for the couple's happiness and the future of the family are at stake. A misstep can have grave consequences. Grandparents, aunts, and uncles are involved; their advice is valued and must be considered. Assuming egos remain intact after the visit and all else goes well, the marriage ceremony and party are held, usually at the expense of the groom's family.

The bride's family delivers her to the groom's home. She leaves her family and joins the family of her husband. She must obey the men in his family as well as her mother-in-law. Often she is treated poorly and has difficulty accepting her new social standing. "A daughter-in-law is a cook for a hundred families" is a Vietnamese saying that speaks to her subservient status.

The status of a man who lives with his in-laws is described by this aphorism, "A husband who lives with his wife's family is like a dog under the table." A middle-aged man told me he would not join his wife and daughter in California because he would have to live with his wife's family. He stayed in Saigon with his teenage son.

After the ceremony, the couple signs a certificate in the presence of the authorities to legalize their marriage. People say that to sign the document without a traditional ceremony is not a real marriage; a ceremony in front of neighbors is necessary.

A wife does not take her husband's name, but keeps her own. Children receive their father's family name.

However, no tradition automatically ensures the desired result and sometimes things go wrong. Folly and passion can thwart tradition and wisdom every time.

YOU ARE A GOOD SON: September 2 is Independence Day in Vietnam. The holiday commemorates the day in 1945 that Ho Chi Minh declared Vietnam independent from French rule. One of my students, Hung, invited me for the celebration in the village where he grew up and where his parents still live. Hung, his younger brother, and I made the three-hour trip by car.

Their parents' three-room house lacked electricity and indoor plumbing. They survived on what they grew and raised and on gifts from their children. That afternoon relatives and friends gathered for a feast, and children were given mooncakes and presents. A patriotic skit performed by neighborhood children lent meaning to the anniversary. Like everyone else in the family, I spent the night sleeping on a bamboo mat under a mosquito net.

During the celebration, Hung, who was 33, announced that he wanted to get married and asked for his parents' approval. He could not ignore this basic traditional value. Subsequently, Hung and his father, Viet, traveled by motorbike to Saigon to meet the girl's family at their home. They arrived at nine a.m., the appointed time, but no one was there to greet them. One hour later Hung's 23-year-old fiancée arrived with her father and uncle. They provided no excuse or apology for their tardiness. No wet washcloth was offered to Viet to clean his face of road dust.

When the meeting started, the insulting behavior continued—food and drink were not offered. The uncle turned to Viet and demanded that he address him as bác, which means uncle. Viet refused because the word designates elevated status. If he had agreed, the other man would be accorded a higher status and could demand of Viet limitless respect and obedience. The two men were the same age and Hung's father, after enduring the insults, did not intend to hold the "uncle" in high esteem or show any respect. At that point, the prospective bride's father and uncle refused to speak to Viet, instead addressing all their comments to Hung. The daughter cried when she saw how badly her family was treating her would-be father-in-law because she knew it meant he would not approve the nuptials. The meeting broke up in anger with the financial terms of the marriage and details of the ceremony unresolved. There were no compromises.

At home that evening Viet told his son that he did not approve of the marriage. Viet said the girl's family was difficult, bad mannered, insulting, and from the North. He explained that it would be a mistake to marry into that family because the marriage would be unhappy. Hung was disappointed but understood what was expected of him. He said he would abide by his father's decision. He was rewarded by the words of praise so important in Vietnam: "You are a good son."

DIVORCE: "But there is a problem," Hung confessed. "We have already had a civil marriage." The girl's mother had insisted; it was a condition of letting the unmarried couple sleep in her daughter's bedroom. The problem was that even though there had been no traditional marriage ceremony, they would now have to get a divorce. It is difficult for divorced women to remarry in Vietnam, so the real loser in this situation would be Hung's wife. Knowing this, I did not know what to make of the behavior of the young woman's family. Perhaps their knowledge of the existence of the marriage certificate emboldened them to be uncompromising and difficult. Certainly, the dislike and distrust that exists between Northerners and Southerners played a part in the unfortunate outcome. The young woman's family had overestimated their position and the patience and tolerance of Hung's father.

Viet's wife and daughters disagreed with him. They said, "Let Hung marry. He is a man now and able to make his own decisions." Five months later, under relentless pressure from the women of the family, Viet told his son to marry the girl if he still wanted to. He would approve the marriage, but instructed Hung to keep him out of the arrangements and away from those Northerners. This time Hung's mother met with the prospective bride's family to make the wedding arrangements.

The damaged relationship between Viet and the bride's family was irreparable, though. The symbolic journey by the groom's family to the bride's house to present gifts took place without Hung's father. He refused to make the trip. For their part, the bride's father and uncle made a show of inspecting and disparaging the gifts.

The wedding ceremony took place at a rural restaurant the following day. As is true the world over, the groom was nervous, disorganized, and confused. The bride, of course, was beautiful, confident, and very much in charge. I watched as she coached Hung through his wedding vows. She found the ring he was fumbling for in his pocket. In addition, while he looked around to see whose cell phone was ringing, the radiant bride reached into his jacket and shut it off. She gestured as if to smash it to the ground, but then smiled and placed it back in his pocket, all this in front of family and friends. Sometimes being a man is difficult.

LOVE IN CAMBODIA: In Vietnam, even mature couples consult with their families, seek their advice, and involve them in the marriage ceremony.

Matrimony in haste suggests the bride is pregnant, and Vietnamese women believe it is bad luck to attend such a wedding.

It is said that the Vietnamese grow the rice, the Cambodians watch it grow, and the Laotians listen to it grow. I have not been to Laos so I do not know if Laotians are really that laid back, but the Vietnamese are a lot more industrious than the Cambodians appear to be. Cambodia is poorer than Vietnam; there are fewer people and they appear to work less.

Clara, my sister's friend, stayed with me in June for three days and then traveled to Siem Reap, Cambodia, where she met and fell in love with Jerome. I went to Cambodia for their August wedding.

At age 65, Jerome was forced to leave his surgical practice in Chicago because his hands shook. He took a job at a children's hospital in Siem Reap.

Unexpectedly and to his everlasting surprise, he met charming, beautiful Clara in the Elephant Bar of the hundred-year-old Grand Hotel while she was in Siem Reap to tour the marvelous ruins of Angkor Wat. Clara, 48, became the director of public relations and a fundraiser for the children's hospital.

The marriage was a modified Cambodian Buddhist ceremony lasting three hours instead of the usual three days. The bride and groom had three costume changes and I, as best man, had two. The ceremony included a symbolic haircut, a monk's chant, feet washing, wrist tying, gift giving, blessings, and flower throwing. Sensuous hand dances and traditional music played by children on handcrafted traditional instruments added to the wonder of it all. A joyous reception for 200 persons was held on the roof of the hospital guesthouse. The day was magical, everything right, no glitches. It was a perfect celebration of two wonderful people and their commitment to one another and to the children of Cambodia.

The rashness and unconventionality of this couple will not surprise most Americans, but such conduct contrasts sharply with Vietnamese traditions.

Jerome and five other doctors work at the hospital, which is funded by an American charity. On an average day, they diagnose and treat 140 children for everything ranging from AIDS, to intestinal parasites, to landmine wounds. They amputate, operate, suture, and medicate. Jerome is undaunted by his palsy. One wonders why he is allowed to operate and how patients fare under his scalpel.

Patients start arriving at the compound at six a.m. The gates are locked either when the site is full or at noon, whichever comes first. Only children who are bleeding are allowed into the enclosure after noon.

As in Vietnam, family members accompany the patient, bringing with them food, water, cooking fires, and sleeping mats. Hundreds of people vie for space in the unsheltered courtyard. Nurses circulate in the crowd to determine whose medical needs are most urgent. The doctors do not leave the clinic until everyone who entered the compound before the gates closed has been cared for.

A few weeks before I visited, the keepers of the Angkor Wat Royal Elephants had disrupted this routine. A baby elephant had been injured; an adult beast had crushed its foot. Naturally, the animal had been brought to the children's hospital for treatment.

Jerome related that it had been a chaotic scene. Sick children had crowded around the swaying baby elephant. The doctors could not help the animal, and by the time it was removed from the hospital precious time had been lost. Patients not treated that day had been allowed to stay overnight and were the first ones seen the following morning.

GREED BREAKS THE SACK: Folk stories, songs, and poems describe the consequences of acting contrary to family obligations. The selfish and greedy are punished. The generous and caring are rewarded. Through these works, be they literature, poems, or songs, children and society are instructed in the traditional values and moral principles of Vietnam, which are inherent to its culture. Children read, discuss, and analyze these tales in school. They are part of curriculums taught throughout the land.

One such story tells of an elder brother who inherits his parents' property. Although he was obligated to be benevolent and caring toward his younger brother, he drove his sibling out of the family home, giving him only a single starfruit tree. The younger son nurtured the tree and subsisted on its fruit. One day he challenged a large bird that was eating the starfruit, explaining that he would have no food and would die if the fruit were eaten.

The bird proposed that if it were allowed to continue eating, it would return the next day to take the boy to a pile of gold atop a mountain. The youth was instructed to bring a bag of a certain size and he did. The next day the bird flew him to the mountaintop where he filled the bag. The flight back was uneventful.

Upon hearing of his sibling's good fortune and new wealth, the elder brother demanded that the starfruit tree be returned to him. Ever obedient, the boy complied. Soon the bird returned for nourishment and was challenged by the elder brother for eating the fruit. Instructions were given as before, but things ended badly. On the flight to the mountain to get gold, the greedy brother brought with him a bag much bigger than he was supposed to. On the return flight, the extra weight of the gold in the big bag caused the bird to tire and drop its load into the ocean, where the elder brother drowned.

THE LAZY AND SELFISH ARE PUNISHED: Another fable tells of twin girls born with humps on their backs. Hoa was sweet, industrious, and altruistic. She loved her father, who worked in the forest gathering wood for sale. Hien, her sister, was vain, lazy, and selfish. Their humps made life difficult. The likelihood of finding a husband was slim.

One day their father became sick and could not work. Without wood to sell, the family would soon have no food. Although an inexperienced young girl, Hoa immediately set out for the forest. Hien was afraid that collecting wood would mar her skin so she stayed at home. Hoa made fagots all day. The following morning she would bring the fuel to her village to exchange for food for her family.

She awoke in the forest that night to singing from a campfire not far away. A band of spirit men was having a party. Hoa politely asked to join them. They were surprised she was alone and impressed that she was doing her father's job. At their request, she sang a love song. They said she would receive a gift from them in the morning. When she awoke, the fire was cold, the men were gone, and so was her hump.

Hoping to be as fortunate as her sister, Hien went to the woods the next day. She encountered the same tribesmen and demanded that they remove her hump. They knew Hien had come not to help her family but to help herself. When she awoke the next morning, she discovered she had two humps. The spirit men had given her the one they had removed from Hoa.

ANOTHER MYTH: After 1975, a group of American Vietnam War protesters, veterans, and irresponsible journalists created a myth they called Agent Orange. They gave this name to the defoliant used by America in the war to deny hiding places to the enemy. The defoliant does not kill trees, only leaves. These people claimed that it poisoned the countryside, thus causing birth defects and disease across generations. Sadly, birth defects and sickness are part of the human condition and have been with humanity since long before the Vietnam War.

The herbicide was developed in the United States and is still used to control weeds. The dioxin in Agent Orange is one part per million. It was not added as a poison but was a result of the manufacturing process. Other common sources of dioxins are enzymes in the soil, forest fires, auto exhaust, and copper smelting. Dioxin in Agent Orange degrades within 72 hours when exposed to sunlight.

U.S. veterans of the war sued the manufacturers of Agent Orange (U.S. Veterans v. Dow Chemical) seeking compensation for a wide variety of ailments that they or their family members suffered from. They were unsuccessful because, in the words of U.S. 11th District (NY) Judge Weinstein, "The most serious deficiency in the plaintiff's cases was their failure to present any credible evidence of a causal link between Agent Orange and the various diseases from which they are allegedly suffering." Further, the judge wrote, "The unfounded and speculative assumption underlying the testimony of plaintiff's experts has no probative value whatsoever. No rational jury could conclude that exposure to Agent Orange caused the alleged injuries."

The veteran groups turned to Congress for compensation and, even without proof of a causal link, a law was passed instructing the Veterans

Administration to make monthly payments to claimants in respect of a long list of ailments supposedly linked to Agent Orange. Astonishingly, this law requires the Veterans Administration to even compensate Vietnam veterans for their prostate and other age related conditions, which they assert were caused by Agent Orange. Prostrate problems are common in men (whether veterans or not) over 60; according to the American Medical Association, one out of six are affected. Without proof, Congress permitted members of a powerful lobby to receive taxpayer money. In 1787 Alexander Tyler, a Scottish historian, wrote that democracy is finished when citizens discover how to access the public purse.

Subsequent studies have found a casual link between Agent Orange and several diseases, but one wonders if the studies and conclusions meet scientific vigor. What organizations have sponsored the studies, one asks?

The Vietnamese government has vigorously pursued Agent Orange claims in the U.S. courts but has been unsuccessful. Logically they tell the court, "If American veterans were injured by Agent Orange then so, too, were Vietnamese citizens." The Vietnamese media has explained its case to the people, and the government has conducted a public relations campaign in the United States hoping to influence the courts and Congress. They have presented thousands of alleged victims' affidavits in support of their case.

Vietnamese authorities visited Phong, my father-in-law, at his house. They pressured him to sign a letter saying he was ill because of exposure to Agent Orange, but, not being sick, he refused. They told him he was not a good Vietnamese. It was a warning. Nevertheless, he still would not cooperate. Phong believes that soon, some way, he will be punished for this. "Lies, all lies," he told me. "They want American money."

Many groups have studied the affect of Agent Orange on the health of Vietnam veterans. Such studies are mainly based on statistical analysis. Many of these studies are contradictory and lead me to agree with Judge Weinstein.

Thirteen

REGIONAL ANIMOSITY

In friendship false, implacable in hate,
Resolved to ruin or to rule the state.
-John Dryden, Absalom and Achitophel

Vietnam has a totalitarian and insecure government. Although ruled by the Communist Party, it is not a doctrinaire Marxist society; private property and profit are permitted and encouraged.

Two million party members govern, supervise, and control a population of 90 million. Some people say they also siphon, extort, and extract money from the public. Corruption, petty and gross, is widespread at all levels. Payments to officials and the police to do their jobs, or to look the other way, are common. I have seen only instances of low-level corruption that directly affect people. Accounts of improbity by persons in high positions are discussed and sometimes published.

When I think about dishonesty in Vietnam, I recall what I saw as a young infantry lieutenant in 1963. Province and district chiefs, military officers and ordinary soldiers, were often venal in their dealings with the populace. Then, as now, I was aware of the corruption. It was so pervasive and public that everyone believed crooked behavior was the norm at upper levels of the military and government. Personnel rosters were falsified to inflate military payrolls; supplies, including munitions, were sold on the black market where the Viet Cong bought them; public works projects funded with United States aid were constructed by conscripted peasants and their wages stolen; gasoline, rice, and other commodities disappeared from inventories; unauthorized surcharges were added at border crossings; and fees were demanded for the right to do business.

Corruption undermined the pre-1975 government's legitimacy in the eyes of the people. One important difference between then and post-1975 is that Southerners stole from other Southerners. However, today, people from the South believe that Northerners, who rule the country, enrich themselves at the expense of Southerners.

In America and other democracies graft is also a problem, but in Vietnam it is entrenched. Perhaps the cultural importance of familial, business, and social ties explains the difference. A Vietnamese man described as "a monkey with no tail" has no family or friends dependent on him. It is difficult to influence him. However, a man who is "a monkey with a long tail" has an extended family and many friends. Such a man is obligated to help them any way he can. He is likely to be corrupted.

The U.S. media routinely reports on legal proceedings against people in positions of power. One such criminal activity resulted in adverse consequences worldwide, even reaching Vietnam 12,000 miles away. The theft of $50 billion from investors by Bernard Madoff, a New York fraudster, caused three of my seminarian students to lose their scholarships to study at universities in the United States. Their benefactor was an American victim of the crime. The U.S. citizen lost most of his money, and thus was unable to honor his pledge. Madoff was sentenced to life in prison.

Given the opportunity, some Americans are also dishonest and unethical, but in the United States it is more likely that such people will be exposed and punished. Democratic institutions, transparency, and accountability are missing in Vietnam. It will be a long, long time before multiple parties, free elections, a free press, and the rule of law are allowed in Vietnam. Until this happens, venal officials will continue to rule, and progress for the people and the country will be thwarted.

Vietnam's leadership understands that fraud and bribery undermine its authority as well as its attempts to raise the population's standard of living. Periodically, it embarks on anti-corruption campaigns that often are derailed by long-standing and powerful personal relationships.

Following the revelation of criminal misconduct involving the leader of the government agency that dispenses hundreds of millions of dollars in foreign aid, senior party members, concerned that grants and soft loans from the World Bank and industrial countries would be curtailed, spoke out on the need to rid Vietnam of this pervasive and intractable problem:

"Corruption threatens the survival of our system."
-General Secretary Nong Duc Manh

"There is now a serious crisis of trust among our people and in our party."
-Former Minister of the Interior, Mai Chi Tho

"The party has become a shield for corrupt officials."
-General Vo Nguyen Giap

"If you don't change the system, if you don't introduce transparency, a counterbalance of power, a real voice of the people, a responsible and independent press, you can hardly stop corruption."
-Ministry of Planning, La Dang Doanh

According to the April 10, 2006, International New York Times, the scandal that engendered these surprisingly candid remarks began with seven million dollars of soccer bets. Millions of dollars of foreign aid intended for construction projects was diverted to purchase grand houses, luxury cars, warm wives, protection money, and gambling thrills. Those responsible were arrested, stripped of their jobs, and jailed.

If the party were to succeed in wiping out venality, it would feel more secure in its right to rule, and the people of Vietnam would benefit.

*****

REGIONAL ANIMOSITY: Occupying 126,000 square miles, Vietnam is the size of Italy. It is over 1,000 miles long and shaped like an elongated "S." In the north, Vietnam shares a long border with China. The geography and climate are diverse and so are the attitudes and traits of the people.

Each region has its own history. Vietnamese from the North and Central regions populated the South hundreds of year ago. The desire for a better life still inspires Northerners to settle in the South. Large-scale migrations occurred in 1945, 1954, and 1975. The 1945 migrants were desperately poor after the Japanese occupation during World War II and came south for sustenance.

Hundreds of thousands of Catholics, as well as the rich, fled the North for the South in 1954 when, pursuant to the Geneva Accords, Vietnam was partitioned into South Vietnam and North Vietnam. The groups that fled south knew that their religion, or their wealth, would cause them problems under the communists.

The Northerners who migrated south after 1975 have benefited from communist rule, and are either members or supporters of the party.

In conversation, people use a code to tell when their family arrived in the South. They say, "I'm a 45, "I'm a 54," or "I'm a 75." Alternatively, if one came in 1945 or 1954 one can say, "I'm a 9," the sum of the last two digits of those years. Similarly, if one's family arrived after 1975 one can say, "I'm a 75" or "I'm a 2," the sum of the last two digits minus ten.

Southerners say that people from the Center are the troublemakers, warriors are from the North, and Southerners are the peacemakers. These words reflect the historical reality of a thousand years of internal strife. Another belief holds that ideas originate with Southerners but are implemented by Northerners.

Today, the three regions are united politically and culturally. However, there is a long history of conflict, distrust, and animosity between Vietnamese from different areas. They view one another with suspicion; it is centuries old.

People from these regions have fought wars against one another. Sometimes the North won and sometimes the South was victorious.

Southerners do not trust Northerners and are vocal about it. I have heard many spurious statements about Northerners:

"People from the North are dishonest, crafty, overly ambitious, greedy, and have ulterior motives."

"Northerners do not honor agreements."

"Northerners say one thing and do another."

Two reasons are given for Northerners' supposed duplicity. They have lived next to China, a powerful and demanding neighbor, for thousands of years. They learned that they had to agree to China's terms or be punished. Northerners developed a strategy of accepting what China wanted but of not living up to all the terms of the agreement. The second explanation is that the weather and the soil in the North are not good for growing rice, so Northerners are difficult because their lives are hard.

Northerners have negative views of their Southern compatriots as well: Southerners are ungovernable, not serious, unpatriotic, lazy, showy, and too direct.

The war's victors hold positions of power in government and business. Their children have access to the best education, housing, jobs, overseas travel, and paths to success. Southerners believe they are second-class citizens. They seethe with resentment and do not conceal their feelings. Gross generalizations about a group of people are common, and as such they are always oversimplifications and usually unfair. Nonetheless, in Vietnam these blanket statements are outlets for intense, strongly felt bitterness.

Ho Chi Minh is idolized in the North. In the South, he is revered as an important historical figure that freed Vietnam from foreign domination and unified the country. School children are told countless laudatory stories about his life. These tales portray him as Vietnam's savior. Sayings credited to Uncle Ho are used to foster traditional values and love of country.

Wise words claimed to be his are displayed prominently in public places and in the media. Government propagandists use them to garner public support for policies and projects. Southerners snicker at this blatant propaganda and make jokes about it. A smiling university student volunteered that, fortunately, the government had recently found a new Uncle Ho saying.

Saigonese enjoy telling the following joke. It begins with the famous words of Martin Luther King: "I have a dream." The joke teller continues with Uncle Ho saying, "I have a dream, too." The first time I heard it, everyone laughed but me. A Dream II is an expensive and much desired Honda motorbike, I was informed. The joke makes fun of the government's attribution of other people's ideas and expressions to Ho Chi Minh. I was cautioned not to repeat this rib-tickler in front of Northerners.

STATE-OWNED COMPANIES: Everyone scrambles for a job, and those fortunate to land one with the government or a large state-owned company are secure, but not well paid. Most people have "small jobs." They have no savings, pensions, or health insurance. A job with a contract is desirable and guarantees severance pay in addition to certain other rights, but most employees have no job security.

Northerners have the best jobs in government and state-owned businesses. With few exceptions, Southerners are not allowed to advance to upper management. Frequently, unqualified people are brought from the North to fill management jobs in the South. My, a friend of mine from the North, described her Saigon-born subordinate in the state-owned utility company where they worked as follows: "Inside he is 100% American. His parents are in California and he has tried to go there. We know. He will be kept down and not allowed to advance in his job. Anyway, top jobs are for the North people."

State-owned companies, which numbered 3,800 in 2004, are the backbone of Vietnam's economy. They are highly politicized and critical to the party's powerful role. The party believes they can be used to steer the country towards prosperity. However, these companies are characterized by mismanagement, inefficiencies, corruption, and lack of accountability. Senior management positions go to party members, relatives, and loyalists.

Vinashin, which began as a ship building company, has expanded into 450 businesses including spas, motorcycle assembly, and real estate. This state-owned company has consistently failed to make a profit, and is on the brink of bankruptcy with $4.5 billion in debts. The state has not honored its moral commitment to repay foreign investors.

In order to compete efficiently with foreign competitors, party leaders have embarked on major restructuring and privatization of state enterprises. Since 1998 the state has sold over 2,000 businesses, but individuals in management who benefit from the status quo have resisted; they do not want to endanger their soft jobs or accept new responsibilities. Most often, the management buys these businesses from the government at a discount, financed with unsound and below-market-interest rate loans from government-controlled banks. As powerful men compete for more power and better positions during this period of change, they have resisted corporate restructuring and undertaken to influence the outcome. Prominent state-owned companies, including Petro Vietnam and Vietnam Airlines, have been investigated, and reports of arrests and dismissals have appeared in the press.

DISTRUST: People lie to the government at every turn. They say telling the truth costs money. They do not believe the authorities tell them the truth, either. The media is controlled by the government, which means the party. I have never met a Vietnamese who takes political or economic news seriously. Heavy-duty propaganda is most evident in coverage of those topics.

Sixty people died in a Saigon building fire in 2002. "If the newspapers write 60 die, it means 120 or 130 people die," a student told me. My neighbors and I could hear the engines and see the glow of flames against the night sky. Thao and I walked three blocks to the blazing building and with hundreds of others watched the flames and smoke. Cries of those trapped inside reached the street where peddlers sold coconut milk, roasted corn, and sweet soup to the crowd. I watched as a burly Western man made numerous trips up the firefighter's ladder, each time returning to the ground with a child or elderly Vietnamese clinging to his back. It was a mechanical ladder, perched atop a fire truck that reached to the third-floor windows of the five-story building. He rescued one hysterical child by holding her to his chest while using his free hand to navigate the descent, rung by rung. Two days later the press carried accounts of the fire. The fire department was criticized for its slow response time. The manager and owner of the disco from which the fire started and spread were condemned for storing flammable material in violation of the law. An American man, a long-time Saigon resident, was praised by name in the press for saving lives.

In 2004, the regime announced that one person had died from SARS in Hanoi, but that other Vietnamese cities were free of the disease. Despite this news, the Saigonese assumed that SARS was killing people in their city as well, but they were wrong. The administration had acted decisively to stop SARS from spreading. Travel restrictions and quarantines were imposed when the health threat became known. Unlike in China, authorities in Hanoi made the difficult decisions early and were able to limit the disease to a few areas. Eventually neighboring countries made the same decisions, but not before hundreds of people had died.

Most Vietnamese eat rice twice a day; it is an essential part of their diet. Rice stores sell the grain from large bags at prices, in 2011, ranging from $.50 to $1.50 per kilogram. The different prices reflect the quality, which is determined by taste, fragrance, texture, and origin. Japanese rice is the most expensive. A store I frequented offers 36 different kinds of rice.

In 2006, the media reported that crop failures had resulted in rice shortages in some Asian countries, but not in Vietnam. Public officials promptly reported there was plenty of rice; the Vietnamese people would have all they needed. Immediately, citizens flocked to the stores to buy as much as they could. They emptied the stores and hoarded the grain. The nation's rice stock dwindled; prices rose and the government imposed price controls and a per person limit of five kilograms of rice per store, per day.

Repeatedly Vietnamese friends would express disbelief about a particular announcement from Hanoi and ask me (the American who should know) for the truth. They listened to the BBC and the VOA and heard news that was different from what the government-controlled media reported. I made sure these people understood that government distrust is universal and that in the United States we do not always believe our leaders or what the media reports.

GO BACK: A wealthy Northern woman I knew had lived in Saigon with her husband and two children for 15 years. They owned two small houses in a nice area. One they resided in, the other they rented to foreigners. Most of their neighbors were also from the North. The motorbike drivers who provided cheap transportation to the residents were all from the South. They and their families came from poor neighborhoods. The woman said the drivers were good, hardworking men. She and her neighbors felt safe around these men and trusted them.

Nevertheless, one of the men was a problem; once a month he would get drunk and, while sitting on his parked motorbike, tell the residents to go back to their country. "Go back to the North where you belong," he would yell.

The neighbors met to discuss how to deal with this man and his insults. To report him to the police or to hurt him or his business might endanger their children. Their solution was to have the largest Northern man in their group stand—arms folded, shirtless, and in boxer shorts—10 feet from the drunken man and stare at him. Other men were at the ready nearby. The insults stopped immediately. "We know how to deal with this man now," the wealthy woman told me.

Of interest is that the man said what he wanted and the people did not turn to the authorities to punish him. They intimidated him instead.

MY EXPENSES ARE HIGH: Traffic laws here regulate the same things that are regulated in the United States: speed, lane usage, traffic flow, safety, vehicle registration, and driver licensing. For the most part people obey traffic laws in America. Education, enforcement, and an instinct for self-preservation are the reasons. In Vietnam, it is different. Enforcement is sporadic and traffic laws are treated as options or mere suggestions.

Many motorbike drivers do not have licenses. It is not difficult to get one, but most people avoid bureaucrats if possible, and with good reason. A student once told me that he had gone to a private driving school before taking his driving test. The test had two parts, written and driving. The school fee covered two hours of classroom study and 10 hours of driving practice. If he failed the exam, he could repeat the course one time free of charge.

When the course ended, the instructor told the student that for $25 he could get his license without taking the test. The student refused, took the test and, of course, failed. His instructor was angry. Students who fail make the teacher look bad and make it hard for him to get new students. The student retook the 12-hour course and refused a second time to pay the bribe, but this time got his license.

Since 2008, motorbike helmets have been required throughout Vietnam. This law is enforced. Unfortunately there are no uniform standards for the construction of helmets. Shops sell helmets made from different materials and of different shapes. Are they safe? Will sunlight degrade the plastic? Will they shatter on impact with plastic shards piercing the brain? Does one that covers only the top of the head provide sufficient protection? Foolish motorcyclists favor thin, fashionable helmets with wide brims, or ones shaped like baseball caps. Still others are made of cloth-covered cardboard.

One Sunday afternoon I was traveling north on Highway 1 to visit a friend. We came upon a line of policemen stretched across the road. Helmeted travelers were let through the line to continue their journey. My driver and others without helmets were directed to a police officer seated at a folding table. Police with sticks, pistols, Northern accents, and supercharged motorbikes staffed the checkpoint, where documents were examined and tickets for driving without a helmet were issued.

The seated policeman gave my driver a ticket and pointed to a nearby bamboo and thatch structure where a long line of other offenders waited to pay the $3 fine. His registration, license, and ID card would be returned to him when he presented a receipt proving that the fine had been paid. The line of 50 people was slow moving and stuck in the sun. My driver called it a two-hour line.

A small, unkempt man worked the queue. He told the people that if they hired him they would not have to wait their turn. "Give me your ticket and $3 for the fine and I will return with a receipt and your documents. You will be free to continue your journey in 15 minutes." His fee was another $3, which he acknowledged was expensive. He explained he had to pay others for this priority service. "My expenses are high."

My driver looked at me and I nodded. We accepted the expediter's services. When the man had five clients, he walked directly into the bamboo hut. Tickets in hand, he marched to the head of the line and dealt with the seated policeman. He returned to his clients, who then paid his fee, and he handed back their paperwork. Many drivers chose to wait, as the $3 fine and $3 fee was too expensive. Angry, they watched while the wealthier travelers paid and the police enriched themselves.

THEIR PAY IS SMALL: This is not a dangerous country for foreigners. Theft is a problem but violence against foreigners is not. It is safe here if one is not foolish. One reason is that Vietnamese are afraid of the police, who are numerous, highly visible, and quick to use force. Plainclothes cops work the streets as well as uniformed ones. Popular belief holds that for every policeman you see, there are two you do not.

People do not obey all the laws, especially traffic regulations, but when spoken to by the police they are cooperative, respectful, and obedient. Fines are imposed and, at times, beatings administered on the spot for uncooperative or disrespectful behavior. Silent crowds watch the street beatings and understand what awaits them if they antagonize the police.

Summary power of this kind always results in abuse and corruption. People accept that street fines supplement the low salaries of the police officers and their superiors. I have heard rationalizations such as "They work hard,"

"Their pay is small," and "They have families to support." Policemen keep bribes low because people will pay small amounts to avoid the detention of their motorbikes until a court hearing takes place. However, a large fine may be contested and this works to the police officers' disadvantage because of the time required for court hearings and paperwork. The system is self-regulating; it is kept in balance by mutual convenience.

It is widely believed that police treat Northerners more leniently than Southerners. One evening I found a wallet on the street near my house. Inside were a young man's photo identity card, his driver's license, cash, and a creased copy of a letter signed by an army general stating that the young man was the son of a former hero soldier from Hanoi. Most certainly, he produces this letter when dealing with the police and other officials. Thao advised that I turn the wallet over to the ward officials.

SOUTHERNERS SPEAKING: In early 2003 it became obvious that America would not tolerate Iraqi intransigence any longer. The United States was going to war to change the leadership of Iraq and we, the United Kingdom, and "the coalition of the willing" would do it without the United Nations, if necessary. I was in Saigon while America built up its forces and prepared for war. It was no secret that we were preparing a preemptive strike. Everyone everywhere knew it.

I supported this decision but regretted the unavailability, for me, of serious, impassioned debate. I wondered how the Vietnamese would react to an American war in Iraq. I braced myself for harsh criticism, but I was surprised.

One of my students explained, "Martin, war is wrong. Many innocent people will be hurt and killed. But if there is a war, I want America to win. America is good and Saddam Hussein's Iraq is evil." Other Vietnamese I knew expressed similar opinions. I do not think they were hiding their real views to make me feel comfortable. These were Southerners speaking.

The opinions of my students whose parents were party members, however, were critical. They condemned the United States' intervention in the internal affairs of another country. Local TV news programs pieced together negative sound bites from the BBC and CNN to show how badly the war was going for the United States.

Shown on television were numerous government-sponsored demonstrations in Hanoi against the war in Iraq. I witnessed only one in Saigon, where 50 citizens were trotted out to announce their opposition to the war. Loudspeakers blared statements critical of U.S. policy to a small group of observers. Placard-waving demonstrators carried peace messages and grotesque cartoon-like images of Uncle Sam. It was surprising to see how few people participated and how quickly it was over. This carefully orchestrated event was shown on television for days.

DVDs featuring comedy routines are popular here. Some are quite humorous. One DVD satirizes Vietnamese marriage brokers. It depicts a 20-year-old, curvaceous woman asking how much a husband will cost. The broker responds that the cost depends on nationality. An American husband will cost $30,000, a Canadian $25,000. The price declines with each nationality mentioned until she hears $2,000 will get her an Iranian husband. To the accompaniment of canned laughter, the broker then tells her that she can get an Iraqi man for free. "They are not civilized," he says, "and they have no future."

RECONSTRUCTION: The American Civil War, which lasted from 1861 to 1865, pitted 11 southern states (the Confederate States) against the remaining Union states. At issue were states' rights, slavery, and secession. From this place in time, the outcome does not seem surprising, but back then, it was in doubt. The Union had vastly superior resources, industry, and manpower. The Confederate States had superior generals, whose brilliance for years trumped Northern advantages and nearly won the war.

The war was brutal and savage. Counting both sides, 500,000 died. This number is more than the aggregate of American soldiers killed in all other wars. Keep counting; it is a running total. In the not too distant future, wars won and lost, necessary and unnecessary, just and unjust will push the total beyond 500,000. It is our destiny; it is humanity's fate to go to war, kill one another, and destroy. It is sad but true that war is part of, and fundamental to, our nature.

The Confederate General Robert E. Lee surrendered his army at Appomattox Courthouse on April 9, 1865. U.S. General Grant allowed Confederate soldiers to return to their homes. None were imprisoned or put in reeducation camps. They were only required to stack their rifles. Officers were permitted to keep their side arms and horses. The Union did not confiscate Confederate soldiers' land. Richmond, Virginia, the capital of the Confederate States of America, was not renamed Lincolnville, nor was Atlanta, Georgia, rechristened Shermanville.

Opportunists from the Union states moved to the former Confederate states to seek their fortunes after the war. They were called "carpetbaggers" because they often traveled to the South carrying a single canvas bag. The canvas material was colorful and to some resembled a carpet. The carpetbaggers had the Union Army's protection. Abuse of power by these men was widespread. Many were dishonest, and were responsible for years of ill feeling and mistrust between the former enemies.

There was no unanimous agreement about how to treat the former Confederate States. Powerful political groups insisted on stern punishment. Eventually, the conciliatory policies of Presidents Lincoln and Johnson prevailed, resulting in surprisingly mild punishment being imposed on the losing side.

The Reconstruction Period lasted 12 years. During that period, full rights were restored one by one to the secessionist states. Their citizens could elect representatives to Congress and vote in national elections. Southerners were granted a full pardon and amnesty for treason. Carpetbaggers either left of their own accord or were sent packing by the people they had abused. They went back to where they came from, to the north.

Reconciliation was successful after the American Civil War because the citizens and former soldiers of the Confederate States were treated, for the most part, humanely and fairly. Although a comparison between post-Civil War America and Vietnam after 1975 is imperfect, Vietnam would be much closer to true national unity if Northern rule had been more appeasing and, specifically, if soldiers and supporters of the vanquished South Vietnamese regime had not been dealt with so harshly and, incidentally, if the North had not changed the name of the South's capital city to Ho Chi Minh.

Today, the North still rules the South's provinces and cities. Northerners and party members own the prime property and major businesses. Southerners feel these people are dishonest and that the success of Northerners in the South is the result of fraud and theft. Deep-seated resentments simmer within Southerners. Successful nation-building is hostage to this anger and alienation.

Fourteen

LAW AND ORDER

The problem with power is how to achieve its responsible use rather than its irresponsible and indulgent use—of how to get men of power to live for the public rather than off the public.
-Robert Kennedy

Laws exist in Vietnam to protect citizens and foreigners. Statutes protect life, liberty, and property, and provide processes to address wrongdoing. Large corporations that generate foreign exchange and jobs can look to these laws to protect their rights. Smaller enterprises and individuals, however, must look to relationships and bribes. They must do so because they are subject to arbitrary and unfair outcomes by decision makers unknown to them. What in the West is called the rule of law does not exist in Vietnam. Instead, the words "rule of the party" describe the reality of justice in Vietnam.

Uncertainty, cost, and delay deter individuals from turning to lawyers and the courts when they have a problem. For the most part, people work out their difficulties informally with the help of ward leaders and the police. This system is less costly and quicker, but like on-the-spot justice everywhere, often it is capricious and subject to abuse. Police power of this kind corrupts; the profit motive replaces justice.

Everywhere, lawyers are considered a bother, an inconvenience, and an unnecessary expense. In Vietnam, where relationships trump contracts, that is an understandable position. However, in countries like the United States, where agreements are zealously enforced and justice impartially applied, the knowledge and expertise of lawyers is important.

*****

IDENTITY DOCUMENTS: The population is monitored and controlled in various ways. Marriages, births, deaths, and abodes are recorded in a government-issued book (hộ khẩu) maintained by the senior family member. He or she is responsible for entries and obtaining requisite stamps and approvals from the underpaid authorities. Every Vietnamese must be listed in someone's family book. However, it is possible to leave your father's book and start your own. To replicate a lost or stolen family book is expensive, time consuming, and frustrating. One must get consent of the authorities both where one lives and where one is moving. If one's family book is recorded in a distant province, it must be presented there to obtain a birth certificate for a child born elsewhere. For the poor and uneducated, it can be a daunting task.

Thousands of children in the cities lack birth certificates because their unregistered parents are migrants who are afraid to, or are otherwise unable to, engage the bureaucracy. Consequently, their children are ineligible to register for public schools. They do not get educated unless they are fortunate enough to attend a free school run by a non-profit organization.

National photo identity cards are issued to everyone over the age of 16. They must be shown to the police upon request and are required for all business an individual has with the government. Hotels, employers, trains, airlines, and banks examine the card and record pertinent data. By custom, males face jail terms if they do not obtain an identity card, but females receive only a rebuke. People say the different punishments reflect the fact that men cause the problems in society. Men fight, rob, and go to war. They have to be watched more closely than women.

The province where one is a legal resident issues identity cards. The issuing province keeps a file of one's activities (travel, job, residence, marriage, etc.). Sometimes things go wrong and licenses are issued that should not be.

When dealing with bureaucrats, gratuities are expected. If the proffered amount of money is too small, the envelope is returned, the paperwork is put aside, and the supplicant is told to return next week. Money is not mentioned, but the message is clear.

MISTRUST STALKS THE MARRIAGE: Alex, a portly 44-year-old German acquaintance, has lived in Vietnam for nine years. He married a divorced Vietnamese woman whose three teenage children live with their father. Alex and his wife have two small children of their own. He was happy in Vietnam, but one day his wife's first husband appeared at Alex's door and demanded money as compensation for losing his wife. There had never been a divorce. The woman had wed Alex while still married to her first husband, who threatened to cause trouble with the police unless Alex paid him to keep quiet. Alex gives a small amount each month, but he realizes it is only a question of time before more is demanded. Naturally, mistrust now stalks the marriage, and Alex's dream of returning to his country with his family is in jeopardy. Among other very personal questions, he wonders how a marriage license could have been issued if there was no record of his wife getting a divorce? Was it incompetence at the province level or had a bribe been paid? Moreover, if a bribe had been paid, who had paid it?

SAFEGUARD FOREIGN MEN: Passports identify you as a citizen of a particular country. A valid passport is essential for international travel and, together with a visa, permits entry into and exit from countries. Governments also use them to limit the travel of their citizens and to have a record that reveals the dates, duration of stays, and countries they have visited. Passports are a privilege and countries regularly refuse to issue them for many reasons.

Every sovereign country exercises the right to control its borders. At airports and border posts, officials inspect passports and visas. In Vietnam, for foreigners, it is done efficiently and with a minimum of hassle. On the other hand, overseas Vietnamese complain that immigration and customs officials treat them poorly, unless they leave a $20 bill in their passport. Without a gratuity, Vietnamese are subject to delays and body searches.

Tourists enter on 30-day visas. It is not difficult to obtain six-month visas. However, qualification rules are uncertain and the cost of the visa mysteriously varies. Unless one has egregiously misbehaved, extension requests are routinely granted.

Foreigners must produce their passport and visa upon request of the authorities and when renting a house or checking into a hotel. The landlord and the innkeeper are required to register the alien with the police. Most hotels try to keep the documents until checkout as security for payment. Unannounced, police visit hotels to review the guest register.

Once a foreigner has registered his residence with the police, he can come, go, and do what he wants, subject to the same laws that apply to the Vietnamese.

I understood the importance of safeguarding my passport. However, one morning on a bus to the coast, I realized that the hotel I had just checked out of had not returned mine. I had arranged to stay in a beach bungalow for five nights and was now painfully aware I might be refused accommodation. Not knowing what to expect, I stayed on the bus for the remainder of the five-hour journey. Upon arrival, I presented myself to the resort clerk and explained my problem. Without any hassle or theatrics, he accepted my New York driver's license in lieu of my passport.

Unless proof of marriage is shown, Vietnamese women and male foreigners are prohibited from staying overnight in the same hotel room. (See Note 5.) Supposedly, the law is meant to protect Vietnamese women. Knowledgeable locals disagree and say it safeguards foreign men. As with all silly laws, it is ridiculed, overlooked, and manipulated for profit.

I have been told some hotels make the couple rent two full-price rooms, though they permit them to sleep in one. Other hotels allow the pair to check into one room, but they only register the Western man. Still others charge a negligible amount for the second room, but do not give them the key. People believe that tip-offs given to the police by informants who are hotel employees lead to late-night evictions of "guilty" couples. At times, the ever-vigilant police will extort a bribe from the Westerner, under threat of jail for the Vietnamese woman.

YOUR FAMILY STILL HERE: Thuy, a 36-year-old nun, applied for a passport to study English abroad for a year and then work in Rome taking care of sick, elderly nuns. It took eight months from the time she filed the paperwork until she was granted her passport, and another four months to get her travel visas.

Sister Thuy was required to travel to her home province for a passport interview. She was seated at a table across from four men who interrogated her about her travel plans. Where are you going and why? Whom will you visit? Who is paying your expenses? They lectured her about the merits of the Vietnamese government and warned her not to say or write anything critical about it while abroad. At the end of the interview, she was required to sign a document agreeing to this condition. As she left the room, the senior man pointedly reminded her that her family still lived in the province.

In another situation, nine nuns who I taught applied for passports in their home provinces to attend a conference in Europe. Four of them received their travel documents, each having to pay $15. The other five women who were from a different province were not granted passports because they refused to pay $300 each. Perhaps the nuns failed to convince their province officials of their loyalty, or maybe the officials misjudged the nun's ability to pay an inflated fee.

TRAFFIC VIOLATION: I felt safe in Vietnam, maybe a little too safe. Vietnamese people were polite, courteous, and helpful to me. I did not lose any property, nor was I threatened, except on one occasion. However, I did wonder what the Vietnamese really thought of me. Did they harbor deep resentment against Americans, against foreigners in general, who, to them, were wealthy and seemed to have everything? So, too, the poor in America.

What do the less fortunate think? How do they feel about their fellow citizens who have had the benefit of luck and circumstances?

Most traffic accidents are resolved amicably and quickly. Initially, after a scrape or collision, there are shouts and raised voices, but within minutes there are serious settlement discussions before one party pays and everyone leaves the scene. Not always, but most times, parties agree between themselves who was at fault and how much to pay. Everyone is in a hurry because if they do not quickly settle and leave, the police will arrive and they have to be paid, too, or they will confiscate the motorbikes and drag the luckless drivers off to the police station.

Sometimes beatings settle traffic disputes, with one of the drivers left in a heap on the pavement. The driver with the most friends wins. The crowd, which has been attracted by the accident, watches as the outnumbered driver is dealt with. It is not pretty. Everywhere it is the same; only in boxing matches and cowboy films do men square off, one against the other.

A local saying informs, "A man without alcohol is like a flag without wind." Vietnamese men prove this observation. Normally they are quiet and reserved, but alcohol changes them, as it does most of us. The Romans, who were accurate commentators on the human condition, said, "In wine there is truth."

"Wine in, talk out" is a Vietnamese axiom. Most restaurants and curbside cafes are crowded day and night with beer-drinking men. Beer bottles serve as ashtrays. Bones and other food scraps litter the floor. Six to 12 men per table keep track of their consumption (and the bill) by storing the empty bottles in cases under their table. As they progress, they get noisier. Frequently they clink glasses while shouting một, hai, ba, yo! (One, two, three drink!) At the party's end, wide-eyed, aggressive, impaired revelers mount their motorbikes for a perilous ride home. Sometimes even expats drink to excess, and their attempts to return home late at night on wobbly motorbikes often result in misfortune.

Vietnamese ladies do not join the men. It is not done. Nor do they usually smoke or drink alcohol. They would get a bad reputation if they did.

Tom was a short, stocky, 30-year-old Australian with a self-assured demeanor. He had asked me to comment on a personal statement written by Tram, a chunky 23-year-old Vietnamese woman who had recently graduated from the Customs College and was applying to American law schools. Tram's personal statement would give her an opportunity to distinguish herself from other applicants. She had arranged to take the Law Scholastic Aptitude Test (LSAT) in Saigon. Since Saigon is not a scheduled testing site, and since she was the only person taking the test, her fee was three times the cost charged in America. Her written statement, school transcripts, and recommendation letters would be submitted to each school together with her application.

Tram had graduated from Saigon's top high school and was accepted for enrollment by the city's most prestigious university. Nevertheless, she enrolled at the Customs College because, according to her 1,500-word personal statement, "Custom jobs are famous for corruption and I want to be rich." Although free of spelling errors, the statement was abysmal. Poor grammar, appalling syntax, nonsensical sentences, and wondrous non-sequiturs would have challenged any reader. I had no doubt that her declaration would distinguish her from other law school applicants.

The three of us were to meet at my house so I could help her rewrite it. As it was, the statement would mark her as having mendacious intentions and offer direct evidence of her poor English. Tram did not come at the scheduled time. Tom arrived instead and explained that he had gotten into trouble the night before and did not have time to spend with Tram until his problems were resolved.

His face was bandaged and his upper lip was split and twice its normal size. A dentist had forced two front teeth back to where they were before he had been slugged. Tom was told he would probably lose them because of nerve and blood vessel damage. He walked to my sofa bent a little at the waist, his right arm tucked close to his body. Gingerly, so as not to aggravate a fractured rib, he lowered himself onto my sofa.

Late the previous evening, Tom had crashed his motorbike into a parked car. A crowd quickly gathered and a man who claimed to be the car's owner demanded $900 to repair the dent. Labor is cheap in Vietnam. Nine hundred dollars was excessive and the Australian did not know if the man was the owner. During the ensuing argument, which Tom described as ugly, a man stepped from the crowd and punched him in the face. Other men joined in, beating and kicking him. He was balled up on the ground when the police arrived.

The police tried to make sense of what had happened. Tom told his story and showed his injuries. The crowd related that a drunken, belligerent foreigner had attacked them when they would not let him leave without paying for the damage. The police impounded both vehicles and Tom's passport. They administered a breathalyzer test, which Tom failed. Both men were ordered to report to the police station in two days, and to bring their driver's licenses with them. Like many expats, Tom did not have a Vietnamese license. He was taken to the hospital to be patched up, and at four a.m. the police drove him home.

He asked the old lawyer, an expert on all things legal, for advice. I responded with caution, saying that I knew nothing about Vietnamese law, but suggested that he could face charges of drunken driving, reckless driving, driving without a license, and creating a public disturbance. Driving while intoxicated is a crime in Vietnam and can result in imprisonment.

I warned him not to go to the police station alone, but to take a Vietnamese with him to explain what was happening. More importantly, it would show the police that he had Vietnamese friends willing to help. He called a Vietnamese-American lawyer I knew who was polite, sympathetic, and unhelpful. The lawyer refused to accompany Tom to the station. He said, "The police would not like me if I came there with you and got in the middle of their business. It would be bad for me and for you."

Eventually, after hurried calls and promises, a friend of mine agreed to go with him. Unbeknownst to me, she brought along her boyfriend, also a policeman. The boyfriend knew the arresting police officer, and this definitely worked to Tom's advantage. At the meeting, Tom was fined $100 for driving without a license and was ordered to pay for repairing the car. His motorbike would be returned when he obtained a Vietnamese driver's license.

The car owner, who was fined $30 for causing a public disturbance, produced a $600 repair estimate. The police advised Tom that he could pay the owner the $600 or get the car repaired at a repair shop of his choosing. The owner objected, insisting that his repair shop would put the car back to its original condition. The police threatened to hold the vehicles until the parties reached a financial agreement. To discourage delay they would impose a $2 daily parking charge until the car and motorbike were released. The car owner was a rock star, nightclub singer, and recording artist. He wanted his car back immediately, and after negotiations, which included input from the police and the Vietnamese woman, Tom paid the man $100 for the repairs. The case was closed and everyone went home.

Tom had dodged a bullet. There was no criminal charge for driving while intoxicated. He was elated. He said the episode was a wakeup call for him and he would change his ways. Perhaps.

Tram, the law school applicant who wants to get rich fast, was rejected by all seven U.S. law schools she applied to. Although, after revisions, her personal statement demonstrated a good command of English and was free of anything calling her character into question, her LSAT score was not high enough for admission.

AN ACCIDENT: A car driven by a 35-year-old American man struck and killed a 16-year-old boy late one rainy night on the highway connecting Saigon with Vung Tau, a beach resort. The boy had been walking on the dark, unlit highway. The expat had a valid Vietnamese driver's license, was not speeding according to a witness, and was judged sober at the scene by the police. The police declared that it was an accident; the driver was not to blame. However, he would not get his car or passport back until he had settled with the boy's family. Two weeks after the accident, at a meeting organized by the police, the family demanded $3,000. The astonished American had been expecting a much higher amount and promptly agreed. He paid, his car was returned to him, and that was the end of his liability.

CENSORSHIP: My sister Eileen sent me a present for Christmas. The customs department at the hundred-year-old Central Post Office intercepted it. This grand structure looks like an old European railroad station. It is a fine example of industrial architecture. The edifice features two huge wall murals. High on an interior wall is a map of the streets of Saigon circa 1890. On the opposite wall, 40 feet across the polished marble floor, a 1936 map depicts the telegraph lines of South Vietnam and Cambodia. A grandfatherly painting of Ho Chi Minh adorns the back wall, welcoming all. The architect of this iconic jewel was Alexandre Eiffel, of the Paris tower fame.

An official notice ordered me to report within 30 days to the customs office for an interview, or my parcel from America would be confiscated. Unaware of what had been sent, I was apprehensive when I arrived a few days later. After waiting an hour for those ahead of me to be interviewed, I was escorted into a small room by two uniformed inspectors. We sat on plastic chairs at a gray metal table. A fluorescent ceiling lamp illuminated the stark white walls. The female inspector carefully examined three CDs that had been mailed to me by Eileen.

"Who is Wynton Marsalis?" she asked. "What does he sing about? What is a Celtic Solstice? What are Irish Rebel Songs?" Her follow-up questions were all silly, too. Although I saw the humor in the situation, I was impatient to leave and told them to keep the CDs. They smiled, said no, and the session ended, but not before they requested, without explanation, a fee ($5.30). I paid, they gave me the CDs, we shook hands, and I left. They offered no receipt.

My Vietnamese friends tell me that censorship is intended to limit pornographic and anti-party tracts from entering the country. However, there is widespread access to the Internet and attempts to limit or block such content are ineffective. Thus, salacious and subversive material enters Vietnam unimpeded. Other than as a source of revenue there seems to be no reason for customs officials to summon people to their offices and inspect their parcels and private correspondence. Drugs are not mailed into Vietnam; they come overland from Cambodia and Laos.

WRONG SONG: Che Linh has lived in the United States for 35 years. He has 17 children with four wives, seriatim. He is famous for his songs about the war. Although from the South, he is popular all over Vietnam. He returned in 2011 to perform in Saigon and Hanoi. The concerts were sold out; ticket holders looked forward to a nostalgic evening. In Hanoi he was required to obtain approval for the songs he was to sing and for the advertising copy for the concerts. Alas, at the first concert he sang one unapproved song; apparently it glorified the South and diminished the North. Furthermore, advertisements had been placed in unapproved places. Outraged, the authorities cancelled the remaining Hanoi concerts and banned him from performing in the North for six months. Inexplicably, the concert in Saigon was not immediately cancelled. However, on the evening of the performance, disappointed ticket holders read the cancellation notice on the theater's door, which was posted mere minutes before the start time.

NEIGHBORHOOD BANKING: Prior to 1975, American dollars fueled South Vietnam's wartime economy, which made many people wealthy. Twice after 1975 the communists devalued their currency, and each time the state limited the amount of old cash an individual could exchange for new currency. The currency exchange limitations wiped out the savings of many South Vietnamese. Those with the foresight to hold their wealth in gold or dollars did not suffer. The exchange limitations caused little hardship in the North, because Northerners, after 20-plus years of communist economic policies and war, had no savings. Thousands of Southerners were made paupers and they have not forgotten.

Vietnam has a well-developed banking system. Both domestic and foreign banks have branches in the major cities. As of 2012, business was conducted in both U.S. dollars and dong (VND). The VND is not stable; it lost 30% of its value between 2002 and 2009. International currency transfers are restricted; one cannot take more than $7,000 in cash or gold out of the country. Interest on VND deposits has varied. In 2005, savings account rates were 8%, in 2009 14%, and in 2016 2%.

Bank loans are difficult to obtain, and when they are available, interest rates are high and repayment terms short. Borrowing from banks is not attractive to homebuyers and small businesses. Instead, they borrow from a consortium of family and friends, agreeing to repayment terms less onerous than required by the banks. Familial ties and extralegal enforcement practices work together to minimize loan defaults.

It is a cash economy; few places accept checks or credit cards. At the end of each month employers withdraw large amounts of cash from banks to pay their workers. Under the watchful eyes of bodyguards, they stuff wads of currency into duffle bags, exit the bank, and return by van to their workplace.

I once stood behind a man at a bank who withdrew $65,000. The amount appeared, for all to see, in large red letters on the face of the bank's money counting machine. He crammed the $100 bills into an old canvas suitcase. Flanked by bodyguards, a quartet of serious-looking men, he left the building on foot. The transaction took place in the open at the teller's window. Everyone in the bank saw what was going on.

The son of a Vietnamese man I know was to travel to the United States on a business trip. His father asked me to go with him to the bank. He was afraid that bank employees would tell robbers on the street that he was withdrawing dollars. The father asked me to carry the money out of the bank for his son. The money would not be stolen from a foreigner on the sidewalk in the middle of the day, he confidently explained.

On the son's departure date, the father, mother, son, and I went to the bank where the father withdrew a large amount of dollars. In front of employees and customers, the money was strapped under my shirt. We left the bank and took a waiting car directly to the airport. En route, the money was transferred from me to the son. At that time, there was a $3,000 limit on the amount of U.S. currency a traveler could take out of the country. I am sure the son declared his stash to the authorities.

Later the father told me his son and the money had arrived safely in the United States. All of this activity seemed silly to me and I wondered if it was necessary. Later I found out that the danger of being robbed when leaving a bank is real and that precautions are indeed necessary.

On Saturday afternoons I taught English to seven Vietnamese staff members of a street children's organization. During the one-hour lessons, they practiced reading, writing, vocabulary, and grammar. In order to make them comfortable, I started each session with the simple question, "How are you?"

"I'm sad," was the answer I got from Loan, a 20-year-old woman. The other students nodded their heads in agreement. Two days earlier Loan had been robbed of $600, which she had just withdrawn from her bank. As she drove away with the money in her handbag, two motorbikes pulled up next to her, one on each side. When she turned her head to respond to a question from one of the men, the second man deftly cut the strap of her bag and sped away with it. The questioner stunned her with his fist and then he, too, sped off. It had taken Loan three years to save the money, which she had intended to give her parents so they could repair their house.

The students speculated that the men had a spotter in the bank. He was probably a bank employee who had used a cell phone to tell the robbers waiting outside about the cash withdrawal and to give them a description of the girl. One student said that bank robberies happen often and most people take friends with them when they withdraw funds "because it makes it hard for the bad men to get money." I sympathized with the young victim. However, I would like to know more about those desperate men and their patrons. If their modus operandi is so well known, why haven't they been apprehended?

Bank customers are easy prey; they need cash, they are exposed, and, because it is daytime and the streets are crowded with people, they discount the risk. Lieu, the 50-year-old daughter of a prominent Viet Cong, had increased her inheritance by savvy land speculation. One morning she and her teenage daughter withdrew $20,000 for a down payment on a parcel of land. Outside the bank, they hailed a taxi. They were seated only a few seconds when the back doors were flung open. Two well-dressed, middle-aged men glared at the women. One of them grabbed the purse from Lieu's lap. They slammed the doors and disappeared down the crowded sidewalk with her cash. The robbery had taken less than 10 seconds.

THE WEAKER SEX: Foreigners have to be careful, too, especially women. They are often victims of theft and petty fraud. In 2005 the brother of one of my students worked as a driver for a wealthy Japanese family that was victimized. The husband owned a motorbike parts factory. The wife cared for their four children with the assistance of a Vietnamese cook, a housekeeper, and a driver. The staff worked eight hours a day, six days a week, at a combined monthly salary of $400.

The wife came home one afternoon after shopping with friends. Frightened and upset, she explained to her staff that while leaving a store a man had ripped her handbag from her shoulder and run away. She had lost $130, her house keys, credit cards, and personal papers containing her Saigon address. Once home she had the house locks changed and cancelled her credit cards.

Two days later a couple came to her door claiming to have bought a handbag from a man on the street and found the keys, credit cards, and personal papers inside. They offered to sell the bag and its contents to the Japanese woman for $100. On the emphatic advice of her suspicious cook she refused and they left—but not before the cook was threatened with harm for interfering with their "business." The next day a different couple rang the bell and said they had found the bag on the street and requested a reward for returning it. The husband called the police, who arrived after the couple had left.

One afternoon I sat next to an older American woman in an Internet café. Her face was bruised and cut, her left arm bandaged. On a sidewalk the prior morning a young man on a motorbike had pulled her to the ground while trying to snatch her handbag. He fled empty-handed. No one intervened or helped her to her feet. She explained that it was the second time someone had tried to pull her bag away from her and that her house had been burglarized twice. In the weeks that followed, I passed her on the sidewalk; her handbag swung freely from her shoulder. Foreign women are frequent victims of handbag theft. They are thought to have money and tend to be easy targets.

Another American woman was in Vietnam to adopt her sixth Vietnamese child. She told me she had hired a cyclo driver to take her to the market a few days earlier. When she noticed the driver was going in the wrong direction she told him to stop. Instead of stopping, he pedaled faster. Fearing that she was to be kidnapped, or worse, she rose to her feet in the open seat and began screaming. For two blocks she screamed without anyone helping her until three Vietnamese men from a wedding party halted the cyclo and lifted her to the ground. They yelled at the driver and placed her in a taxi to continue her journey. Through the car window she watched the cyclo move slowly away, its driver eagerly scanning the crowded sidewalk in search of another passenger.

Vietnamese are slow to help someone who is injured or being beaten, or they do not help at all. It is disturbing, but quite common. They do not want to get involved, which could be due to a cultural reluctance to interfere with fate. More likely, they do not want to incur the wrath of strangers or involve themselves with the police. They are just too concerned with self-preservation to help. Kindness is a universal virtue. We all want to help others if we can, but for the poor and others at risk it is a luxury. Often, it is a dangerous luxury.

A GOOD MAN: Truth is elusive, especially when hidden by conflicting information.

I asked Em Thy what she knew about Khanh, the director of an orphanage I had agreed to work at.

"I think Khanh good man, but his reputation have problems. He jail for selling extra babies to Americans. Don't sign anything. Martin, you must learn refuse jobs."

"I'm not being paid."

"He tell his contributors that he pay you and then keep money."

Later Khanh told me he had had trouble with the government and was jailed for 23 months in the early 1990s on a false charge of not complying with adoption laws. Khanh's sister, whom I knew well, said she had to pay two bribes to get him out of prison. Relatives in California had sent her the money. The first payment of $7,500 did not secure Khanh's release. "Police keep money and brother," she said. In time, she found an "honest" policeman who, for another $7,500, finally freed her brother.

CHRISTMAS: Christmas is celebrated throughout the land. In this Buddhist country with a communist government, Christmas lights adorn the city streets, messages of peace and love are exchanged, and scenes of Mary, Joseph, and baby Jesus are displayed in public places. And Santa Claus, too. He is everywhere. The contradiction is explained in part by commerce, in part by the desire of these very tolerant people to show solidarity with their Christian neighbors, and in part by the party's desire to appear to allow religious freedom.

Masses on Christmas Eve and Christmas Day are crowded. Those who cannot find room in a church stand in its courtyard. The large public square surrounding Notre Dame Cathedral in the center of Saigon is jammed on Christmas Eve with thousands of people, mostly families. Early in the day, police cordon off the streets leading into the plaza. The crowds, I have been told, consist largely of non-Catholics who go to participate and celebrate with the Catholics. On the evenings of December 23, 24, and 25, the Saigonese ride their motorbikes around the city in celebration. Late into the night they circle the major streets and boulevards, families of three or four to a motorbike. It is a festive time.

YOU GET TOO HOT: Soccer is popular in Vietnam. Both professional and amateur teams play in domestic and international competitions. National pride is at stake when the opponent is from another country. The matches are broadcast on television, and when Vietnam wins, gangs of young people consume the last of their beer, don headbands, bedeck themselves and their motorbikes with Vietnamese flags, and race around the city. The streets and sidewalks are more perilous than usual as these drunken revelers speed, weave, and dodge; people all around are endangered. They cheer, shout, and intimidate, like soccer fans worldwide, in a patriotic frenzy.

One evening at Christmas time I was walking home alone after dinner. The Saigon streets were crowded with families on motorbikes. The merry crowd rode around in celebration of the holiday. Suddenly, several young men on motorbikes zoomed onto the sidewalk, turning, dodging, and swerving to avoid (just barely) pedestrians. The men wore red and yellow headbands, carried the national red and yellow flag, and loudly cheered the Vietnamese soccer team, which had just defeated a foreign team. They were boisterous and belligerent. It was dangerous for everyone, particularly those walking on the sidewalk. On that night, according to the media, this confluence of holiday celebrants and drunken soccer enthusiasts resulted in nearly 300 emergency admissions to hospitals. Most victims were young men with head injuries. Seven died.

That night, the handlebars of a motorbike hit my left arm. I meekly complained to the driver who immediately cursed and pointed at me. I politely reprimanded him for driving on the sidewalk while drunk, and gently knocked his hand aside. At that moment, the season of peace and love was forgotten. Traffic stopped while onlookers stoically watched. We remonstrated, postured, and exchanged insults in our respective languages.

Then I heard one of his mates say, "Let's kill the foreigner," words which chilled me.

A middle-aged woman in the billowing, lovely native dress emerged from the crowd, touched my arm, and said in perfect English, "Come with me. You will be hurt." I did not argue; what man would? She led me away, against the traffic and away from the inflamed soccer fans. "They won't leave their motorbikes," she said.

They hurled more insults at me and I turned, raised my right arm in front of me and hit its biceps with my left hand.

"Don't do that," she said. "You get too hot for an old man. Calm down." Before leaving she advised me, "Don't walk tonight. They will look for you. Take a taxi home and stay there."

I did both. I have no idea who the woman was but obviously I am indebted to her.

Ulysses was foolish many times, too. It is well settled that discretion is the better part of valor, but it is not an option when the demon Anger is loose. I could retire, and maybe I should, to the shade of a leafy tree where Anger rests and valor resides only in the mind.

THE INTRUDER: Although foreigners are generally safe from physical attack, their property is not safe. It is believed that foreigners are rich and careless with their property. Thieves target them.

At four a.m. Thao heard a noise on our roof terrace. Minutes later a shadow on the wall showed something descending from the roof to our bedroom balcony. Thao investigated and found a man dressed in black crawling into our bedroom. I had left the balcony door open! Her shouts awoke me. I got to her side to see the intruder jump from the balcony to the tiled courtyard 36 feet below. Amidst our cries of "Thief! Thief!" he scrambled over the 20-foot, spiked iron fence and made his escape. A hue and cry from the neighbors followed him as he limped out of our alley. A flowerpot thrown by a neighbor crashed at the thief's feet.

Immediately, people came out from their houses to discuss the incident. Our 80-year-old next-door neighbor found on her balcony the following items the thief had left behind: a cigarette box, matches, black pants, and a five-foot pole with a grasping claw on the end. On examination it was found that the pole telescoped to eight feet and was used, she explained, to reach through barred windows to steal things. She was sure the robber had first tried to get into her house. Dangling from the roof terrace to our balcony was a cloth rope fashioned with foot loops.

Thao's nephew slept in a room off the terrace, and his cell phone had been taken from his bed next to an open window. He claimed not to have been awakened by the thief or the clamor. He explained to Thao that the thief had thrown "magic dust" in his face and, thus, he could not get out of bed. The police were called and a lone policeman arrived 30 minutes later.

The nephew was living with us while attending a computer college. Each semester his father, a hardworking motorbike deliveryman in the countryside, gave him tuition and an allowance. In the evenings, the young man said, he worked at an upscale restaurant. Thao became suspicious because his college had a lot of holidays, he had no books, and his working clothes were not right for a first class eating-place. The boy's father asked Thao to investigate. She went to see him at work. All the workers wore uniforms, and no one knew who he was. At the college the following morning, Thao was appalled to learn that he had never enrolled. For a year, the nephew had left our house for school at eight a.m., returned at three p.m., and left again at five p.m. for work. He was home by 10 p.m. every evening. It was all a lie. Thao sent him back to the countryside that same day.

The errant nephew spent his tuition money on foolishness, and lost his chance for a decent future. In a factory far from Saigon, he now works for a small wage.

SQUATTERS' RIGHTS: Most houses in urban areas are attached 2- or 3-story brick structures. They are long (10 to 12 meters) and narrow (3 to 5 meters). People describe the size of a house by its width. They say, "I own a 4-

meter house," or, "I live in a 5-meter house." Houses are dark because there are no back or side windows, only front ones. Rooms are small by Western standards but adequate.

A showerhead and hose is affixed head-high to the bathroom wall, between the sink and toilet. Shower water flows to the floor drain. All know that to avoid wet bottoms later they must raise the toilet seat when showering.

Interspaced among the row houses are villas and demi-villas—walled compounds with front gardens, and windows on four sides. Location, privacy, light, and space determine the property's price, as in the West.

I have heard many stories about buying a house in Vietnam. As in America, everyone wants to own his or her own home. The well-off also buy houses to rent; landlords are vilified, distrusted, and envied. A house that leaks sells for less than one that does not. People caution one another never to buy a house in the dry season and never sell one in the rainy season.

The confusion, fraud, and disruption that occurred in society after 1975 still affects land transactions. A deed from a prior owner whose title can be verified by an unbroken line of deeds provides evidence of ownership. America had this same system decades ago but abandoned it because it was cumbersome and subject to fraud. In America and many other countries, buyers register their deeds with a central registry. Land ownership is a public record and title insurance is available.

Many Southerners burned house deeds and other important documents days before communist troops arrived in 1975. They were afraid that proof of house ownership would single them out for punishment. Still others fled the country taking ownership papers with them. Houses were confiscated by the new regime or stolen outright by people from the North. Some families have lived rent-free for 35 years in houses they do not own. They claim that lengthy possession (or fraudulent deeds) has given them title.

In 2008, a religious order of priests filed a lawsuit in an attempt to reclaim valuable land in Hanoi it had been forced to lend to the government many years ago. Corrupt officials had divided the land and sold it to individuals, who thereby received "legal" title from the government. The officials kept the money. Houses and businesses now occupy the land. The government says it has documents signed by a now deceased superior of the order, which purport to convey the land to the state, but it refuses to produce the papers.

The authorities resisted pressure from foreign countries and international bodies, as well as from noisy Vietnamese demonstrators in Hanoi, to pay for this state-sponsored fraud. Not unsurprisingly, the government-controlled media supported the authorities. Its unfair, biased, and untruthful coverage was all the public knew about this dispute. Eventually, the court ruled in favor of the government. At the same time, it disbarred the lawyer representing the religious organization and sentenced a group of the demonstrators to jail.

In 1991, the National Assembly passed a comprehensive law stipulating that the state would return houses it took from private owners before July 1, 1991. In addition, individuals and organizations that confiscated private houses prior to July 1, 1991, were required to return them to their original owners. The law was an attempt to deal with a complicated situation fairly and equitably. Owners, or their heirs, of houses confiscated since 1954 in northern Vietnam, and since 1975 in southern Vietnam, were entitled to either the cash value or return of their property.

In a blow to those who fled the country after the war's end, housing transactions conducted before July 1, 1991, involving either Vietnamese people living abroad or foreign entities were specifically excluded from the law's provisions. Since 1998, various interpretations of and amendments to the law have tried to clarify land rights. However, it is necessary to have a powerful patron on your side if you are attempting to retake confiscated property.

Today, a struggle between long-term squatters and rightful owners takes place within the parameters of a venal judiciary and an all-powerful Communist Party. Even when officials strive to find the truth, and even when the truth is known, it is difficult to achieve a just result.

Saigon is becoming a modern city. Bridges, highways, subways, and other infrastructure projects are being built or are on the drawing board. Zoning laws apply and building permits are required for private construction. However, for many years houses and buildings were constructed in violation of building and zoning laws. People ignored the law and built on city property, or they bribed corrupt officials for permission. They infringed on streets and parks to enlarge their houses, and constructed five-story buildings where only three stories were allowed.

The government must deal with this situation if Saigon is to evolve successfully. It strives to develop policies that are fair and conducive to prudent growth. The authorities must decide if prior illegal construction should be torn down, and if current owners must pay for the demolition.

In spite of these problems, a brisk real estate market exists. Land changes hands frequently and prices escalate. Although difficult to accomplish, foreigners can now own land. Mortgage loans available from banks are short term and expensive. Most land purchases are for gold or for cash measured against the price of gold. There is no capital gains tax on the sale of one's residence. Annual residential property taxes are between $10 and $20; taxes are determined by multiplying the square meters of the land by the market price of a kilogram of rice. A 1% land transfer tax is payable by both buyer and seller. Prior to 2009, a strong economy and favorable tax policies resulted in aggressive land speculation.

Property buyers must be careful, however. A German I know discovered that a house he was going to buy had one floor more than the law allowed and a second house he wanted infringed three meters into a public right-of-way. No one was able to explain how these infractions would affect him if he were to purchase either of the houses. He prudently declined to buy. Subsequently, he learned that in both cases the houses had been sold with Vietnamese buyers taking the risks, but confident, one way or the other, that in time the problems would be resolved in their favor.

In order to bring certainty to land transactions, a process to obtain a "red deed" has been instituted. If a seller can produce a good chain of title, if there are no building or zoning violations, and if all taxes have been paid, the authorities will issue a red deed to the buyer. Ownership of a house with a red deed is registered with the government and is a matter of public record. Depending on the local authorities, the process can take months and may be costly. At the end of the process, the seller may be denied the red deed because of title defects or gross zoning violations. Without a red deed, property may be sold at a discount, if the buyer is willing. Fingers are crossed and a search for an influential friend is initiated. Nevertheless, the government's efforts to simplify land sales and eliminate fraud have made land transactions less risky.

EXPAT FRAUD: After the war, Hoa spent eight years in Russia where she studied Marxism and secret police work. She was a good student and her understanding of the principles of intimidation, betrayal, and negotiation served her well back in Vietnam. Her Saigon utility company position was not demanding, allowing her time for her "people-helping business." In her second job, she collected overdue loans and gambling debts. "It easy job," she stated. "I get police help. All day they stand in front of house. Sometime family afraid, sometimes they hurt."

Hoa helped my friend Steve who first came to Vietnam as an American soldier in 1969. He returned in January 2001 with the intent of starting a business. He met Judy and Allan, both Californians, who had lived and done business here for 10 and 12 years, respectively. Steve signed a contract they had prepared, which purported to give him legal rights to a fish farm in a far-off province. Pursuant to the document, Steve invested $400,000 with the Californians to acquire land and build out the fish farm. However, the land transfer never occurred. Three years later, after repeated inquiries, Steve learned that the title to the land and fish farm had been issued to a Vietnamese national. Judy and Allan refused to meet with Steve or give him an accounting of his funds.

Unable to get the Vietnamese police or courts to help him, and desperate to recover his investment, Steve recruited Hoa. She was hired because of her police background, aggressive personality, and her sister's position as a judge on the economic court. In return for 20% of any assets recovered, she has relentlessly pursued the Californians. She was able to get from Allan a dying declaration. On his hospital deathbed, he signed an affidavit admitting to his part in the fraud and implicating Judy and the Vietnamese national as knowing participants in the swindle. Three Vietnamese, one a police captain, witnessed the affidavit.

Hoa called Judy and told her she was writing an article for the Police Gazette about economic corruption involving foreigners. She read Allan's affidavit aloud and asked Judy if she would like to respond to it because it would be described in the article. Judy declined. Hoa was lying; she didn't write the article. It was a ploy to pressure Judy.

Allan's dying declaration was delivered to the court, the U.S. Consulate, charities Judy was a board member of, and a long list of Vietnamese and expat executives.

To humiliate Judy, Hoa prepared wanted posters with Judy's picture and a description of the fraud charges. The posters were hung on the walls of Western restaurants and expat pubs. On the street, well-dressed men gave the posters to passersby.

This matter has not been resolved. Like most things in Vietnam (and in life), the outcome is uncertain; the two sides compete for influence. In America, lawyers try to convince the court with arguments. Often in Vietnam, litigants compete with cash. Steve should prevail on legal grounds, but his resources are now limited. Hoa and her connections are his only hope.

Fifteen

NON-GOVERNMENTAL ORGANIZATIONS

It is justice, not charity, that is wanting in the world.
-Mary Wollstonecraft

It is reasonable for governments to be concerned about organizations that provide help to the poor.

In Vietnam, religious institutions must obtain government approval for their activities. This way they can be monitored and, incidentally, controlled. The Catholic Committee of the Socialist Republic of Vietnam and the Buddhist Committee of the Socialist Republic of Vietnam are state agencies responsible for supervising these religions. The committees influence the personnel decisions and internal affairs of these religious groups.

Similarly, state officials oversee the activities of non-religious NGOs. Throughout the country, charities provide food, shelter, healthcare, and education, among other things, to the poor. The variety and scope of charitable projects is impressive. Many are large international NGOs represented by foreigners, while others are small operations staffed by Vietnamese. Almost all are funded by donations from abroad.

After 1975, education and medicine were exclusively government sectors. Private schools and hospitals were confiscated and their services were provided by the state. The poor quality of such services, the need to attract overseas investment, and the interest of party officials in securing every possible advantage for the well-being of their children forced the government in the late 1980s to allow the reopening of non-religious private schools and hospitals. Only the well to do can afford them.

*****

SERVING THE POOR: Many Vietnamese from abroad return to sponsor their own charitable undertakings. A Việt Kiều woman I knew spent one month a year in Vietnam where she led a small medical team. Beginning in 2001 they traveled to the countryside to perform cataract operations for $30 each. For those who could not afford it there was no charge. During the other 11 months of the year, she solicited donations and recruited volunteers from the medical profession in the United States. After 30 years of working for a California healthcare provider, she had compiled a long list of contacts that supported this worthwhile cause.

By the end of 2004, sight had been preserved or restored for over 2,000 patients. However, in 2005 when the surgical team returned, they discovered that, contrary to prior years, the hospital management had not selected any patients for the operation. The medical team was prepared to operate on 300 people over six days. The local officials wanted Vietnamese doctors to perform the operation at a rate of three per day. They persisted in their position even after being told by the highly trained foreign doctors that their local counterparts lacked the requisite expertise to remove cataracts. The Việt Kiều woman was told to leave the money she had raised with the local hospital; the authorities would make sure 300 cataract operations were performed in her absence. Concerned that corrupt officials would steal the money, she refused to release it. The medical team returned to Los Angeles without having performed a single operation. As frequently happens, venal authorities thwarted good intentions and the poor suffered.

The dedicated leader of one NGO told me he undertakes three types of charitable projects: joint ventures with the government, solo ventures when approved, and illegal ones. The illegal projects help the people but are not sanctioned due either to unsatisfied financial demands or adherence by local authorities to doctrinaire interpretations of communist principles. With advice and help from influential persons in various sectors, his NGO carries out unapproved activities in the south, where those in charge are usually more flexible. Unable to get approval from a northern province to take 20 poor children to the United States for vital, cost-free surgery, a high-ranking party official advised the NGO leader to send the children to America from Saigon. He did and no one interfered.

STUDYING MARXISM: One of my students was a 40-year-old doctor whose ambition was to attain a high administrative position at a public hospital. The post Xuan aspired to, however, was reserved for party members. He studied communism one night a week in order to satisfy membership requirements. He knew it was a failed system and wondered if Marxism was studied anywhere else in the world. Xuan confided to me that there was a risk in party membership because if democracy ever replaces communism he might lose this job.

Though the Communist Party governs Vietnam, I did not meet anyone who believes in the doctrine. Although party members control all branches of the government, police, and military, they are communist in name only, and certainly not in an ideological sense. It took decades for people everywhere to come to the understanding that communism was an unsound creed. Its essential beliefs conflict with man's nature, values, and hopes. Its strictest tenets have been abandoned everywhere, except for the troubled nations of Cuba and North Korea. Vietnamese condemn the corruption and abuse of power that comes with a one-party system but say, "We can do nothing about it now. When China change, Vietnam change." Indeed, Vietnam has always been anxious and wary of its powerful neighbor.

THE DEAD BISHOP: Communism is antagonistic to religion. There is an uneasy relationship between the party and Vietnam's 90 million inhabitants, most of who believe in a higher spirit and practice some form of religion. The Vietnamese constitution guarantees freedom of religion, but as Americans know, constitutional protection of any kind is only as effective as those in power allow.

Catholics make up about nine percent of the population, and Buddhists and followers of other religions and beliefs account for the rest. In reality, all Vietnamese to some extent worship ancestors, assorted spirits, the wind, the sun, and the rain. Animism is an important ingredient in the folk religion of Vietnam. Every home I have been invited to has a shelf supporting an ancestor shrine. Buddhism and Catholicism have had to accommodate the ancient practices and beliefs associated with ancestor worship.

Charismatic Christian sects complain of harassment. Since they did not exist in Vietnam prior to 1975, they are treated differently than those religions that did.

Organized religions are watched and reported on. In many ways they are restricted and controlled. Suppression is not uniform countrywide, however. Authorities in Saigon and certain southern provinces are not as rigid as their Northern counterparts.

The rules are often petty, and sometimes verge on harassment. A nun traveling to Hanoi reported that she was not allowed to spend the night in her convent but had to stay in a local hotel. She could visit the other sisters all day but had to return to the "safety" of the hotel after dark.

A bishop in the far north was allowed by the government to oversee a multi-province diocese. The authorities knew this frail, elderly man could not adequately serve this huge area. Maliciously, they did not permit other priests to help him. His only assistance came from a nun who pretended to be his housekeeper.

Religious groups are not officially allowed to operate schools and hospitals. Nevertheless, with winks and nods, and the intercession of righteous party members, religious organizations are providing more and more services to the poor.

Police show up unannounced at convents and pagodas to count the monks, nuns, and priests. Buddhist and Catholic clergy are summoned to local police headquarters or Hanoi for lengthy interrogations about their activities and the activities of their religious counterparts. Inconsistencies result in additional sessions.

Young men who wish to become priests attend university and then study philosophy and theology at a seminary.. After six years they become eligible for ordination. However, government approval is required before a man can enroll in a seminary or be ordained. The state limits and attempts to control this dangerous profession.

Afraid that too many priests will undermine party rule, each year the state permits the ordination of only a small number of those who have completed their studies. Those who have graduated from the seminary but have not been ordained are added to the growing list of deacons who patiently wait. For years, the deacons teach catechism, tend the sick and poor, and hold administrative posts, until, and if, the government allows their ordination, at which time they can say Mass, hear confessions, and administer the other sacraments. Sometimes, however, the deacons do not wait. They ask to be ordained secretly. Out of police sight, a bishop ordains these men. When in time it is reported to the authorities that a certain deacon is saying Mass, he is called in for investigation.

One priest told me the story of his secret ordination and subsequent interrogation at police headquarters. After several hours he realized they were not going to imprison him, but that they wanted to punish the bishop who had illegally ordained him. At the end of the day, after repeated questions and threats, the priest gave them the name of a dead bishop. This information satisfied the police and the case was over. The young priest was released and today he publicly performs his priestly duties. The Jesuits taught me long ago that not every untruth is a moral wrong. We are not obligated to give accurate information to those not entitled to it.

Government measures to control religious organizations wax and wane depending on party politics and circumstances. Beginning with Vietnam's liberalization of policies (Đổi Mới, literally "change to something new") in 1986, foreign investment has increased and there has been a gradual but noticeable reduction in religious suppression. There is more religious freedom now than at any time since 1975. However, the apparatus of control is still extant, and to believe that the current liberality is permanent would be unfounded.

It is difficult to understand exactly why the government is so concerned about organized religions. The restraints seem so small-minded, and hardly worth the authorities' time and effort. I am aware of the doctrinal and historical strains, but this is Vietnam where the communist model is discredited and almost everyone embraces some form of religion.

Will The Sisters Turn A Profit?: Catholic nuns run an AIDS hospice about one hour northwest of Saigon. It is a clean, bright, open place staffed by four nuns. They feed and clean patients and administer painkillers. One afternoon a week, a doctor from Saigon sees the patients. Only medicines for treating opportunistic infections are available. AIDS drugs used in the West are too expensive.

The handyman at the hospice was a former Viet Cong. After showing me his war scar he told me that he is still using soap and other things left behind by the Americans long ago. "Americans make good thing," were his words.

Government hospitals send the very sick to the 12-bed hospice. Every patient dies. Notwithstanding, two patients told me they were getting better. One month there were eight deaths. The head sister confided that psychologically the work was very difficult. The nuns got depressed and needed counseling. In preparation for three months of training at an AIDS clinic/medical school in England, I gave her English lessons two evenings a week.

The hospice relies on donations. The state provides no money and contributions are uncertain. One nun now spends most of her time trying to raise funds. It is not what she wants or was trained to do, and it is inefficient.

In order to supplement donations and create a steady cash flow, the sisters decided to raise shrimp and grow orchids at the hospice. The venture required little capital or labor. Their business plan consisted of:

- Buying one shipment of shrimp and one of orchids and keeping a portion of each harvest to start the next cycle.
- Using the healthiest patients as workers.
- Selling the shrimp and orchids to hospice visitors, restaurants, and hotels.

They hoped the project would give the patients a sense of purpose and provide cash for the hospice.

The nuns had never run a business; they knew nothing about shrimp or orchids, either. My words of caution were met by, "Yes, Martin, we know. But we must try, and we pray for God's help."

On schedule, the starter shrimp arrived from New Zealand and the starter orchids from Thailand. The nuns were in business.

The shrimp all died from a disease they had brought with them from New Zealand. On the other hand, 250 orchid plants thrived under the patients' care. Cuttings are sold after one year of cultivation to hotels and high-end tourist attractions. The orchids provide a small but reliable source of revenue.

Bill, an American veteran of the war, was an orchid expert. A mutual acquaintance put us in touch. He had arrived in Saigon a month earlier and had been meeting with officials in order to start a business. Getting approvals from the authorities proved to be difficult. He wanted to meet me and discuss my activities and how he could do something similar. He was determined to help the Vietnamese in some way. We met the following evening at a local restaurant. He was six feet two inches tall, heavy, and sported a crew cut. Perspiration dripped from his nose and chin the entire meal. He left the table several times to smoke and make telephone calls. His pale skin and heavy breathing caused me to worry that he might collapse at the table.

Bill had sold his assets in Hawaii to move to Vietnam for a different life. Of interest was that the business he sold in Hawaii and the one he wanted to start in Vietnam were both orchid farms. He had 25 years of experience growing and selling orchids. He agreed to assist at the hospice and went there on several occasions, providing invaluable help each time.

Orchids are air feeders, sending their roots into the air. Only a few roots penetrate the soil or tree bark for stability. The nuns had placed each plant in a coconut shell and added a mixture of sand and peanut shells. Bill was impressed. He explained that a coconut shell is a natural herbicide and fungicide.

"A very small operation," Bill said after his first visit to the hospice. He examined each plant with a magnifying glass. They were all free of disease and bugs. Bill measured the PH in the water, the chemical composition of the soil, and the amount of sunlight able to penetrate the green plastic awning. Orchids die in direct sunlight and from too much water. He told the nuns they had done everything right and that the plants were healthy. He gave them a Vietnamese translation of a book he called the bible of orchid growing. Bill asked if he could return in a week to "clean up" the plants and give them a superior fertilizer. The trip was productive and I felt good about bringing Bill to help.

However, I had one nagging question, which I asked on our return to Saigon. "Will they make any money? Will the sisters turn a profit?"

"Maybe, maybe not," he answered. "It's too small an operation and the numbers don't pencil out. You should tell them."

He explained that the Thai market was fully developed and currently exported orchids to Vietnam. The Thais would crush Vietnamese growers if they perceived a threat to their income. In other words, they would cut prices to force local growers out of business. I am hopeful that without labor costs the nuns will be able to compete.

Bill is in Thailand now. "It is too difficult for a foreigner to do business in Vietnam," he said. "Thailand is easier."

ORPHANAGE FOR THE BLIND: The state runs schools for the blind, but only for children who have birth certificates. Newborns are issued birth certificates if their parents have a residency permit from the local governmental unit.

For eight months in 2002 I taught English at an orphanage administered by a religious-based NGO. Some of the orphans had been born blind, while others had lost their sight playing with, or scavenging for, abandoned munitions. The orphans had the bad luck of being blind and of having parents who moved to Saigon without permission. Officially, they do not exist and are not entitled to government services.

Twenty-seven blind children, ages five to fifteen, and four nuns lived at the orphanage. The children were clothed, housed, fed, educated, and counseled by the nuns, all without government funds. In addition to academic subjects they studied music (guitar, drums, flute, and traditional Vietnamese stringed instruments) and played sports.

The school was a 45-minute motorbike ride from central Saigon. The compound was walled with brick, 10 feet high all around. Bits of broken glass embedded atop the barrier discouraged intruders. A large fishpond and 16 evenly spaced fruit trees in four rows provided the children with food, adventure, recreation, and serenity. They climbed the trees for fruit, fished in the pond for dinner, and relaxed in the shade while they talked among themselves. A cemented area near the school furnished space for soccer, ping-pong, volleyball, and foot races. All of these activities had equipment and rules adapted for those who were blind or had limited sight. For example, the soccer field was small, the ball had a bell in it, and a handheld rope guided the players.

The seven-year-old, one-level building had classrooms, bathrooms, a kitchen, and a dining room. There were sleeping cells for the nuns and two single-sex dormitories with a Murphy bed and closet per child. Each child had housekeeping chores; the nuns said the girls' dormitory was the neatest.

One nun confided that the older children try to meet at night and the sisters must stop them. "A pregnant student would have a bad life and would cause police-trouble for the orphanage and sisters."

The children were brave, resilient, patient, and humorous. They helped one another and they helped me. A Vietnamese had written the book I used for teaching English to sighted children. With the help of the sister who taught them how to read and write Braille, the students had translated the book from Vietnamese into Braille for their own use.

They sat in front of me and read with their fingers. They repeated aloud each English sentence I spoke. Embedded in each sentence was a grammar lesson. To teach this way was frustrating, and it was not a good way to learn, but they were enthusiastic and seemed to enjoy our time together. I know I did.

The classroom was small, with 12 chairs lined up in four rows. The boys sat up front and tended to dominate the class if I let them. They called out the answers and wanted to speak as often as possible. At first I thought the girls did not understand as much as the boys, but I found this was not so. Even though they spoke softly and did not volunteer answers, their English was just as good as or better than that of the boys.

One day a boy in the front row was nervously moving around in his seat. He looked like he was trying to control himself from speaking out. Finally, losing restraint, he blurted out, "What is your wife?" Another pupil was reading aloud from her Braille book and the question was disruptive. I knew the boy wanted to know my wife's name but his interruption annoyed me, and to discourage further speaking out of turn I answered, "My wife is a woman." The boy who asked the question became quiet and serious while he tried to make sense of my answer; the other boys did, too. The girls in the back immediately saw the humor in my response. They smiled and laughed softly and one of them said in English, very quietly, "Of course, of course."

May, June, July, and August are uncomfortably hot in Saigon. Since I did not take siestas, the nuns insisted that I spend the hour after lunch in the computer area, which had air conditioning. The narrow room had six computers and chairs pushed against a wall. The nuns gave me lemonade, turned the air conditioning on, and left me to read and write. It was comfortable but not quiet because some students used the computers instead of resting.

When a student struck a key, a computer voice, first in English and then in Vietnamese, gave instructions on how to proceed. The voice would say what key had been struck and what the computer had been instructed to do. Proficient students taught others. I was constantly amazed that these children were able to do things that I thought required sight.

Two of the nuns had private lessons with me as well. They were kind-hearted, bright, and practical. Before coming to the blind school, the head sister worked for 10 years at the hundred-year-old leprosarium. Soft-spoken, slight, and about 40, she was formidable. Prior to 1975, the leprosarium was owned by her order of nuns. Now they staff it, but it belongs to the government.

One of my lessons required the sisters to discuss the following statement: "Schools should teach children to think for themselves." I was surprised and disagreed with them when they said that schools should not teach children to think for themselves. We had a lively discussion; a difference of opinion, I thought, until I heard one of them say, "Schools should teach children to care for everyone, not just for themselves." We were not disagreeing, only expressing different ideas.

MARY WAS HAVING THE FLU: The dry season in the south ends in May. The approach of the rainy season comes up in almost every conversation. The rain should break the heat, but it does not. In the monsoon season, the heat and humidity were a trial. Perspiration dripped from my face and neck while I taught. My shirt and pants were stained dark by the wetness and clung to my body. I could feel beads of sweat rolling down my back and chest. Sometimes I was a little lightheaded and then I appreciated the bottled water and washcloth the students always placed before me. The bottled water and the cloth, each on its own small dish, were served to me on a tray. The cloth was wet, with ice chips on top. After I sipped from my glass, a blind student refilled it. They used a finger to determine the height of the water in the glass.

"Are you tired, teacher?" they asked. The way they showed their concern and respect was charming. All the while, I knew they, too, were uncomfortably damp with sweat.

There were problems, though. We were unable to discuss grammar issues because my Vietnamese language ability was limited. Frequently, the students lost their place while reading with their fingers, and there was a lot of page turning and talking until it was found. Sometimes I spoke too quickly or indistinctly and so the students repeated gibberish back. Moreover, the English in the book was not always perfect.

During one class, the students repeated a two-page dialogue between Mr. White and Dr. Brown: "Mary was having the flu. Will she be having the flu? Why was Mary absent from class? Mary was absent from class because she was having the flu." I used the words from the book even though I flinched every time I heard them repeated.

One afternoon the students wanted to have class outdoors. It was over 100 degrees with high humidity. There was no electricity that day, no fans. They led me to a cool place under a tree and then went back to the classroom to get two small tables and some chairs, all this without sight. They had different strategies for getting around. With arms outstretched, some took small steps; others purposefully strode from place to place relying on familiar landmarks, their memory, and their senses of hearing and touch. The students held hands, touched things nearby and grasped the clothing of others. They made their way and got around, but most of them had bruised arms and shins.

At a height of 12 feet, enormous webs stretched between the fruit trees. Yellow and black, finch-sized spiders guarded the corners of the webs, awaiting vibrations from trapped insects. The webs were studded with silk-wrapped bugs stored for later consumption. The unwary are easy to ensnare.

Although there were no Vietnamese teachers in the room, we always got through the day's lesson. However, I never knew if they learned anything from me. It was hard for us to communicate. Their English was quite limited and my Vietnamese, I am convinced, got worse day by day. We struggled; we persevered; we got by on good will, humor, and dogged determination.

Teaching the blind children was difficult, uncomfortable, and frustrating, but I was not going to quit. If the nuns and the children thought the lessons were worthwhile, I would continue teaching. One morning, eight months after starting the class, the sister in charge told me that the blind children did not want to study English anymore. "They want to study more Vietnamese history. Do you mind?" I most certainly did not.

A NEW NAME: It was one p.m. at the orphanage. A Vietnamese man and woman had joined us for lunch. They were from a Japanese NGO that was sponsoring soccer matches between blind teams from Japan, Korea, and Vietnam. The matches were to be held in Japan. They brought a video of last year's games, which the orphans and staff watched during lunch. The man gave a running commentary, including cheers.

The game was played on a small field covered with foam rubber. Since many blind persons have some sight, all of the players were blindfolded. To help the players, the ball had been designed to beep as it rolled around. The game was played fast and aggressively. The players were fearless.

After the meal was finished, the man invited the blind school to send four boys to Japan to play on the Vietnamese team along with two nuns to accompany them. Their teammates would come from government run schools for the blind. All expenses would be paid by the NGO. The sisters accepted, and then picked the boys who would go on the two-week trip.

One boy, though, had a problem that would make it difficult for him to obtain a passport. His family name was different from his father's and he had no birth certificate or other official records. His parents had divorced and disappeared and no one knew his history.

"What will you do, Sister?" I asked.

"I think we will give him a new name and somehow get a birth certificate for him, otherwise we must choose a different boy to go to Japan. Sometimes God needs help. And we must pray."

The boy went to Japan. With the help of authorities friendly to the orphanage, he obtained a passport and necessary approvals. Nuns may be defenseless but they are resourceful.

The Vietnamese team lost the four games it played, but the players gained confidence and the nuns obtained knowledge about ways to help the blind.

MASSAGE: An ongoing concern of the sisters is finding employment for the orphans after graduation. The blind are vulnerable. They and the nuns know it. The students asked me what jobs the blind have in America. They said there were only minor jobs for them in Vietnam. Some hope to be musicians and others train to be masseurs. The blind are reputed to have superior hearing, which enables them to be first-class musicians. It is also believed they are better masseurs than the sighted because their fingers are more sensitive and the customer's modesty is intact.

Massage is a traditional form of therapy that reduces muscle pain and induces relaxation. In Vietnam, as is the case everywhere, there are both legal and illegal massage parlors. Illegal ones are thinly disguised prostitution businesses. They flourish in Vietnam.

Advertisements proclaiming "Hot Massage Here" are a common sight. Cyclo men and motorbike drivers pimp for massage girls. In addition to established parlors, freelance masseurs work the neighborhoods and restaurants in the evenings. Men (no women) on bicycles circle the streets and alleys shaking bottle caps affixed to a long stick. The distinctive noise advertises their trade and availability. Those interested call the men into their homes and for $2 receive a 30-minute massage.

Massage ladies, uninvited, give two-minute neck and shoulder teaser-massages in local eateries. Restaurant patrons enticed by the promotion are free to make an appointment at their home for later that evening.

The blind students say they will only work in legitimate massage parlors. The sisters and I pray for it to be so.

A SUPERIOR PUBLIC PURPOSE: In Vietnam the state owns all land, but individuals can own the use of land in perpetuity.

The government provides generous economic incentives for foreign companies to locate export-oriented facilities in designated areas. These industrial parks benefit Vietnam in many ways, mostly through the creation of jobs.

The purchase of land and subsequent construction of the orphanage were funded by a wealthy Swiss man. When built, rice paddies surrounded the complex. Today a large industrial park abuts the compound. The industrial park has been a success. It has attracted companies that would probably have located in some other Southeast Asian country and it has created thousands of jobs.

The authorities wanted to expand the park by tearing down the blind school. Governments all over the world have the power to take private property for a public purpose. It is an important, necessary power that in the United States by law requires a determination of what constitutes a public purpose and what is fair compensation to the owner who has been forced to relinquish his property.

The school's land was purchased in 1995 for $2 per square meter. In 2002 land near the school was selling for $10 per square meter. The state offered the nuns undeveloped land located two hours by car from Saigon. This land was smaller than the blind school's compound, and was equal in value only to what the compound had cost in 1995. The nuns would receive no compensation for the value of the school building or for the increase in the land's value from 1995 to 2002. What this meant was that they would not be able to replicate the school unless a donor was found.

Even assuming the compensation was fair, someone had decided that at that location job creation was a more important public purpose than a free school and home for the blind. I would be inclined to agree with the decision if a similar facility could be built somewhere else, but this could not happen given what the nuns were offered in compensation. The nuns said no.

An influential friend of the nuns successfully interceded on their behalf. It has been many years since they rejected the offer, but they remain vigilant and concerned.

NO BOYS ALLOWED: Few jobs are available in rural areas other than watching water buffalo and working in the rice fields. Unaccompanied children and teenagers make their way from the countryside to Saigon, where safe opportunities are limited. Once in the city they often provide for themselves through self-destructive and/or criminal activity. They sleep on the sidewalks, defecate in the gutters, wash in the rain, steal, and sometimes sell themselves for the price of a meal. Many people, Vietnamese and foreigners, have dedicated themselves to helping these boys and girls.

Three nuns operate a home for such teenagers in a poor Saigon neighborhood. A German man paid for the house and contributes part of its annual expense. He had intended that six boys be housed on the ground floor and six girls on the top floor. Two years passed before the ward leader gave his permission to build the house, but he insisted that only girls be allowed to live there. The neighbors said that boys would cause trouble, and certainly they would. Just think of the copious flow of hormones coursing through the bodies of 12 coed teenagers all living under the same roof. The situation would have been nuclear. The ward leader did the sisters a favor.

Today, 12 girls share the house. They eat and sleep there, and learn how to sew and use computers. The nuns teach them about their bodies, men, babies, values, and health care. They tell the girls it is natural to want to go with men, but a bad idea to do so if not married because men might get them pregnant, or sick, and then go away.

The girls are required to obey an 8 p.m. curfew. If they do not, they must move elsewhere. When I visited the house, classes stopped and they sang and performed traditional dances for me. The German who funds this project and the sisters who care for the girls have given them a chance for a better life.

DRY WELLS: Most people who help the poor, the marginalized, and those at risk are Vietnamese; in most cases the supporting funds come from foreigners. A vast cadre of local social workers and volunteers tend to the needs of their fellow citizens. They are the ones who interface with the needy, donors, police, and government functionaries. They must accommodate these constituencies or the poor will not benefit.

The effort and money foreigners contribute to charitable causes in Vietnam is amazing and laudable. Foreign governments, institutions, and individuals run or fund charitable projects throughout Vietnam. It is heartening to see, but sometimes there are obstacles to success.

I was asked to draft a letter to a German NGO that had donated $35,000 to a local religious organization to finance the construction of water wells in a poor village. The letter's purpose was to explain how the contribution had been used and to report on the project's status. The NGO needed the letter for its report to the German tax authorities. If the money had not been used for a charitable purpose, then the NGO would have to pay a tax to the German government.

All the funds had been spent building the project. The wells had been dug, installed and encased, and had produced water. The letter would be easy to write, I was sure. However, I was quite wrong.

Local authorities had destroyed the newly installed wells because the nuns had used a low-priced contractor instead of the high-priced one favored by those in power. It was obvious that some portion of the higher price had been destined for area officials.

The nuns were obligated to report to the NGO, but they did not want to explain that the wells had been destroyed or why, for fear that it would be made public. The charity would have a problem with the Vietnamese authorities if that happened. I explained in the letter that the $35,000 had been spent on the project, but more funds were necessary to complete it because of unanticipated cost overruns related to contract bidding problems. It was true (kind of), but incomplete. I hoped the Germans could not read between the lines. Eventually, after another source contributed funds, the contractor favored by the local officials repaired the wells. The wells now provide uncontaminated water. However, they were completed nine months late, and the total cost was one-third more than the original contract cost.

ROYAL REFUSAL: In 2004 a member of royalty from a European country paid an official visit. In the company of diplomats and officials, he attended concerts and state dinners and visited charitable institutions. At the offices of an NGO dedicated to helping street children, the Prince announced that he would contribute $30,000 to help the poor. Within days the government officials responsible for supervising the NGO claimed one-half of the donation. When the Prince was informed, he refused to release the funds unless all the money went to the charity. Unable to get the assurances he wanted, the grant was not made.

Sixteen

EXPATS AND MIGRANTS

Throw your dreams into space like a kite, and you do not know what it will bring back, a new life, a new friend, a new love, a new country.
-Anais Min

Vietnamese are at a loss to explain why foreigners (the overwhelming majority of whom are males) leave their rich countries to live out their lives in Vietnam. "Why are you here?" I was asked numerous times. They wonder. Of course, there are as many reasons as there are expats: a desire to help others, nostalgia, adventure, a comfortable life at low cost, a business venture, a broken relationship back home, and chance—fate's companion. For many the explanation is no deeper than it is damn fun here. That is reason enough, and why not? Once here, men stay because the women are beautiful, exquisite, non-judgmental, compliant (well, kind of), and determined to please.

Vietnamese leave their country for opportunities and freedom. The United States is home to more than 2,000,000 of them. After the fall of Saigon in 1975, they came by boat via refugee camps, and then by immigration, legal and otherwise. Most have prospered in the U.S. and most are good citizens. Their relatives and friends hear stories about freedom and opportunity in America, and when they compare them to what's available in Vietnam many choose to emigrate. Every Vietnamese I have spoken to either knows someone in America or knows someone who wants to go there. It is a dream of many. They go themselves or they send their sons and daughters, perhaps never to see them again. Their schemes for obtaining visas are varied, complex, and often fraudulent.

"Can I get a job in America?" they ask. I tell them, yes, but you may not like what you have to do, or that you do not earn enough money, or where you have to live, or that your family is far away. My words of caution do not dampen their desire.

My students tell me that it is better to emigrate to Australia or the United States because there is less chance of success in Europe. They think European societies are more rigid and less open to them.

*****

MIGRANTS: The Vietnamese, like others, have developed strategies to cope with the restrictive and complex immigration law of the United States. Untruthful affidavits and fraudulent documentation commonly support visa applications. The United States Immigration and Naturalization Service (INS) and the U.S. Consulate in Saigon investigate each application and turn down many either because the documentation is not believable or the examining officer believes the applicant, if granted a visa, would not willingly return when it expires. Instead, the illegal alien would hide and, if caught, use the courts to fight deportation.

A marriage of convenience is a common way to get a visa. The Vietnamese national, a young woman in the stories I have been told, marries a U.S. citizen. Her family pays the man $30,000 to $40,000 in two installments, part when the visa is granted and the rest years later when her permanent legal status is confirmed. The second payment is waived if the pair falls in love. After the couple arrives in America, the INS may conduct surprise home visits and open closets, drawers, and medicine cabinets, looking for evidence of joint housekeeping. The visa can be revoked for fraud if the INS discovers that the couple does not live together or if they divorce soon after arrival in the United States.

Many marriages are arranged via the Internet. Decisions to wed and emigrate are based on personal information exchanged via email. Unfortunately, such data is notoriously unreliable. Lies about age, marital status, employment, and finances are common. Deception works both ways. Sometimes a man is surprised at the airport arrival gate when his Internet fiancée does not match the beautiful young Vietnamese in the photograph he had been sent. Prudent people on both sides of the bargain must be cautious. Relatives and other parties are asked to verify information and determine bona fides.

Inquiries, however, can end a budding relationship. A woman asked me to investigate her Internet fiancé. She thought my background, as a lawyer would help her determine if the man was "real." Initially, the man agreed to answer my email questions, but he would not give me his place and date of birth, the name of his employer, or the name of the university he claimed to have graduated from. Subsequently, he broke off contact with the woman, who became annoyed with me. "No good deed goes unpunished" is a saying I remember from my law practice.

The INS office in Saigon is very busy. It is a high-pressure job for the American civil servants who work there. The man who for years made the final decision on all visa applications attended the same Sunday Mass at Notre Dame Cathedral as I did. He was 6'4", trim, and about 50 years of age. He came alone each Sunday and sat 10 pews in front of me. I never met the man but I knew his name, what he looked like, and where he sat during Mass because the applicants knew and several of them told me these things when they learned I attended Mass at Notre Dame, too. Women (often not Catholic) who had visa applications pending sat near him at Mass hoping for his recognition, interest, or sympathy. Indeed, I saw him accosted as he left the church by comely, demure supplicants pleading their case and trying to influence its outcome. Nevertheless, I do not think they succeeded, because every time I heard him spoken of he was described as difficult, which to me meant he was doing his job correctly.

Many successful visa applicants are woefully unprepared for and misinformed about life in America. Two of my students, 16- and 18-year-old sisters, received visas while I was teaching them. Their mother and stepfather already lived in Atlanta and the sisters were soon to join them. These concerned teenagers asked me many practical questions: "Will we be safe in our house? Will the house have furniture? How will we find the Vietnamese school? Do we have to begin high school again? Is there Vietnamese food in Atlanta? Should we bring a rice cooker on the airplane? Our clothes are thin, should we bring them? Will America help us? Since we speak bad English, will we be able to find a job?"

I was sure that within a year they would adjust to life in America. Like millions before them, they, for better or worse, will become part of the American immigrant experience. I hope they are not disappointed.

WOMAN DANGEROUS IF LUST NOT GO AWAY: Vietnamese love to sing. In restaurants and classrooms, during casual conversations or upon request, one or more persons will, with confidence and self-assurance, sing for their pleasure and the enjoyment of those around. Thus, it is no surprise that karaoke clubs are popular here. Men and women, young and not so young, take turns singing to recorded music. They meet, they talk, they sing, and they drink (beer for men, soda for women). Applause and single stem roses await the performers.

I accepted an invitation to a karaoke party from two of my students. It would begin at 12:30 p.m. and end at 3 p.m. The party straddled lunchtime and the midday rest period, which seemed odd. Who would come then? The students picked me up at my house and told me we were going to a famous karaoke hotel. It used to be a "massage hotel" but its 20 bedrooms had been turned into daytime singing rooms. Rates were $2 an hour during the day and $6 an hour at night. By way of explanation, one student said, "Other things happen at night."

I was introduced to 14 young women in the lobby of the former massage hotel. They paid for the room, as I was their guest. The hotel was rocking:

music blared, cell phones beeped, elevators clanked, doors slammed, and everywhere was laughter and singing. The place buzzed.

The room had a long, horseshoe-shaped sofa and a rectangular, black, knee-high table. A telephone for ordering food and beverages and, according to one of the women, "to call help" rested on the table. At the open end of the horseshoe, against the wall, was a big screen television.

For two hours the women took turns singing. The lyrics of the song selected from a 20-page laminated list appeared on the screen in large letters. Evocative video scenes accompanied the words. There were no sex scenes, only images mirroring the emotions that the singer and lyrics conveyed. Pictures of roaring rivers, sedate streams, combat, ocean waves, mountaintops, babes in arms, beautiful women and handsome men, waving fields of grass, and majestic trees helped set the mood. After each song, the singer, with help from friends, would translate the words into English for me as best she could. "Woman dangerous if lust not go away" was the collective translation of one song.

An electronic gadget automatically graded each singer and awarded her a score, which appeared on the screen. When this happened, the girls giggled and told me what they thought of the automated scoring.

"TV fake."

"It not real."

"How it know?"

"It just for fun."

During the party, they changed seats so each could speak to me about what was on their minds.

"I no marry yet," one girl confided to me. "I live alone in room in District 7."

"I came alone Saigon six years ago," another girl explained shortly after the next song came on.

A pattern emerged as I spoke to each girl in turn.

"My family live Da Nang."

"I alone. I work in store. I alone."

"I work in a store. I married. No baby."

"I go university."

"I work for Japanese company."

"I have four-year-old son. I clean house. Can you introduce me foreign man?"

"My father won't let me go out alone with men at night. I must go with my brother or nice girlfriends, but during day he no watch."

Encouraging me to sing, they read the list of English songs hoping to find one I knew. One of them pointed to the title "Danny Boy" and asked me to sing it. In a flash, I recalled the answer Louis Armstrong gave when I asked him if he liked my rendition of that song. It was in 1961 at the officers' club in Fort Knox, Kentucky. He and his band were entertaining the commissioned swells, and at my request Mr. Armstrong gave me the microphone. He played Danny Boy on the piano and I sang. Afterward he told me, "I ain't heard nothing like that before."

Five of the women spoke in detail to me about their plans to go to America. Their schemes were elaborate, in advanced stages, and all constituted immigration fraud under United States law. I described the consequences if their fraud was discovered and told them not to do it. Their schemes included fake engagements and marriages, false military records and family relationships, changed birth certificates, and sham adoptions.

Two of the women were seeking fiancée visas, which they believed are easier to obtain than marriage visas because fiancées are not entitled to social security benefits, whereas surviving spouses are. Marriage within 90 days of the beneficiary's arrival in the United States is required; otherwise their visa will be revoked. Cash was paid to secure partners in the United States and for false documentation to support their applications. These women did not plan to marry; they would get a job in a nail salon and hide. They knew the U.S. government would not chase them once they entered the United States. "Not enough police", one said.

The last step in the application process is an interview at the consulate. Questions to prior applicants, and recommended answers, are studied in preparation for the meeting. The names and personalities of interviewers are known and the chances of success diminish if a difficult person conducts one's interrogation. The applicant can request that the interview be held in Vietnamese and, naturally, many do. Months after the karaoke party, I learned that each of the five had failed their interview. Their paperwork had been dubious and their answers not believable.

One of these applicants was named Bi. Still desperate and determined to leave her country after failing her interview at the consulate, she finally made her way to England. Her friend Liz, a British male who had been surgically modified to become a female, had sponsored Bi's English visa. They married and now live north of London. Bi does not like the cold or the food and she complains that there is "not enough noise." Her English is poor, she has no friends, and her family is far away. She dislikes Liz's friends. "I don't like how I live. I am not a lesbian," Bi e-mailed me. We must be careful what we wish for.

Bi's former boyfriend, a German, was disappointed but philosophical. He remarked, "Bi married a guy who has nowhere to put a condom."

VISAS ARE A GOOD BUSINESS: Obtaining a visa to enter the United States can be difficult. Applicants who seem qualified to me are routinely rejected. Those turned down blame random chance, or capriciousness, or, bless them, a mistake. They try repeatedly, becoming more desperate each time. With each successive application, less attention is paid to the truthfulness of information they submit.

Chau worked in an upscale cyber-café where he met many foreigners. His spoken English was good but his written English poor. I had hired him to turn the handwritten manuscript of this book into typewritten copy. He guessed at individual letters when my handwriting was not clear, and he sometimes engaged the computer's grammar check option and selected an offered correction. I learned from the pages he returned to me that the grammar option is useful only if the typist can read and write Standard English.

Chau befriended a couple from Portland, Maine, who volunteered to sponsor him for a student visa. They offered to feed and house him and pay his tuition for four years. He submitted an application to the consulate together with a non-refundable $100 application fee. Attached to the application were an acceptance letter from an accredited American college, a sponsorship letter and bank statements from the couple, and laudatory reference letters from two American executives working in Vietnam. His application included a signed statement that after completing his education he would return to Vietnam to take care of his mother. I told Chau I thought he qualified for a visa.

On the day of his interview, four of the 40 interviewees received visas, but he was not one of them. Consulate policy is not to give reasons for rejections. Naturally, Chau was disappointed. "Visas are a good business for the U.S.," he observed later, noting that the consulate had collected $4,000 in one day.

The consulate charges Americans for some services. For example, to have one's signature notarized by a consulate official costs $50. However, the fee is waived for a government employee. Millions of people around the world, including servicemen, politicians, and federal workers, are exempt. Congress, in its wisdom, decided that all citizens should not be treated the same, and that the exemption should not be based on a means test.

The State Department considers Vietnam a hardship post; consequently, U.S. Foreign Service Officers stationed in the country are entitled to their salary plus hardship pay. Their job is to advance the interests of the United States and to assist U.S. citizens. I was annoyed when a consulate official told me, "Saigon is a great city to live in, but the American expats make our job difficult. They have problems and do things they should not do, and they think we should and can help them. They expect too much from the consulate."

A DIRE SITUATION: Ann and Gene returned to Saigon when they were both 80 to supervise the cataloging and installation of their 30,000-book library, which they had donated to Can Tho University. According to Gene, they had been hustled out of South Vietnam by the U.S. government shortly after President Diem's assassination in 1963. Gene made the dubious claim that he'd had an office in the Presidential Palace, where his job was Diem's Foreign Press Secretary. When he died in Saigon after a botched heart operation, his wife Ann refused to pay the surgeon or hospital. Months later, destitute, she ended up literally living on the sidewalk. I asked the consul general to help Ann. (See Note 6.)

Vietnamese who knew this couple were shocked that neither the U.S. Consulate nor family members in America would move Ann back to the United States for proper care. Eventually, a concerned U.S. Senator asked the State Department to help Ann; his request was forwarded to the consulate, which contacted local authorities.

Poor Ann; her end was not nice. The Vietnamese government arranged to put Ann in a home for the destitute, mentally impaired, and drug addicts. The police asked me to go with them when they collected her from her sidewalk hovel. They reasoned that Ann would be easier to deal with if a countryman of hers was present. Ann, social workers, government officials, police, and a doctor were waiting when I arrived.

The travel agent who had arranged for Ann's visa (long expired) was forced to pay for the move and for a portion of Ann's care at the home. She explained that the authorities held her responsible because she had sponsored the 80-year-old woman's Vietnamese visa; the agent was annoyed with me for introducing Ann to her.

Ann had a big room; all her boxes were stacked against a wall. It was better than living on the sidewalk, I was sure. The Vietnamese officials called me several times to report on her condition. They complained that Ann could no longer speak; she made noises and grunted, but it was not a language. Ann would not shower or eat. "What does she like to eat?" they wanted to know.

After a few weeks, she fell in the bathroom and broke her leg, which later had to be amputated. She languished in a hospital bed for six weeks before she died.

EXPATRIATES: There are three main expat groups: Asians, French, and other Westerners. Socially, there is little intermingling. The French look to the sky, bless them all. They actually think the Vietnamese like them. Happily for all, Vietnamese women are willing to socialize with everyone.

The Westerners are mostly men from Vietnam's former enemies: America, France, and Australia. This exotic land and its wonderful people exert a powerful, magnetic pull. Among the Americans living here is a small group of war veterans like me. They are drawn, no doubt, by a sweet nostalgia for a time in their lives when they were young and strong and part of a great adventure. These men come to Vietnam alone. Most are entitled to military disability or social security payments, which are deposited directly into offshore bank accounts. ATM cards are used to obtain local currency at the official (unfavorable) exchange rate. Some are serious-minded men with serious pursuits. Others chase the local women, party hard, and sleep late. They live in the backpacker district of Saigon, either in $10-a-night rooms with ceiling fans or $12 rooms with A/C. Some even drink alcohol.

Young women jokingly say that the best place to meet Western men is at the airport when they first arrive. They do not know how to drive a motorbike or deal with the Vietnamese, so they need help. They are still sweet because other women have not yet cheated them. After six months, however, these men no longer need much help and become difficult.

In this culture, age differences do not deter relationships. It is common for a young woman to be romantically involved with a Western man who is 30-40 years her senior. The men are unattached and financially secure. The woman benefits economically and the old guy gets to live out his fantasy. "An old water buffalo likes to eat young grass," is a Vietnamese saying that describes these pairings. The old buffalo has bad teeth. Young grass is sweet and easy to digest. This humorous saying also recognizes that young women are easier to live with; they want to please.

One thing Western men do not understand is that when they marry or live with a Vietnamese woman, they are marrying the bride's family as well. In-laws, siblings, aunts, uncles, nieces, and nephews arrive to share the happy couple's abode and food. They take up space and do not work or contribute to expenses. Often, the relationship teeters on cultural expectations.

Life is not so sweet for single Western women; Vietnamese men are not interested, or are afraid of rejection. Western men favor the young Asian grass. Usually, no matter how good a job she has, after a year or so, the Western woman moves to another country seeking a normal social life.

Other Westerners come to Vietnam to fill jobs for which Vietnamese do not have the training or experience, or to protect the interests of foreign businesses. Still others secure teaching jobs in private English schools. Some come with cash and a dream of starting their own business. Physically, foreigners are safe in Vietnam, but when it comes to business, all too often dishonest Vietnamese partners swindle them.

There are laws to protect foreign investors, police to enforce them, and judges to interpret and adjudicate. However, it would be foolish to do business in this country without a well-connected local partner who will deal with venal officials and act as an intermediary and advisor. Hanoi legislates, but the local authorities that control business in their jurisdiction frequently must be paid to issue the necessary approvals.

MULTIPLE WIVES: The western women who live in Vietnam usually cater to the poor and needy. Joan was one of them. I met her at the orphanage for blind children where we both volunteered. She told me about her husband who had been a travel agent in NYC and had died in a fall from his office window. This information surprised and made me cautious because Billy, my NYC travel agent, had died this way. Joan's husband and my travel agent were one and the same. We were both surprised by this chance meeting years after and 12,000 miles away from his death. We did not speak about why he killed himself.

Billy ended his live because he had too many current wives. That happens, don't you know? Upon discovery, the wives complained to the authorities. To escape the situation he jumped from his office window in lower Manhattan. He too was a migrant. He traveled from one wife to another and from life to death- looking, looking, and looking.

As a young lawyer, I traveled a great deal. Billy went "beyond the call" and took good care of me. He was my friend, and he always took my call, no matter when or where I was calling from. I wanted to be home to be with my sons and he knew it. He'd arrange it so that I could arrive at JFK at 6 AM, so as to get home by taxi at 7AM, have breakfast with them and then get the 8:30 AM train to my office.

Once I told Billy to put me in 1st class on a flight to California because a senior investment banker who was a possible client was in 1st class on the same flight. I wanted to befriend the banker and hopefully get business from him. What an ambitious fellow I was then. Billy got back to me immediately and said, "All the 1st class seats are taken."

"But," I insisted. "I have to sit in 1st class." Within a ½ hour he'd confirmed that I had a 1st class reservation. The airline had bumped someone with a 1st class ticket back to coach and had given me the bumped passenger's seat. Yes! I called the banker to tell him I would be sitting near him and that I had some business ideas for his consideration. He replied, "Fine, let's talk." Regrettably, I also told him about Billy, my wonderful travel agent.

When I got to the airport, the banker was irate. He had been downgraded to coach. I had his seat in 1st class and he knew it. He refused to switch seats. I think Shakespeare said something about plans not working: a slip between the cup and the lip.

Comfortable but uneasy, I traveled to Los Angles. Weeks later the very same banker called and said, "Martin I want you as my lawyer. If you have the ability to bump me from 1st class to couch, you can do wonders for my business. Let's do deals together." And we did. You never know where circumstances might lead, but in this case it was to satisfaction and prosperity for both of us.

Poor Billy, I'm sad about his choice and fate.

The line between instinct and rational behavior is unclear. How close are any of us to his desperate choice? For the most part, our lives are not planned. Opportunity and chance, and their companion, risk, govern our lives. Prudent decisions, although important, are a minor contribution to what we call success and happiness. Everything is dependent on luck, fortune and providence.

BEER BUS: At 9:30 p.m. on a Saturday night, I returned from teaching the nuns at their convent. The end of the week, and 20 hours of volunteer work, was at hand. I had a great thirst and went to Murphy's.

In the middle of this Southeast Asian city, Murphy's advertises in its window, LIVE IRISH MUSIC ON SATURDAY NIGHTS. It is a small, dark pub, decorated with photos of Ireland and Irish heroes. I got a jar and settled in a corner seat. A group of four musicians played instruments: violin, fiddle, flutes, and tin whistle. In addition, there was a Celtic war drum. The owner, an Irishman, sang a rebel song. The band played jigs, reels, and ballads of old. A beautiful young woman in a black T-shirt and pants, and sporting a man's short haircut, sang in a clear, sweet Irish brogue. It was a friendly crowd of 30 or so. Not surprisingly, the Vietnamese customers broke the rhythm of the evening by stomping, clapping, and swaying at the wrong times.

The musicians were all Vietnamese, as was the lovely singer with the enchanting brogue. Their faces were expressionless and their bodies motionless as they performed. They sang detached from the typically irresistible, Irish-style vibrancy that filled the bar. The night was surreal and riveting. I had a second jar to keep my thirst at bay and then settled in to think about the surreal. I pondered with relish the old Irish proverb: "Live horse and you will get grass."

The Vietnamese band had been playing the same songs for three years. They had learned them from Michael, who owned the place, and from his collection of CDs. They wanted to perform new songs but he would not let them. According to one of the singers, Michael had told them, "You don't have the old ones right yet." They felt insulted and angry, rightfully so I think. "Maybe we strike," the singer said to me.

The table area where pub food was served shared the musicians' space. Behind the musicians and to their left was the bar, visible to all. On most nights, older Westerners and a table of young Vietnamese out to experience some exotic music would sit in this area. Conversation was only possible during the infrequent 15-minute music breaks. Most of the time I sat surrounded by familiar tunes, lost in savory recollections of growing up in America with my Irish-born parents.

Suddenly a patron by the door shouted, "Beer bus! Beer bus!" Customers drained their glasses as the female singer announced: "Drink up lads, drink up. It's the beer bus." A tall, shapely blond woman entered the pub followed by a muscular six-foot-tall man with a half-keg of beer strapped to his back. They were Australians.

A short hose ran from the keg to a nozzle in the young woman's hand. Amidst coarse jokes about what she was squeezing, she filled each customer's jar—but only once; that was the rule. White sashes worn from shoulder to opposite hip identified the beer bus as a Carlsberg promotion. Quickly they finished their job and made for the door to dispense free beer at other nightspots on their route. A quartet of beefy Westerners noisily blocked the door and demanded more beer as an exit price. Michael intervened and escorted the Carlsberg twosome out the door. His motive was clear. More free beer would mean less beer sold at his pub.

A GARDEN TO ROMP IN: The crowd at the pub is friendly and non-competitive, very different from the customers at other expatriate saloons where one often finds "Masters of the Universe": tall, muscular, clean-shaven, well-dressed, well-spoken, overpaid, handsome, cash-flashing, expense-account-privileged, testosterone-driven, 40- to 60-year-old Western men. They sport impressive titles from the foreign companies for whom they work and brag that they are on the ground floor of a once in a lifetime opportunity. Somehow, they entertain one another while competing for taproom dominance and the "liberated" Vietnamese women who flit and flirt among them. For these men, Saigon is a garden to romp in. When fully charged they venture foolishly into the night to test their endurance, wits, and health against the offerings of the city. It is a loser's challenge. They would be safe only if they stayed at home chained to a cement-embedded iron ring. So, too, all men under 60, everywhere.

A DOCTOR OF NUTRITION: In the 8th century B.C., the Celts settled Britton, Ireland, Scotland, Cornwall, and Wales. Each developed a national identity and distinctive Celtic language and songs.

Pierre, from Britton, France, sings and plays the flute and the bodhran, the Celtic war drum. He is 45 years old, 5' 9", has hips aplenty, dresses in black, and wears Velcro-strapped sandals. A shirt barely covers his ample, slopped belly. He has a handsome face, glinting blue eyes, a strong nose, and a full jaw, all of it crowned by short, salt-and-pepper hair. It is a face yet unmarked by time or excess. His glowing cigarette and open beer bottle are always nearby.

Standing with legs apart and grasping the microphone in both hands, Pierre sang songs from Britton in a deep baritone voice. Although no one understood the Celtic words, his facial expressions, body language, and intonations identified the songs as laments for lost love. The pub would fall quiet when he finished, then everyone applauded and saluted him with their glasses. For a short while Pierre would stand with his arms at his sides and his head stooped, then he would reach for his smoke and drink. He was always dramatic. I wondered if he had been away from Britton for too long.

He lived in Saigon on the weekends but during the week he traveled throughout Asia advising corporate clients about animal nutrition and health. He boasted, "Martin, I'm a doctor of nutrition."

LOVE SONGS: An American of uncertain years took his place in front of the microphone, strummed his guitar, and in a voice roughened by age sang Vietnamese love songs. One song lamented the thousand years of war against the Chinese, the hundred years of war against the French, and the 20-year civil war involving America. The ballads were wartime classics. Vietnamese soldiers in both armies sang them during the 60s and 70s.

When he finished, he sat atop his stool, head bent, until the applause stopped. Vietnamese were enthralled by the songs and enchanted that an American veteran could sing in their tongue. The singer had returned to Vietnam in 1984, and has lived for years with the original inhabitants of central Vietnam who are ethnically different from the Vietnamese.

A SHRILL, PENETRATING SOUND: A man entered the pub just as I was arriving one Saturday night. The irregular shape of his canvas bag did not help me identify its contents. Michael greeted him with laughter and an embrace, and he was soon introduced to everyone as Sean, the bagpiper. This 35-year-old man was of medium height and trim all around. His head was a little big for his body and sported a crew cut, very neat indeed. Khaki shorts revealed he was wide at the knees.

Bagpipes are a demanding musical instrument, difficult to play and to appreciate. They are best listened to in a field or large hall. If the venue is wrong, such as in a small pub, the shrill, penetrating sound sets the eardrums twittering and pierces the soul. When Sean began to play, tables emptied and the bar crowd hurried to the street. Customers stood on the sidewalk talking, drinking, and waiting for the disturbance to end. The Vietnamese musicians stood there, too, bemused and thankful for the break. It was obvious that Michael cared more for the bagpipe music than 15 minutes of lost revenue. He knew it would be quickly recouped when the customers returned.

SHORE LEAVE: Saigon, which is 50 miles inland, can be reached from the sea via the Saigon River and is a port of call for navy ships from many countries. The sailors and their officers spend weeks at sea, mostly in the company of other men. Stops are arranged to obtain provisions and to let the men explore the cultural highlights of exotic cities. Liberty privileges are determined by the relationship between the countries and the discipline record of a ship's sailors on prior visits.

Six large men in the white tropical uniform (shorts and short-sleeved shirt) of Her Royal Highness's Navy were at the bar. The ship's crew had a 10:30 p.m. curfew. The crowd was friendly; everyone was in good spirits and no one had said anything nasty yet about the Queen. The men sang nautical songs and told stories of their sea adventures. Moreover, they drank some beer; had been all day. At 11 p.m. a seaman whose face was as pink as a ham started photographing the scuffed checkered tiles of the pub's floor. After each flash, the crowd applauded and he sidestepped a bit to take another. At this point, while everyone was still well behaved, the pub owner inconspicuously made a telephone call and within minutes a group of sober, serious, uniformed men from the British ship arrived to retrieve their mates. Michael had not wanted any trouble in his pub.

In November, 2003, the first American warship since 1975 entered the Port of Saigon. The USS Vandergrift, a guided missile frigate, was invited to pay an official three-day visit. American sailors, dressed in their tropical white uniforms, were on their best behavior as they sampled the city's offerings. Bars, restaurants, and other businesses advertised discounts and special promotions for the United States seamen. An official reception and wreath-laying ceremony had been scheduled. The visit was publicized in the local and national presses. One can only imagine the duration and intensity of the high-level talks preceding Hanoi's approval of the visit.

Michael, the Irish owner of Murphy's, is a longtime resident of Vietnam. He is keenly aware of the political and financial risks that arise from his activities and status as a foreigner. However, some things cannot be planned for, nor understood.

On the morning of the ship's arrival, Michael hung a 10' x 2' banner on the front of his pub. Bold black letters proclaimed:

WELCOME UNITED STATES NAVY

Several hours later the police arrived and tore the banner down. Michael and his Vietnamese partner were criticized for hanging the banner.

"We are Vietnamese and this is our country," the police said. "We do not honor America or their sailors."

The police had acted contrary to the clear policy and directives of the state. Vietnamese and foreigners considered their reaction inexplicable. People wondered why an example was made of Murphy's, a popular expat watering hole.

GREEN-SHIRTED LAD: Murphy's is near Notre Dame Cathedral, which is Gothic, faced with honey-colored bricks, and dates from the 1880s. The 9:30 a.m. Sunday Mass is for foreigners and Vietnamese. Prayers are said in Vietnamese, and then again in English, so it takes twice the time (the prayers, sermons, and songs go on forever). When I first came to Vietnam in 1962, there had also been a 9:30 a.m. Sunday Mass for foreigners at the Cathedral, but it was in Vietnamese and French.

On Easter Sunday 2003, the priest told us that the Queen Mother had died at 101 years of age and asked that we all pray for her. She had witnessed the events of the 20th Century and was revered worldwide, but I was still surprised to hear her remembered and prayed for in a Catholic cathedral 10,000 miles from England.

A few nights later I entered Murphy's and saw at the bar a man in his early twenties with short hair and a bright green t-shirt. I noticed him because he was too low on his stool, a great lopsided slouch, really. Michael came up to him and said, "Time for you to go home, lad." His dismount was unsteady and memorable. He slipped on something, or perhaps misjudged the distance between his feet and the floor. He fell against the wall and brought a near table down with a crash. The beer-splashed customers were not angry. The man was only drunk. "Came in that way," Michael repeated several times, motioning to the door. The man's apologies were loud and in an American accent. The waitresses brushed him off, toweled him dry, and led him to the door. Before he left they advised him: "Go home. Be careful. Take a metered taxi. No cyclo man, no girl, no massage."

They watched him walk unsteadily to the curb and then called him back to give him his wallet, which was found on the bar. He left the pub a second time and waited on the curb for a taxi. Quickly a man whose business was sex appeared and engaged him in conversation. One of the waitresses left the pub and positioned herself between the two men, hailed a taxi, and saw the young man off. I caught her attention as she came back through the door and mouthed, "Good job and thank you." She smiled at me and said, "Someone had to. It was the right thing to do." All of this took place while the musicians stoically played Irish jigs and reels.

At Mass the following morning I saw the green-shirted man from the pub. He was seated in front of me, alert, confident, and unscathed; his foolishness from the night before forgotten, I am sure. I wondered if he remembered his guardian angels from Murphy's in his prayers. Vietnamese ask, "Does a cake have bones?" when the answer to a question is obviously no.

These questions appear at the end of an old folk tale about an evil stepmother who favors her own children: "Does a stepmother ever love her stepchildren?" "Does a cake have bones?"

Perfidy is a human trait. In this country, when a person cheats, or lies, or says one thing and does another, people say of this person, "A tongue has no bones."

Although I took seriously the various warnings I received about my safety and activities, I think the dangers were overstated. The good deed of the barkeep and his staff toward the green-shirted lad, and the daily assistance and pleasantries I received are the norm.

GUEST WORKERS: The nuns awoke at 4 a.m. and by 6:30 a.m. they had prayed, sung, and breakfasted. Sometimes they telephoned me before 7 a.m. We would discuss my teaching jobs and their work. They gave me advice and extended invitations. Moreover, they sometimes asked for assistance, which I always tried to provide.

One morning I got a call from a sister who asked, "Do you remember agreeing to let three young Germans stay at your house while they explore Saigon?" She reminded me that the request to find beds for these university students had come from a German priest whose nephew was one of the travelers.

Years ago Em Thy, my landlady lived in Dresden as part of the East German guest worker program to assist impoverished Vietnamese. For two years she cleared tables and washed dishes in the cafeteria of a Workers Paradise munitions factory. Em Thy has no fond memories of that experience. She did not like the cold room she shared with four other guest workers, the way the German workers treated her, or how she and other Vietnamese were insulted and hassled on the street by "anti-Asian hooligans." Her feelings about Germans were not ambiguous.

Today, thousands of Vietnamese work abroad, mostly in menial jobs. In the media they are referred to as export labor. To relieve domestic unemployment and lessen trade imbalances, the state encourages this export.

Two of the visiting Germans (a male and female) were tall and blond, just like the stereotype. The other German, short and dark, had been born in East Germany of Vietnamese parents who had been guest workers. These 25-year-old architecture students were about to begin their final year of university. My fears about how they would behave, and about Em Thy's reaction to them, were unfounded. They were intelligent, curious, and grateful for the accommodations. They charmed Em Thy and I noted a hint of nostalgia when she told them about her experiences in Germany.

Four nuns escorted them from the airport to my house. It was an outing for the sisters. They brought fruit. We celebrated the students' arrival with mangos and tea. Their first order of business after the nuns had left was to confirm that they could stay without charge. The nuns had told them so, but they wanted to make sure. I gave them a set of keys and cautioned them about cultural differences and what the Vietnamese expected of them. I told them to stay together.

The Vietnamese-German was carrying a large sum of cash, a gift from his parents to both their families—examples of family loyalty and export labor remitting money. Keeping money in the house worried me, but there was no realistic alternative. It took him two days to make contact with his relatives and deliver the cash.

AN EXTRA FEE: One of my students, Hoang, had recently returned from Russia where she had worked for six years. At 26, she arrived at her parents' house in Saigon with baggage, gifts, and two sons. Their father did not want to leave his country and she did not want to stay in Russia. It was early August, one month before the start of school. Her children needed birth certificates to enroll and the school would not accept their Russian ones. The authorities told Hoang they could not possibly process her applications for Vietnamese birth certificates in such a short span of time, unless...unless she paid an "extra fee," which she did. Hoang believes that even if she had applied for the birth certificate in January, they would have asked her for extra money because their positions allowed them to, and because they assumed that she, having worked in a foreign country, must be rich.

VIETNAMESE WHO RETURN: Every year thousands of Vietnamese who fled the communist takeover and the difficult times that followed the war return. They are called Việt Kiều and are further identified by adding the name of the country they settled in. Việt Kiều Mỹ are Vietnamese who live in America. Those from England are called Việt Kiều Anh, returnees from Australia are Việt Kiều Úc, and French-Vietnamese are Việt Kiều Pháp.

Ho Chi Minh, who led Vietnam to independence, left Vietnam in 1911 to work and travel the world. He worked in London and Paris, and even visited the United States. In Moscow, he studied Leninism and returned to Vietnam in 1941 as a dedicated communist (some say as an agent under Soviet control). Uncle Ho was one of the first Việt Kiều.

Since 1987, economic necessity and a desire to reconcile have resulted in some government policies conciliatory to overseas Vietnamese who wish to do business or live in Vietnam again. Thousands have returned, bringing with them their money, experience, and a can-do attitude. Many have United States pensions, which enable them to retire in Vietnam, where the dollar goes a long way.

Most come for a short stay to see family and friends they haven't seen in decades. Others come with uninhibited enthusiasm and bold schemes to better Vietnam and enrich themselves. Notwithstanding why Việt Kiều return, their memories of Vietnam have been clouded by time. Coming back, their expectations are unrealistic. Vietnam has changed and so have they.

Unfortunately, local residents view them as having condescending attitudes and contradictory Western values. It explains why many Việt Kiều come and go, never having accomplished anything in Vietnam.

Lien introduced himself to me on a Sunday morning as I exited church. He was 5' 4", nattily dressed, and articulate. He had left Vietnam by boat in 1976, at age 21, alone. One year later, by way of Thailand, he landed in Arkansas and began working on a chicken farm. Somehow he made his way to Louisiana where he attended public schools, cleaning offices at night. In addition, for room and board, he slept next to a sick elderly man and assisted him during the night.

All his classmates in the postgraduate business school he attended were foreign born like him. Lien pointed out to me how this showed that Americans did not want to do business or work hard. I bit my tongue and did not tell him that the poor reputation and lower admission standards of that particular business school might just explain the absence of native-born Americans.

At age 51, he was wealthy after succeeding in the food business. His wife managed a small business in America and his two children had finished university. He was trolling at the church doors that Sunday morning for a native English speaker to teach in a new school he had founded. I turned him down, telling him I had been a lawyer and now was doing charity work. Lien countered with an offer to start a law firm in Saigon where he would get the clients and I would do the legal work. In Vietnam, he told me, a non-lawyer could own a law firm. I declined again, but immediately he suggested that I work for and invest in a charcoal-making company. All of his offers and my rejections took place on the church steps in the span of 10 minutes.

A few days later I became intrigued by the charcoal investment and gave Lien a call. I attended three meetings at which the original investors tried to sort out their problems. A Vietnamese woman had mortgaged her land to finance the $800,000 project. Her French partner was paid $200,000 for proprietary charcoal-making technology and had agreed to buy the project's output at a price sufficient to repay the bank loan in three years. The Frenchman would make a profit on the charcoal's resale and the woman was to make a 20% return on her investment. Everyone would win. Or so it seemed. However, there were problems.

The technology was not proprietary. In other words, the Frenchman had sold what he did not own. He also defaulted on his obligation to purchase the output of the charcoal factory. The woman would lose her land to the bank unless a new investor put up cash and guaranteed the loan. I was interested because charcoal is the country's primary cooking fuel. I was sure that restructuring the debt would put the project on a solid financial footing and I would recoup my investment with a profit. I stopped my financial analysis, technological investigation, and business plan development when I learned that the charcoal to be produced was not charcoal for cooking but activated charcoal to be used in gas masks destined for the Middle East. I reasoned that if it took me one month to learn that I was investing in gas masks, what else was I unaware of?

STARS IN THE NIGHT: Although I would not teach at Lien's school, I agreed to give the welcoming speech to the first class.

I stood in front of the students, many of them Communist Party members, and wondered about their backgrounds and what they had done in the war. Perhaps I had crossed paths with some of them back then. I mused that they were having the same thoughts. "Who is the American? Was he a soldier? Why is he standing in front of us?"

I was there to introduce them to the course, give them a test to determine which ability group they would be assigned to, and demonstrate enthusiasm for the project. The unstated reason for my presence was to lend credibility to Lien and his English language school. I was a senior native English speaker associated with the school. They would be impressed because most English teachers in Vietnam are Vietnamese who speak English poorly.

Ron, a 6' 4", 30-year-old self-described black American from Alabama stood by my side. Subsequently, I learned he was not a U.S. citizen, but an African who had immigrated to Alabama when he was 22 to live with his mother. Ron confided that as an American he received a better reception in Vietnam than as an African. He was going to teach the course. Ron was to be married soon and I had been invited to the wedding reception. In keeping with Vietnamese tradition, his fiancée insisted that they get her parents' approval. No one from Ron's family was available to speak on his behalf, so Lien acted as a proxy for Ron's father. They visited her family, presented them with symbolic gifts, and discussed the wedding plans. Lien steered the conversation away from difficult issues, extolled Ron's virtues, and successfully negotiated the wedding responsibilities. Although an uncle who had been a Viet Cong in the war objected to the marriage because he did not want an American in the family, the woman's father approved.

At the wedding party, the couple greeted guests at the banquet hall door. Ron and his bride wore white—she in a Western-style wedding dress, he in a tuxedo. During the three-hour meal, the bride changed her dress three times. Trusted family members sat at the gift table. On one side of a cardboard box, a mail slot had been carefully fashioned. After guests deposited envelopes containing cash (typically $12), they received an immediate acknowledgement and smile. Thank you notes were not sent or expected.

The 300 guests were served an eight-course meal and beer. The bride, groom, and a photographer visited each table. Glasses were raised, best wishes conveyed, and photos taken.

The band was loud. In turn, beautiful female singers crooned sweet love songs for $10 each. After three songs, the entertainers left the wedding party bound for another gig. Alluringly attired, with legs crossed and hair elegantly coiffured just so, they perched sidesaddle on the passenger seat as their motorcycle driver sped them from banquet hall to nightclub to disco. Stars in the night were never as breathtaking.

HISTORY IS TOO OLD: The West offers more opportunities for a better life, especially for women. Industry, politeness, and proper behavior are virtues Vietnamese women are expected to cultivate. These qualities are found less often in Western women, some of who are actually wanton.

Passion Sunflower, an American woman, visited in January 2003. In the wake of her departure were anxious nuns, disappointed seminarians, happy street children, and one very relieved 65-year-old American.

Before ever touching foot in Vietnam she lost her passport. Near the Great Wall in far-off China, it disappeared. The U.S. embassy told her it would take seven days to get a new one and the necessary visas. Upon hearing the awful news and the over-the-top distress in her voice, I sought paperwork for her in Saigon and thought of chartering an airplane to rescue her (yet again). However, it proved unnecessary because within hours of Sunflower's call to me her passport was turned in to the Chinese police.

Sunflower arrived in Saigon one day later than planned, contrite but unbowed. In the taxi from the airport she barked, "Does this here country have cows? And what is a Sai?"

"What do you mean, sweet Passion?" I asked.

"I want to know what is 'gon,'" she responded. The questions one asks can be quite revealing. They often lead to silence and confusion.

Sunflower was on a one-year sabbatical from a former growth company that had lost its way. I sold my stock in it when I learned that the human resources department ran the company. She was trying to find herself—and a husband, too. During one of our conversations she stated that she did not like history. "It is too old for me," was her reasoned explanation. Unexpectedly, she then proclaimed, "I wish my father wasn't a man." I quickly changed the subject.

This wonderful woman was very busy. She spent each day shopping, napping, sightseeing, regaining her strength, chilling out, emailing, resting, and enjoying "eating experiences." In addition, she taught English to street children at a residential shelter run by a non-profit organization. On Fridays, Passion accompanied me to the seminary where I taught English to 15 young men. She and they had a great time, and they learned some English, too. Twice the seminarians came to my house to cook Vietnamese meals for her and twice they took her to restaurants.

One evening two of my students, a nun and a Vietnamese teacher of English, prepared a meal in my kitchen. Two Irishmen, friends of Sunflower from her hellacious Dublin days, and who were sightseeing in Saigon, joined us. The wide-ranging conversation extended our dinner and twice the good nun called her superior to get permission to stay longer.

On another day, Sunflower sped off by motorbike to a recording studio. She had agreed to provide the voiceover for a script I had edited for a documentary on poverty in Vietnam. The documentary will be used outside Vietnam to help raise funds for the Vietnamese poor. Her melodious voice will open many a purse.

We had only one disagreement during her stay in Vietnam. On her arrival, I explained that I had entered her in the All-Catholic Vietnam Beauty and Swimsuit Contest. It was a fundraising event and her $62 entrance fee had already been paid. Sunflower was outraged. She did not want to parade around Saigon in her bikini. Eventually, after reminding her that the contest was a charitable event, she agreed to endure the awful experience.

Of course, there was no All-Catholic Vietnam Beauty and Swimsuit Contest. It was a practical joke that I thought Sunflower would enjoy, but instead it made her suspicious of me and vengeful. Sad to say, she would not have won the contest even if there had been one. However, I am sure she would have gotten a prize for quantity. She is a foot taller and bigger all around than Vietnamese women are. Shortly after I admitted that there was no contest, she told me that my American publisher had called to inform me that they had decided not to publish my book. It was not true, but I skipped a few heartbeats. Women always know where and when men are vulnerable.

Before her arrival I had been concerned that she would not like Vietnamese food, but I was wrong. She ate it for lunch and dinner each day. "I don't get sick," were her words of praise. However, it took me a while to learn what she was eating for breakfast. One of the first things she did when she arrived was buy a supply of Coca Cola, candy, and whipped cream. She marked these treasures with her name and placed them in my refrigerator.

I encountered her in the kitchen one morning. Her eyes were vacant and her cheeks bulged; she was eating candy topped with whipped cream and washing it down with Coca Cola. A simian grin crossed her face. "It's what my mother used to give me for breakfast when I was a child," she said. Sunflower gave up her mother to avoid my scorn.

The days before her departure were a whirlwind of activities. She was invited to a party given by the staff of a medical clinic. Sunflower, ever watchful, ever opportunistic, targeted a possible husband, but instead of the doctor she came home with the door prize: an MP3 player. It was a different kind of plaything.

She bought clothing for 200 street children and agreed to fund scholarships for several of them. Her generosity with her time and money has helped the poor of this country.

My son Tim and sister-in-law Daisy Mae visited me in December 2003. They were good and responsible citizens, easy to satisfy, no lying about, no outrageous dietary demands, and no entanglements. They arrived with their travel documents intact.

We spent two days at a beach far from Saigon enjoying the water, food, and quiet. Tim and I traveled to Hanoi where we won a singing contest in a sedate Vietnamese restaurant. The father and son team was unbeatable that Christmas season.

Upon returning to New York, Daisy Mae summed up her impressions of Saigon with these memorable and now oft-quoted words: "Saigon is busy and crazy, like Martin."

Seventeen

HANOI AND BEYOND

Deep in the human unconscious is a perverse need for a logical universe that makes sense. But the real universe is always one step beyond logic.
-Frank Herbert

The Lac Viet (People of the Valley) emerged in the Red River Delta during the third millennium BC. In time, they united with other tribes from southern China who had also immigrated into the Delta. A single ethnic group, the Vietnamese, resulted from the merger of these clans. Over the centuries, values, traditions, and legends that are central to Vietnamese culture took root in the delta among these people. By the 16th century, Hanoi had developed into the urban center of northern Vietnam. Today, it is the capital of Vietnam and has a population of nearly three million people.

Hanoi is smaller than Saigon, more orderly, and not as busy. People there seem more reserved than in Saigon and more traditional. Wide, tree-lined boulevards and colonial buildings decorate the city. My Saigon friends do not understand why I like Hanoi. They do not want to spend time in the North.

*****

BARGAIN-SEEKING COMPANIONS: Doi was a thin 75-year-old man with long, bony fingers and a drawn face. We shared a compartment on the Unification Express from Saigon to Hanoi. Although we were strangers, we conversed easily.

The room was advertised as having four berths with soft mattresses. The cost was $55 for the 33-hour train ride. Two less expensive accommodations were also available: a six-bed hard mattress chamber, and a bench car without cushions.

The train lurched and then gained speed as we left the Saigon station. Doi commented on our luck; we were the only two in the four-bed compartment. We took the lower bunks and stored our luggage on the top ones.

It was going to be a comfortable journey. The small room was clean. The bedding was fresh. We had a sink and running water. There was a toilet at each end of the car. The one marked "Western" had a seat and the other was tagged "Squat."

Shortly after departing, the conductor opened our door, looked around, and then left without a word. He was back in five minutes with a couple and their two small children. After lowering our luggage to the floor, they quickly climbed to the top berths. A child and parent shared each bunk. We now had six people in a space meant for four—not so comfortable anymore. Doi explained that the conductor had taken a bribe to upgrade the four from the car with uncushioned wooden benches to our luxury class. There was nothing we could do about it. The man and two children were quiet, but the woman was a talker and she was loud. During the day she was merely annoying, but at night I could not sleep.

The lights were out and she was in the bunk above me talking at her husband across the narrow aisle. She went on and on. The husband was quiet. Doi said nothing. Finally, I shouted at her in Vietnamese to stop talking. Her husband admonished her, "I told you to be quiet. This man is angry and he understands what you say. The foreigner is going to do something if you talk again." Thankfully she said no more, and we all slept.

The next day Doi and I talked as the land flashed by. He was going to visit relatives he had not seen in 50 years. Like many people his age, Doi had fled the North in 1954 when, pursuant to the Geneva Accords, Vietnam was divided in two. He chose not to live in the North under the communists, but his three brothers stayed in Hanoi. By 1975, Doi was a captain in the ARVN.

Doi had been touched by the war and its aftermath. One brother never came back from the war. Doi's seven years in post-war prison were a lost lifetime. He believed the communists made a mistake in the way they treated their Southern countrymen after the war ended.

During the long ride we discussed many things. Doi's English was good and I wondered where he had learned it and how he had maintained his fluency. He explained that after being released from jail in 1983 he could not find work, so he helped his wife in her small shop where she sold old things. Today they sell 60-cent CDs and $1 DVDs to tourists. He learned English at the store.

The discs are copied in Vietnam and China and sold without royalties paid to the copyright holders. The quality of the pirated product is uncertain. Many DVD movies are perfect, but some are out of focus, with garbled words, missing segments, and jerky movements. One memorable DVD I purchased had English subtitles from a different movie. Dissatisfied customers can exchange discs of unacceptable quality. The returned items go back on the shelf.

At one point I told him that as I get older I spend more time alone, away from family and friends, and that solitude, the bitter fruit of age, invites unwanted reflection and introspection. I am troubled not by fantasy, but by reality. He replied that as he ages he knows more about life, but is less able to influence those around him. He often knows what the outcome of situations will be but cannot stop his family from making mistakes. I, too, can only voice warnings to those close to me, and they usually go unheeded. Assets, genes, and social status can be transferred to one's children, but not wisdom.

Doi was noncommittal when I told him that Americans do not believe the family is the center of their life. Instead of looking to family for strength and guidance, Americans largely rely on themselves.

The train stopped briefly just before entering Hanoi. The conductor appeared and told the parents in the upper beds to come with him but to leave their children. Within minutes, an inspector who had boarded when the train stopped entered the compartment to count the passengers. Doi would not confirm or deny that the children were his. The inspector took one look at me and did not ask. He left but returned shortly with the parents. Everyone was smiling. The parents joined their children and the train continued to Hanoi. I asked Doi if the inspector had been bribed. He said, "Yes, of course."

Our bargain-seeking companions hurriedly left the compartment as the train pulled into Hanoi Station. Doi and I lingered, talked briefly, and finally said our goodbyes. We did not exchange contact information; we would not be in touch again. Doi left the train to look for his brothers. I detrained, walked through the station, and hired a taxi. I wondered about the combination of fate and circumstances that had brought us together.

TAXI DRIVER: In cities all over the world, taxi rides can be an adventure for tourists. Passengers hope to reach their destinations safely and at a reasonable cost. Drivers try to maximize revenues.

Vietnamese do not tip. Nevertheless, drivers demand tips from unknowing Westerners, and sulk and carry on if they do not get one. One must be vigilant hailing a cab. Unlicensed taxis, "Mafia taxis" with crooked meters, patrol the streets looking for the unsuspecting. To hail one of them, especially for a foreigner, can be a harrowing experience. The drivers get physical if you object to the inflated fare, I know.

Reputable taxi companies compete with each other and have policies to protect their customers and businesses. Drivers are financially responsible for accidents and are fined for mistreating customers. Repairs and fines are paid from a substantial deposit the driver leaves with the company when he is hired. I prefer the Mai Linh Taxi Company because the meters are reliable and the drivers polite. The drivers have a 24-hour shift followed by a day off. The trunks of many taxis hold a metal pipe, thick stick, or knife for use during all-too-frequent traffic disputes.

Saigon has its share of dishonest drivers who take roundabout ways and try to charge more than the meter indicates. Nevertheless, they are angels compared to taxi drivers in Hanoi.

I had a dustup with a taxi driver who picked me up at the Hanoi train station. He would not turn the meter on and took off when I wanted to exit his cab. He wanted $5 for a $2 trip and when I refused he tried to force me out onto a dark street. I locked the back doors and explained, gently, why he was a difficult person. The situation became ugly with raised voices and provocative gestures on both sides. Finally, he took me to my hotel but would not let me out until I paid, but I would not pay until my bag and I were on the sidewalk. Hotel staff intervened to end the standoff. He did not get the inflated fare. That is how this driver makes his living—with deceit, intimidation, and confrontation. It is a well-practiced routine.

WADDAYOU WANT: One of Hanoi's famous landmarks is the badly weathered St. Joseph's Cathedral. The French built it 120 years ago on the site of an ancient pagoda. Communists closed it down in 1954 in an anti-colonial, doctrinaire spasm after the Catholic Church refused to allow the government to control its affairs. After many years church-state relations improved and the cathedral re-opened on Christmas Eve, 1990. Exactly who relented, and how a compromise was achieved, is not publicly known.

In May 2006 I attended Sunday Mass at the cathedral. Its interior is more attractive than its drab exterior. Stained glass windows, arches, a high-vaulted ceiling, touches of marble, and candlelight greeted me as I walked up the middle aisle to a pew on the left-hand side. A few moments after Mass began; a large Western man seated himself across the aisle from me. An old woman, her spine bent and her face parallel to the ground, was seated behind him. Her age, cane, traditional dress, and hair bun marked her as someone deserving of special respect. In wonder, I watched her poke the man in the right kidney with the top of her cane. When he did not react, she did it again. The man sighed audibly. Clearly agitated, he turned at the waist, looked down at the frail woman, and in a gravelly voice reminiscent of Leadbelly bellowed, "Waddayou want?"

A young woman hurried from the rear of the church and explained to the man that the woman wanted him to move to the pews on the left side of the basilica because that was where the men were supposed to sit. He was the only man on the women's side of the church. He moved, quickly and quietly, without theatrics, across the aisle. Amused parishioners shared looks of understanding and humor with the old woman. She beamed a triumphant, toothless smile to all.

Segregated seating at Mass is a Vietnamese custom. It is still practiced in Hanoi and in rural areas of Vietnam, but not in Saigon. The people I have asked do not know its origin.

FOREIGNER DISCOUNT: Although not as prevalent as in years past, many businesses employ a two-tier pricing system. Non-Vietnamese are charged more than Vietnamese for the same service or product. This reality, plus the currency, language differences, and negotiability of most prices, makes many transactions uncertain and often frustrates foreigners. I tended to get a little too involved in the process. Other than the effect on my ego, bargaining did not make any difference because everything was so cheap, even at foreigners' prices.

Until 2003, Vietnam Airlines, the national carrier, charged foreigners double the Vietnamese fare. The government maintained that this discrimination was justified because insurance costs more for aliens. The explanation was unsatisfactory and the unfair pricing was criticized and ridiculed. The airfare policy was changed so that a single fare applies to foreigners and Vietnamese alike. Everyone now pays the same to fly from

Saigon to Hanoi. However, the locals grumble that it is not fair because they pay more than before and foreigners pay less.

On prior visits I paid $10 for a taxi from the Hanoi airport to the city center. Fortunately, a friend told me about a 12-passenger van that would take me there for only $1.25. Before departure the operator collected fares and gave each passenger a ticket. From me he demanded $3. I responded politely in his language that I would only pay $1.25. However, he persisted, so I asked, somewhat louder, "Why?"

"You are a foreigner, you pay more," was his reasoned answer.

After having been paid by the other passengers he again demanded $3 from me and said he would put me off the van if I did not pay.

I reverted to English and told him he would need police help to do that. "I want a foreigner discount," I demanded.

An elderly man enthusiastically translated my words into Vietnamese for the benefit of all. People turned, grinned, and looked at me with interest. The driver settled for $1.25, gave me his winter face, and the trip began. As the van moved into the city, we glared at one another in his rearview mirror. A young Proctor & Gamble employee seated next to me showed me her ticket with $1.25 stamped on it. This slight Vietnamese woman said I was right not to pay more than the other passengers.

"Driver keeps extra, not van company, that's why police not come. Vietnam wants to become a strong country. We must stop cheating foreigners."

LEGENDS: In olden times, people in every part of the world saw many things they did not understand. They looked to nature for answers and when none was forthcoming, myths involving the supernatural were crafted to instruct and clarify. Fables related earlier in this book about the Man in the Moon and the Milky Way are two examples. Zeus, Pandora, and the Olympians are ancient Western myths.

The Vietnamese of long ago were ignorant of the fact that moisture collected by winds traveling over the ocean caused the annual monsoons. The rain's yearly three-month advance and subsequent three-month retreat was an enigma to them. It was explained through the fable of the princess who was loved by both the prince of water and the prince of mountains. The king told these rivals that he would give his daughter to the one who arrived at the palace at sunrise the following morning with the best gifts. The mountain prince arrived before sunup, presented his gifts, won the princess and immediately took her to his mountain citadel. The water prince arrived on time and with better presents, but the king's daughter was already gone. He felt cheated because his rival had come to the palace before the appointed time. Determined to capture the princess, the aggrieved noble and his allies, rain and ocean, attacked the mountain prince with great force. After three months of being furiously assaulted, the rains gradually ended, the mountain prince regained his strength, and peace returned to the land. Each year at the same time, the water prince renews his attack. For three months he fights his way up the mountain pursuing the mountain prince and the princess, but then he loses his strength as the monsoons end and slowly retreats to the ocean.

In antiquity, there was no explanation for the differences between the ethnic Vietnamese (Kinh) and the minority tribes (Montagnards). They looked unalike, their languages were dissimilar, and their cultures were different. Yet they lived interspersed in the same areas. The legend of the dragon and the fairy princess explained this mystery.

The dragon is a mythical creature common to ancient Eastern and Western legends. In the West it is a malevolent, giant, lizard-like monster that does harm to mankind. Grendel, the man-eating night prowler featured in the 8th-century A.D. heroic epic Beowulf, is an example. In contrast, the serpentine Eastern dragon is benevolent towards people. It symbolizes good fortune and is central to the origin myth of the Vietnamese.

Legend has it that the people of Vietnam are the children of a marriage between a lonely dragon that wandered south from China and a fairy princess. Their union produced one hundred eggs. The dragon took fifty to the seashore. The remaining fifty went to the mountains with the fairy. The children who were born and settled on the seashore are the Kinh; they make up 85% of Vietnam's population. The eggs raised by the princess in the mountains produced the 50-plus ethnic tribes that live in the middle and northern regions of Vietnam. This fantasy teaches that the Vietnamese are a distinct, related people and, interestingly, that Chinese blood flows in their veins. China frequently refers to Vietnam as its "younger brother." "A drop of blood is more important than a lake of water," is a Vietnamese aphorism.

Notwithstanding their often-violent historical relations, the Vietnamese are fully aware of their cultural debt to China. They also recognize that its vast size and power limit Vietnam's actions. Vietnam would be unwise to advance ideas with which China disagrees. Her polices are not likely to veer far from China's.

ETHNIC TRIBES: The French called them Montagnards, meaning hill people. Today Vietnam's government refers to them as national minorities or ethnic tribes. Nevertheless, many Vietnamese call them mọi (savage), reflecting a mindset that considers the hill people culturally and intellectually inferior. During the war, my Vietnamese counterpart and the soldiers of the battalion called my ethnic bodyguard mọi instead of his given name. This feeling of superiority and contempt is ancient.

In reality, the minorities were the original inhabitants of Vietnam. They were here before the Lac Viet. Their geographic origins remain uncertain and are disputed. It is known, however, that they settled in the fertile lowlands near the sea but were forced into the less desirable and less productive highlands by the Lac Viet.

The Montagnards are Vietnamese only because they live in Vietnam, not because they share a common culture or ethnicity with the descendants of the Lac Viet. Linguistically and racially they belong to the Malayo-Polynesian and Mon-Khmer groups. The minorities differ in appearance and culture, one group from the other, and from the Kinh. They all speak different languages.

Sapa, in the mountainous north near the Chinese border, is home to several ethnic tribes. Having heard accounts of the region's beauty and the unique Montagnard culture, I traveled there.

The night train from Hanoi to Lao Cai Station was delayed while a dispute over my accommodation was sorted out. As in many such instances, the argument of a foreign man like me was listened to and then summarily overruled. The conductor called the police because I would not let more than four people in my compartment. I stood in the door. "I arrest you soon," the policeman promised. As with the train from Saigon to Hanoi, I ended up with less space than I had bargained for, but I learned that if you do not move they will not push. I got a small refund, enough to soothe my ego.

The Vietnamese have treated the ethnic tribes similar to the way Americans have treated the Native Americans. Notwithstanding agreements to reserve their land for them, and programs intended to integrate them into Vietnamese society, the ethnic tribes have been marginalized and their land taken. There is no love lost between these two groups. Many of the minorities supported America during the war. Their dubious loyalty and strategic location in the mountainous regions bordering Laos, Cambodia, and China cause ongoing security concerns for the government.

Afraid of what priests might teach the tribes, and concerned with where the tribes' loyalty lays, the authorities prohibit clergy in some areas and limit their activities in others. In Sapa, I visited four churches while trekking through H'mong villages. The villagers told me that they were "special Catholics" and could not have priests. "We can only pray together on Sundays."

As I passed through these hamlets I flashbacked to my life as a combat advisor. My bodyguard then was a H'mong named Han. He was 28, short, loyal, and usually conducted himself like a soldier. In 1963, we walked together through Kinh villages in the Mekong Delta searching for Viet Cong. American advisors ironically called those treks "a walk in the sun." On jungle trails and through streams and waterways, Han walked ahead of me, alert and quick to react. He had a strong sense of self-preservation. If he perceived danger, he would not advance. Sometimes I went alone and later he would catch up, muttering softly and glancing disapprovingly my way.

It is possible that 40 years later I had trekked through Han's village. These were his people. He was not with me on this walk; I do not know his fate. This time it was not dangerous. It was peaceful, pleasant, and enjoyable. It was a different kind of walk in the sun.

LANDLADY'S SURPRISE: Upon returning to Saigon from the North I found that Em Thy, her two children, and her servant girl had moved into my house. They had settled (with all their furniture) on the third floor. The owner of the small house she had been living in had suddenly taken it back. He was demolishing it to build a modern one. Em Thy needed a place to stay and I was away and…and "Why you come back early?"

She explained that she could not move to another house until her monk fortune-teller told her which date would be lucky for moving. She then proposed that we share the house; I would only have to pay one-half the rent.

"It not crowded," she said, "and my husband come home once a month, sometimes."

I put my bag down, found a chair and, although I do not remember exactly, probably buried my face in my hands.

Nothing ventured, nothing gained. We negotiated. Thao and I would have an en suite bedroom and office. Em Thy would cook, clean, and pay the utilities. The reduced rent appealed to me. Although it is common practice to rent a room in a private residence, I wondered aloud about the colonel husband and his reaction.

"When you agree, I tell husband," Em Thy replied.

I agreed, not really knowing what it all meant. Thao had doubts about the arrangement.

The next day Em Thy, her entourage and furniture moved out. "Husband say no," she sighed. Thao exhaled; she did not want another woman in the house.

BELOW THE STOMACH: In November 2005 I gave up my lease and returned to New York for two months. I wanted to see my American children, fall, and the Internal Revenue Service. In trepidation, Thao inquired, "You come back?"

Em Thy volunteered to hold the house rent-free until my return. "You good man, do charity work for Vietnamese. You no trouble man." However, my return date was uncertain and the house she had been renting us was too big, so I declined.

A Japanese man wanted to rent the house from Em Thy. I agreed to let them use my living room to negotiate the terms. There were two sessions. He agreed to pay $600 a month, six months in advance, plus a $600 down payment. Em Thy agreed to pay for new slipcovers for the sofa and chairs, a new refrigerator, and an interior paint job. She told me after the second meeting that he was a difficult man.

When he asked for a third meeting, she told me not to smile when he came and to say they must use the less comfortable kitchen. The man explained that his company would not approve the lease. When she refused to make further concessions, he asked for his deposit back. Em Thy said she would think about it. She had already spent $300 to comply with his renovation requirements. To her disadvantage, the house had been off the market for two weeks during the negotiations. I told her to keep the $600.

"My husband say same thing."

When told that he was to get none of his deposit returned the man asked Em Thy and me to dinner. We agreed to meet two nights later at a popular local restaurant. I had eaten there several times, most recently one week before when the chicken legs, rice, and vegetables I had carefully chosen from the lengthy menu turned out to be a heaping plate of boiled chicken feet and rice.

The Japanese man arrived with an interpreter who spoke English, Japanese, and Vietnamese. As it turned out we did not need anyone who spoke Vietnamese because Em Thy did not come. "You go, you go," she insisted at the last minute. "I mad. No deposit, you tell him."

When asked, "Where is Em Thy?" I, always truthful, replied, "Not here."

It was a grill restaurant where customers cook meat at their tables. In the center of our table, a three-legged clay pot held burning charcoal, which spewed sparks and ash with each pass of the rotating wall fans. Unwilling to expose myself to the germs of the hundreds of previous users, I asked the waiter for a clean grill, but was turned down. "Fire clean, fire clean," was the exasperated response. Worriedly, I placed the ruler-thin strips of beef on the blackened, food-encrusted grill.

The interpreter explained that the pot cooking on our table contained goat stomach soup, but after a minute of reflection, he corrected himself. "Below the stomach."

As an appetizer, we were served "chicken egg before it come out." Floating in the steaming broth were two egg sack organs, each containing about 30 eggs in various stages of development. Pinhead-size eggs were at the top of the sack, while larger eggs were located at the bottom ready for laying. Since shells are formed just prior to laying, there were none in the soup.

The eatery brewed its own beer, which sold for three cents a glass. Customers could fill two-liter bottles with beer to take home at a cost of eight cents. Partially covered with a tin roof, the restaurant seated 400 people on one level. At the entrance, goats and pigs roasted over charcoal fires.

During the soup course, the man argued his case once more and asked me to press for the return of his deposit. I dutifully explained why he was not going to get it. The next day the man complained to the ward leader who told Em Thy to return $100. She was allowed to keep $500 because of her expenses and the trouble he had caused. The official explained to Em Thy that it was good for the ward's reputation to give him something back.

A PAIR OF SOCKS: Upon my return to Vietnam, Thao and I checked into a local hotel. The room was dirty, dark, and tiny. A small, naked window faced the hallway, which serviced stairs, an elevator, and seven other rooms.

Late into the night intoxicated men from the North used the hallway to praise loudly the merits of communism and the women they shared that night. They bounced against my door as they stumbled from room to room.

Rent was $10 a night, laundry not included. The Vietnamese paid less, I am sure. The laundry charge was 12 cents per piece and ironing cost double that. The launderer told us that a pair of socks was two pieces. Thao negotiated and succeeded in getting a lower rate for ironing, and by tying the socks together they were treated as one piece.

The fridge did not work. I complained. For the next three days a number of men inspected it and consulted with one another but the fridge was never fixed. I complained again and was told it was unnecessary to fix it because I was not using it. They looked perplexed and a little anxious when I heatedly explained that I was not using it because it did not work.

We left the hotel the following morning and moved into a pleasant rooming house. I was offered a comfortable, bright room for $12 a night, or, if I chose to pay monthly in advance, the rental would be $10 a night. Thinking it would take at least a month to find and rent a house we liked, I paid the monthly rate to save $60. Surprisingly, the owner returned $40 when we moved into a new house 10 days later.

THE BATHROOM EXHAUSTS INTO THE KITCHEN: I asked Em Thy to help us find a house to rent. She enthusiastically agreed but warned me that rents had gone up since I had left. She volunteered not to charge the owner a commission and explained that would keep the rent down. At one house I looked at, the 65-year-old owner and I spoke over tea. It was a spacious, nicely furnished villa with a courtyard, but he wanted more than I was willing to pay. He talked about his four years in East Germany where he had worked during the 1980s supervising Vietnamese guest workers. He was surprisingly candid and critical of the government. Although a former Viet Cong and present party member, he said, "I don't know why I came back. I should have stayed in the West. Here the government steals too much and the people are poor." Moreover, in speaking of the Vietnamese media he remarked, "One-third true, two-thirds lies."

We finally rented a two-bedroom house in the center of Saigon. It was not as nice as the house we had the previous year, but it suited us. It had air-conditioning and a desk. However, it was dark and the only windows faced the street. One bedroom had no window. The bathrooms had exhaust fans; downstairs they vented into the kitchen and upstairs they vented into the bedrooms. An Indian restaurant, motorbike parking lot, and beer distributor were my near neighbors. Noise started at six a.m. and continued until one a.m. The exhaust fan from the restaurant kitchen blew onto our bedroom balcony, where our laundry was hung to dry. Our clothes smelled of curry.

I was back in Vietnam, this beautiful country with these wonderful people, where at every turn the unexpected happens.

★

CONCLUSION

I have come to the conclusion that my subjective account of my motivation is largely mythical on almost all occasions. I don't know why I do things.
-J.B.S. Haldane

A Vietnamese adage, probably derived from a saying attributed to Heraclitus, informs, "No one swims twice in the same river." The water constantly changes so it is never the same river, and so, too, with life. People and circumstances change and no two experiences are identical. Generally, old sayings are reliable, but not always.

My year as a soldier in Vietnam had a profound effect on my life. It shaped me in ways I did not appreciate back then, and I would need years to understand its totality. Although my experiences this time differed vastly from 1962/63, some things were the same. I had been a volunteer both times, and both times I departed feeling good about myself.

It was in my self-interest to volunteer 15 hours a week with the poor, the blind, and the homeless. As before, my life was an adventure and I benefited from the experience far more than those whom I had come to help. This time I had the opportunity to act in ways that accord with how I think about myself. This time I attempted to live up to my aspirations. At my age, this was my last chance to be who I wanted to be. What I was doing was neither a sacrifice nor praiseworthy. My effort on behalf of these people was a small thing and it was for me. I know that.

My life in Vietnam was good for me. As with my military tour, it was more than I expected or deserved. I was doing exactly what I wanted to do and I was being formed by what I was doing. We are what we have done, for sure.

At times, the Irish in me came out and I wondered how I could be so happy, but that bell did not ring often. Sometimes I struggled, but it was internally; there were no out of control situations and no malignant fantasies.

Everything seemed more natural in Vietnam, less forced and stressful than in the United States. I was useful and appreciated. I attached myself to the Vietnamese quite easily. It was what I wanted. I do not want to forget any of the happenings that are part of the best years of my life. Soon none of this will matter. Soon I will be another old lawyer repetitiously tidying up his room, searching the neat arrangement of his sparse possessions for memories, passions, and meanings.

I had no serious trouble of any kind in Vietnam. In fact, I was treated with great respect because I was an old man, a teacher, and an American. Why Americans are shown respect I am not sure, especially given our two countries' 50-plus years of contentious history. The Vietnamese like Americans and our culture. Notwithstanding, school children have sung the following rhyme as they passed me by: "Chinese, Japanese, Vietnamese; Donkey, Monkey, Yankee." A chant informed by familiarity, perhaps. Just as we have grouped them together and given them the same "-ese" name ending because we cannot or will not distinguish among them, sometimes they put us in a category where they think we belong.

Even though many of the foregoing stories in this book are negative, I have a high regard for the Vietnamese. What I like most about these people are their virtues, which flow from traditional values that emphasize family, character, and respect for authority. If fortunate, wisdom arrives unannounced; it cannot be learned or inherited. On the other hand, virtue has to be cultivated. Without care and diligence, one cannot acquire it.

The family is at the heart of Vietnamese motives, plans, and actions. Concern for the family, as well as for its protection and support, largely explains why and how they conduct themselves. Woe to the child who acts contrary to the wishes of his or her parents or grandparents.

I hope traditional values will prevail in the contest with Western ideas. Even though this has not been the case in other countries in this region, I believe it will be so in Vietnam. Not because their values are superior to Western ones—they are only different—but because they account for these wonderful people.

The Vietnamese are determined and they endure. These qualities are cousins; one sets the goal, the other provides the strength to reach it. They are warm, resourceful, hardworking, patient, and pragmatic. We in the West should aspire to these virtues. Although perhaps not evident to foreign tourists fearfully quivering at curbside, at the very core of Vietnamese behavior is their individual generosity. A greeting, a nod, or any sign of respect will draw out this admirable quality. They quickly and readily show their interest and concern, and share whatever they have.

Vietnamese are optimistic about their future. They are born entrepreneurs. Many have small businesses that sell, produce, or provide a service. The confidence is warranted, but real progress for the people has to await a free press and the rule of law, as well as the formation of multiple political parties, consumer advocacy organizations, environmental agencies, and other pressure groups.

There is a lot of suffering, poverty, and injustice in Vietnam, but it is not a grim place. It is vibrant and exciting. I keep thinking there must be a way to improve the lives and circumstances of those who are unfortunate, to help bring about positive change. I know I cannot do a lot about it, but I wish I could. There are too many obstacles, including corruption, greed and government policies.

Those who are successful and happy fool themselves if they attribute it to a careful plan. Prudent decisions, although important, play a small part in achieving happiness and prosperity. In reality, chance and its traveling companion, risk, govern our life's journey. We neither know nor control our destination.

Wealth and poverty do not level out unaided. Time guarantees nothing; it fashions and disposes as it pleases. Some people are left wanting while others have more than they need. For some, suffering brings wisdom and hope. For others, it just humiliates and angers.

The poor, the needy, and the unfortunate will always be around us. We must act to reduce poverty and suffering by bringing about change. Arguments for the well-off that are based on merit or birthright are not persuasive in the face of dire need. Without change, the poor will remain in the unmerciful hands of suffering and grief. We are all responsible and we are all at risk.

Despite its ancient roots, Vietnam is a young country whose leaders have ignored the virtue of mercy and economic law in favor of corrupt monetary rewards. The government acted cruelly and ill-advisedly in the wake of reunification. Injustice and abuse of power are prevalent. Policies to correct some of the wrongs and help the country develop have been instituted, but it is uncertain if the government will or can take the actions necessary to better people's lives.

There is little harmony in Vietnam today. The yin and yang are not in equilibrium. The delicate balance of opposites, which makes life satisfying, is missing. Equilibrium is destiny. It is nature's goal. Excess gives rise to its opposite. This process is evident today in Vietnam. The ruler is not benevolent. The moral order of the universe has been disregarded.

★

NOTES

NOTE 1. p.19

MAN'S LETTER TO MRS. CLINTON

Her Excellency 1998

Dear Madame,

As I understand, you are very busy person and not have enough time to do all that you do. I am honour to have your email address from one of the American family especially from the day your family had visited Vietnam last year. Congratulation for the successful meaningful trip. I have no chance to see you in person, but I am very happy to see all over the places you have visited on the television. I keep wonder if I should write to you or not for a long, long time. Finally I decide to write. As I understand you are a wonderful person and do many good things for many people.

May I take this opportunity to present to you my story, it might or might not interest you, but I hope it does. It is one of a very typical story for many Vietnamese families who work with America and are left behind the war. I am a child growing up in one of the family that my father do service for the American army since 1964 to 1975. We are still survive and enduring the hard time.

Being a very famous and powerful person like you, I wonder if your life ever go through a very difficult situation. I learn you were, because I had read one of your book was public about your personal life. It's a very interesting book. Read your book it help me to understand more that to handle everything in one life is not so easy, we need to try our best to go through everything.

Dear Madame, to return to my story, my name is Man, I was born in 1967 after a very famous year 1968 when the South of Vietnam almost fell into the hand of the North Vietnam. Luckily it not fell, so I can spend 8 years in love and care of my parents till 1975. Even though, I understand from my father that there are many big events that was happened then in 1972.

April 30 1975, I was eight years old, a child, you might think I forget all the past but the fact, the truth is everything is still deeply in my heart and it causes suffering. I am a child with a father who work for the fallen Government, so all my brothers and sisters and my mom, in a very horrible situation by then.

My father was put in jail right after the 30 of April in Lam Son one of the area in the South of Central Vietnam. After one year and some more months when he was so sick they release him to die. We all be send to the "Economic Zone" call Hoa Nguyen. It also locate in South of Central Vietnam, where is the place that inside my home I called it a house but in fact it is a roof with the leaves. My family was in safer place but my father lived and we were forced to come to "Economic Zone" in order my father not be put back in jail. I can look through the forest and I can see the wild animal like tiger and bear. We all got malaria and had days without food. I remember a day all my family with six people only have 250 gram of rice. We have to well cook it in order to get the glue from it to mix with the manioc powder to service our meal for whole day long with salt, one week we can afford to go to the market to buy the bottom of the leg of the cow to cook in order to make the soup better taste with instant noodle or have one meal with rice no vegetables. All my brothers and sisters jump happily and call that a 'Party', because our stomachs were burned for the whole week without food. I even remember one day we are out of food we try to dig the vegetable under the ground it call 'Cu Nan'. Some one told us to keep it in the salt water several days in order to get the poison away. We keep for three days and then cook it. My father try first as he think he is responsible for our family if something happened he will manage it but children and wife too weak now. But it not happened as he thought. After he ate it, his head start turn around like the circle, and he can see one person become two in his eyes. Then we know the poison on the 'Cu Na' still a lot inside, and his body could not except it. Luckily no one died that day by food poisoning. We had to escape the Economic Zone to get out. We took the train from Nha Trang to go to Dong Nai province because we could not stand it any more with no food and sickness, we continue fight with our life, the area we come is not a good place but it just seem we have no choice, that area call --------------- District, ----------- Province. It away from Saigon many Km. Malaria was still in our blood so it continues acting and make all of us so sick. We had no money to buy medicine to treat it. My oldest brother fall all his hair out because of the sickness.

In town where we live there is one nurse name Mr Lanh, when we are so sick by malaria we can come and ask him to give us a shot to stop the fever but we have no money so we could not come to see him all the time. When we did go, we never paid at the visit until we have money later. This nurse know about that so he never ask just remind us when ever we can pay we need to pay him.

Our life was still so hard without rice, but we can plant some corn to replace 'Cu Nan' the name of the poison food that I never forget in my life, so scary, so painful. It is a long, difficult story how we survive. The point I would like to present to you, the reason I write, I have questions and would very much appreciate your concern and answer what can I do:

Question 1: As an officer to service the American army, my father was sentenced to an undetermined jail time. He was released from jail after one year plus 2 months because of his sickness and with the Humane Organization arranged by American Government we could not be considered to qualify as a family to American to immigrate in HO program. The program asks for three years jail, when we first try to fill out papers we were told if not three years, no matter the reason circumstance and many years of working with for America, it must be three years. I hope and pray there is way to explain terrible conditions, sick and worse than more jail time, my father who serves so bravely with America, can he and all my family be helped?

Question 2: If we are not allow to go with HO Program to America with the other Vietnamese who served with America, can the American Government give compensation for the Vietnamese soldiers who work for American Government that are left behind the war, as we are one family left without concern after war ended and treated like prisoners, even my brothers and sisters and my mother when we are put in the "Economic Zone" that we escape.

Question 3: My brothers and sisters and other children of the war who lost everything and treated badly with fathers in jail like us suffering with the war and no opportunity to learn or do anything even now we have some friends in America willing to help us but we can not get the visas to go to America to learn or do something useful for the rest of our life. We need help to get the visas to be able to accept the help that American citizens who are our friends want to give us.

Question 4: Where is the place or person that we can contact and get some help for all these matters?

I am so need of help now. Each year that goes by, it is sadder for us and the end of this does not happen. I hope you can help me in any way and I thank you for your concerns in advance. My family teach me to work hard to make life better, I am want to work and to make life better for others too. All help is highly appreciated, and for you to take the time to read my story and know my heart. Looking forward to hearing from you. I wish you and your family all the best.

Good thank you.

Man

* * * * *

NOTE 2. P.29

LETTER SUPPORTING MAN'S VISA APPLICATION

2004

To Whom It May Concern:

I am a 65-year-old retired lawyer. I was born in the United States and since 2002 have lived in Saigon, where I work as a volunteer with the blind, street children, and AIDS patients. I served in Vietnam during the 1960s as a lieutenant of infantry (serial #____).

During this stay in Vietnam I have had the honor of becoming acquainted with Phong and his family. One of his daughters, Man, has applied for a student visa. I write this letter to recommend Man and her family.

Her father served in the South Vietnamese Army, rising to the rank of major (soldier number: ________), and was imprisoned after the war. He was loyal to his government and to us, the Americans, to the end. He has been told that he and his family, unto the third generation, will be suspect and will have limited opportunities in Vietnam.* Indeed, this has been true. They have been denied education, healthcare, and employment. Twenty-seven years after the war, they still suffer. Man's parents live in the jungle, from which they are forbidden to move. I have spent much time with them and with their four children. They are honorable people with the kind of values we in the United States aspire to.

The daughter, Man, is honest, determined, god fearing, hard working, and possessed of intellectual integrity. She wishes to look for opportunities in the United States that she cannot get in Vietnam, which is the same reason my parents emigrated to America in 1927. To the readers of this letter I ask that she be given every and any possible help and accommodation as she pursues her student visa and education in America.

Respectively yours,
Martin J. Dockery

*Questions on the authorized government CV form, which is required of job applicants for government and company employment, ask: "What did your father do before 1975?" and "What did your grandfather do before 1975?" These questions are intended to weed out those applicants whose families supported the South and America during the war.

* * * * *

PHONG'S THANK YOU NOTE

Dear Martin

I have receive your recommendation with great pleasure, I do hope that it would be most helpful to Man to show official U.S.A government her legal status and makes her much more easier to pursue her student Visa and education in America. We also appreciate all your help that make us a little easier. Indeed, my word is true. After the VN war until now we have contrived to live on a small income on 8 million piaster ($526) for a couple of me, for a year; but this year we have more income from Cassava, but only more than a million.

Martin! Please come with us for Tet again, you and me, we are two old soldiers have a chance to meet and talk again, and we are fond of you. Thank again all your kind assistance. Good luck to you, God bless you.

Phong

NOTE 3. p.153

HIEN'S THANK YOU NOTE

2005

Dear Martin

How are you? I hope you are well. Do you have any new thing in your activities? I have good news. On Sunday, I received my father's email. He said that he had received my rosary, which is sent from your sister Una, with him. It is really a wonderful birthday gift, because his birthday is July 14th. Thank you very much. Truthfully speaking, even though I remember the birthday of my father but I did not dare to think that the gift arrived at an opportune moment. It is really out of my expectation. I also tell that to Una and thank her for her kindness. I think she will be very glad to know about it. She is really nicer than what you said. (Hmm! Unfair! Is that right?) Once more, thank you for all you have done for me.

Martin, I would like to ask you a favor. If you don't mind, would you please recommend me to someone who is in the same sense of purpose as you are? Do you think that it is better for me to have a chance to learn more for my English? I hope I can have a kind-hearted teacher like Una or you. And I also think that God should serve me fairly. OK? Nothing is urgent but whenever you can please, think of it. Thanks a lot. And I also heard that your brother had a heart attack. Is he still in the hospital? How about his state now? I am very sorry to hear it. I hope it was not a serious case and he will get better soon. I also hope that his intention to visit VN will not be given up but only be delayed, so I can have opportunity to be acquainted with another member of your family. I wish you will have good news from him soon and I'm really glad if you will share it with me.

I look forward to hearing from you.
Your student,
Hien

NOTE 4. p.169

SOMERSET HOTEL APARTMENTS, HO CHI MINH CITY

Dear Resident,

Vietnamese Government's Regulation on Local Visitors.

According to the Decree issued by the Vietnamese Government (08/2001/ ND- CP), all local Vietnamese visitors are not allowed to visit after 10.00pm or stay overnight in the hotel/apartment unless they are proven to be the spouse/husband (with valid Marital Certificate} of the resident.

Therefore the management and staff on duty have the right to refuse entry to any visitors after 10.00pm.

We seek your kind understanding and cooperation on this matter.

Yours sincerely,

Asst. Resident Manager

NOTE 5. p.205

MARTIN'S 2003 FORTUNE TELLER'S REPORT

- Before 30, you had many problems because a bad star stopped the good star. Before 30, you traveled many places in the army. After 30, you have had a good life because the good star has had power over the bad star.
- You are helpful, open, intelligent, sensitive, and independent, and have many dreams of success. You love your family, relatives, and friends and are always thinking of them.
- You have a lot of money. You spend and give it to others who need it. You do not spend it on yourself.
- You have scars from accidents and fights but the good star has prevented serious injury.
- You were not satisfied in the army because you could not develop. The bad star was responsible because it covered you. You became a lawyer after 25 and traveled a lot. You are not a corrupt lawyer. The best time for your occupation was at 53 and the worst was at 62. It would be better for you if you became a writer or fashion photographer than to join in business with others at 63. At 72, you will be a great contributor to humanity in medicine.
- From 63-72 you will still have the ability to make a lot of money. You will spend it for other people. Be careful about guaranteeing loans for others, especially in the years of the pig, cat, and goat. You will get a bad reputation because borrowers will not repay the loans. Do not take gifts from ladies because, again, you will get a bad reputation.
- You will spend more than you earn.
- If you are rich you will have hand, leg, and digestive problems.
- You will have four more sons.
- Don't travel by plane when you're 70.
- Your wife works in a clothes shop or a bank and is a little bit big and a little bit modern. She always wants you to obey her, but you won't.
- You have three children, two boys and a girl. The first child has a good star because it is a boy. The two boys are educated, hard working and respectful to you. Your daughter is a big problem; she does not listen to you, is independent, and has a bad reputation.
- You may have a heart attack in the years of the buffalo and goat so you should not work, think hard, or swim in those years. Do not drink alcohol in the years of the tiger, buffalo, and goat.
- Your liver and kidneys will be weak. Eat carefully in the years of the monkey, dragon, and mouse.

- If you are rich you will die at 72, but if not you will have a long life. You will not die in the United States, but somewhere else.
- You sort out problems by yourself.
- If you spend money on travel and business you will not have to spend it on healthcare.
- At year 65 be careful of burns because the fire star is shining on you. If you change business, your car will be stolen.
- From 73-82 you will be happy and will have sexual power. You will be happy with nature and the earth. The front door of your new house will face northwest. Don't build a house near the beach. At 73 the government will take your old house but will compensate you.
- In May 2005 be careful of burns, robbers, and police.
- In June 2005 you will have a sweet, cheerful girlfriend.
- In July 2005 you will have a bad automobile accident and bad news from your wife.
- In August 2005 you will have a bad reputation because of ladies.
- In September 2005 do not go to bars or restaurants because of trouble. You will start a new business in September.
- In October 2005 you will encounter a big problem if you travel alone, so stay away from ladies because of possible trouble.
- At 66 you will have a child with your number two wife.
- At 67 do not go to discos or make friends with bar girls. Do not go swimming or go on a boat. You will buy land and will get into trouble with the economic police.
- At 68 you will have to spend money to solve land problems. You will have a good maid but she will want to be your boss and have your baby. Tell her to go away and get a new maid.
- At 76 you will almost drown in the sea but you will be saved. Be careful of water.
- At 78 you will move to a new house.
- At 80 you will be happy with children and will win the lottery.
- At 81 you will be sick all year.
- At 82 you will die of a heart attack, but if you don't die then you will die instead at 83 in a horrible accident. It would be better to die at 82.
- Avoid people born in 1953, 1965, and 1977.
- Make friends and do business with people born in '54, '62, & '76.
- Avoid people born under the sign of water or the sign of the tree.

NOTE 6. p.252

A DIRE SITUATION—ANN SMITH

July 25, 2007

Consul General
United States Consulate
4 Le Duan Street, District 1
Ho Chi Minh City, Vietnam

Dear Consul General:

I write to you about a grave situation involving an American citizen. Ann Smith is 84 years old and alone in Saigon. Her husband died here last October. She was evicted from her house for non-payment of rent in June. For the last six weeks, Ann has lived on the street in front of that house under a construction tarpaulin. The blue, white, and pink tarp is 10' x 20'. She sleeps in a hammock next to her belongings. The big covering barely shields the cardboard boxes, which contain her treasures. One box contains hundreds of restaurant menus from Tokyo where she once lived. She is protected in her hammock from the rain, but not her property, which is sodden from water flowing under the tarp. Notwithstanding the smoke coils she burns, Ann is covered with insect bites. At night, people try to steal her things, she says, and perhaps she is right.

Ann defecates and urinates next to her hammock. She does not wash. A saintly Vietnamese couple cleans up her mess every morning and brings food and water.

I do not know Ann's financial condition, and she is not forthcoming when I ask her, or perhaps she does not know. However, three months ago I saw a joint bank statement of hers, which indicated a balance of $1,500. The statement seemed to show a $700 a month deposit from the United Nations. There was no evidence that she receives social security payments. A handful of $120 VA disability checks payable to her husband were visible. He was a WWII veteran. He told me he worked off and on for the U.S. government in Saigon from 1950 to 1963.

Ann allowed that she had nieces and nephews in Florida and Missouri, but they would not help her because she had not been in touch with them for 30 years.

Ann believes that she works for Can Tho University and that they pay all her bills. She has told me the university has a nice house for her and she will soon move into it. I traveled twelve hours round-trip to Can Tho and spoke with Dr. Anh Tuan, the rector of the university. He denied any responsibility for Ann. He said she does not work for the university and never did. In the past, she and her husband were volunteers there. "She is crazy," he said. "Ask her to stop telling people the university will pay her expenses and tell her to stop calling my staff at night."

Life on the street is not safe for Ann. The ward leaders have told her so. The police have taken her to a local magistrate. She yells at them all and refuses to cooperate.

The neighbors object to this spectacle (and stink) at their doorsteps. They ask me if the American government knows about Ann's condition.

You have an important job with many responsibilities. Nevertheless, I implore you to involve yourself in this situation. Over the last six weeks, I have spoken to five Americans who work at the consulate; one has been reposted, two are on vacation, and the others are new to their jobs. They have been uniformly sympathetic of Ann's plight and polite to me. However, nothing happens; she continues to rot on the sidewalk.

Ann has told the consulate people that she does not want to go back to America and your staff has told me she cannot be sent back unless she agrees. If she were competent, I would concur. However, Ann is non-compos mentis. She is not legally capable of making decisions.

She defecates in her tent; lives with her excreta. In the United States, that alone is prima facie evidence of mental incompetence. Her imagined university job, housing, and sinecure are other clear signs of delusion and dementia. If the consulate were dealing with a 5-year-old girl, would her desire to stay on the streets of Saigon be honored or would it be overruled?

I am a U.S. citizen, 69 years old, an army veteran, retired lawyer, and author. I have been in Saigon six years. I teach American history at a local university. In the public schools, I teach English to small children. I tell you these things to enhance my creditability, to the benefit of Ann, I hope.

I live in Phu Nhuan District near Ann's hovel. I met Ann and her husband at Skewers where, incidentally, in early July, Tristan introduced your wife and you to me.

I am not able to help Ann. I do not have the resources, contacts, and creditability that are necessary for the task. The consulate does.

If you like, I will take you to see Ann. In any event, please do something.

Respectfully yours,
Martin J. Dockery

* * * * *

July 27, 2007

Martin:

Thanks for your note. This situation is genuinely dire but our ability to intervene is virtually non-existent since U.S. laws "protect" Ann from our intervention. Nonetheless, we are making another emergency appeal to Washington, D.C., to ask for their advice or suggestions concerning anything that we can do. I hope to have news for you soon.

Thanks,
Consul General

* * * * *

July 27, 2007

Gentlemen:

On July 25 I sent the consulate an email letter to the consul general about Ann Smith, a demented 84-year-old U.S. citizen who has been living on the streets of Saigon since the middle of June. I know the consulate people are good folk and that they care about Ann. I am sympathetic; Ann is not an easy problem to solve.

This email describes events that occurred this morning at Ann's tent. For your records, her address is the pavement at 139E Nguyen Dinh Chinh, Phu Nhuan. She, together with her belongings, lives in front of the house she was evicted from. I am making you aware of today's events because the consulate has her fate in its hands.

At 9 p.m. today, I received a call from a Vietnamese man who brings Ann food. He and his wife worked for Ann's deceased husband. "A truck is coming to take her things and dump them in the river," he said. "Come help Ann." Minutes after I arrived, a truck and four men stopped in front of the tent. The men did nothing. I am sure it was not this 155 lb, 69-year-old man that gave them pause. It was Ann, disheveled with uncombed, shoulder-length hair, standing beside me holding a bug spray can. They were afraid of the junkyard dog. She cussed and threatened. They left and so did I.

An hour later, I went again when the man called to say that the truck was back with the police this time. Upon arrival, I saw Ann chasing the policemen and truck driver. They had removed the tarp and were taking her things into their truck. The aggrieved house owner told all that Ann's boxes would be put in the river. Ann was yelling that they were guilty of trespass, unlawful entry, and destruction of her property. She screamed, "Where are your papers? What are your names? Who will pay for my damaged property?" The police, unwilling to restrain or hit her, left but not before telling me they would be back. One said she could not stay here. They put the tarp back up, but did not move her boxes under it. Her hammock was taken so that now she must sleep atop the boxes.

I asked Ann once again if she would like to return to America. Her strong response was, "No!" Nevertheless, she is not competent to make decisions. She must be sent home. I am not able to do that.

I close by asking that you do what you can for Ann. She desperately needs your intervention and help.

Very truly yours,
Martin J. Dockery

* * * * *

September 26, 2007

Consul General: After we spoke this morning, the immigration police called a second time to say they were taking Ann to a government old people's home. They asked me to meet them at Ann's tent. About 15 people were waiting when I arrived: police from the District and the Immigration Department, two nurses, several men in white shirts, and representatives of the tourist company that had sponsored Ann's visa when she first came to Vietnam 5 years ago. An English-speaking policewoman explained that the tourist company was financially responsible for Ann.

It took about an hour to convince Ann to leave her tent and go to the room the government had for her. Most of the convincing was done by the policewoman, who carefully and politely explained to Ann why she should go with them and where they were going to take her. She resisted; she did not want to leave. Many times she asked, "Why do I have to go?" Eventually, of her own accord and without force, she got into the van.

I rode with her to the home, where four caregivers spent an hour processing Ann. They asked me questions you would expect: What medical problems does she have? What will she eat? Who are her relatives? Is she difficult? Who will visit her? What languages does she speak?

She is the only foreigner at the home. Ann's room is large and she has access to a toilet and shower. Her room faces a central courtyard which is spacious, partially shaded and has potted plants. The compound is gated. She is not allowed to leave on her own.

I returned to Ann's tent where the police were taking inventory of her things, which they said they would store for her. Her TV and computer would be put in her room this afternoon.

Ann is better off in the government home than in her tent. She will be dry and safe. She will be fed and cared for. Her address, without the marks, is:

Trung Tam Ho Tro Xa Hoi
463 No Trang Long-f13
Binh Thanh
Tel: 5532082

All of the government people were professional. They were polite and they treated Ann with dignity. They carefully explained to me that Ann's stay at the home was temporary, until the U.S. Consulate made other arrangements.

If you have questions, either call or email me.

Best regards,
Martin

* * * * *

September 27, 2007

Consul General:

There were two things I forget to mention in yesterday's email.

Ann's passport was not found in her belongings, and as of this morning it is still missing. If I hear it has been found, I will let you know.

The second was to thank you and the consulate staff for your efforts on Ann's behalf. I know that without your conversations with the Vietnamese government nothing would have happened.

I wish you well.

Best regards,
Martin

★

BIOGRAPHY

Martin Dockery was a First Lieutenant, United States Army, from 1960-1964, serving as a combat advisor to a Vietnamese infantry battalion for nearly a year in 1963. Shortly thereafter, he participated in the funeral of JFK, supervising visiting Irish cadets. After leaving the army, he practiced municipal bond law as a partner at various law firms in New York City. He returned to Vietnam in 2002 as a teacher at a charity for blind orphans, street children, public school children, university students, seminarians, monks, nuns and foreign NGOs. Ten years later, he moved back to New York with his wife Thao and their two children.

Dockery's previous book was Lost in Translation: Vietnam: A Combat Advisor's Story. Random House, 2003.

CPSIA information can be obtained
at www.ICGtesting.com
Printed in the USA
BVHW031921050619
550272BV00001B/26/P

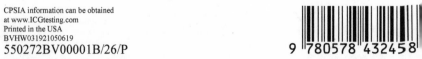

9 780578 432458